MARCELLO MASTROIANNI

the fun of cinema

Matilde Hochkofler

MARCELLO MASTROIANNI

The fun of cinema

Foreword by
Federico Fellini

GREMESE
INTERNATIONAL

Acknowlegdements
The author and the publisher would like to thank Marcello Mastroianni for his generous assistance in the preparation of this book, and for his cooperativeness in reviewing the typescript and suggesting amendments to it.

Author's note
The statements made by Marcello Mastroianni that are quoted in this book come from interviews with the actor in June 1980; March 1981; May 1984; April 1987; 4, 5, 7 July 1990, and December 1991. I have also drawn upon our extended interview, which has already been published in Claudio G. Fava and Matilde Hochkofler: *Marcello Mastroianni* (Gremese Editore, 1980). The discussion of Mastroianni's tax situation is taken from an interview with Stella Pende, which was published in *Panorama* (25 October, 1977). His view of the Oscar award comes from an interview with Lietta Tornabuoni which was published in *Corriere della Sera* (1 March, 1978). The account of Mastroianni's meeting with Greta Garbo is taken from an interview with Alain Elkann, which was published in *Chorus* (9 October, 1990).

Original title
Marcello Mastroianni

Translation from Italian
Jocelyn Earle

Introduction translated from Italian by
Patricia Cavagnaro

Edited by
P.E. Fogarty

Jacket design
Antonio Dojmi

Phototypesetting
Graphic Art 6 s.r.l. - Rome

Photolithography
Bielleci - Rome

Printed and bound by
Conti Tipocolor - Calenzano (FI)

© 1992 - GREMESE INTERNATIONAL s.r.l., Rome
Casella Postale 14335 - 00149 Rome

ISBN 88-7301-011-3

CONTENS

Foreword

Marcello ... yes, he's great. And a very dear friend. Loyal, faithful, and full of good sense, the kind of friend you only come upon in stories, or in certain American films of the Thirties.

Marcello and I rarely see each other, almost never, in fact. Maybe that's one reason for our friendship, a friendship that imposes no demands, never obligates, makes no conditions, and has never known either rules or boundary lines. It's a true friendship, of a quite wonderful kind, based on total, reciprocal distrust.

Working with him is pure joy. Sensitive and intelligent, he is so open and aware that he is able to ease into the characters he portrays, as if entering on tiptoe. Without having asked them any questions at all, not even so much as a 'by your leave?'. And there's no chance he's read the script.

"Where's the fun if you know what happens in advance?" he says. "I'd rather find out day by day, just as my character does."

He lets them do his make-up, arrange his hair, dress him up; he never objects to anything and asks only those few questions that are absolutely unavoidable. Everything about him is calm, malleable, relaxed and natural, so natural in fact that he sometimes dozes off during shooting, right in one of his own scenes, and even when he's being taken in close-up.

And it is precisely this capacity to keep his distance, almost a sort of absence, which allows him to give himself completely, without vanity or the usual professional nerves. In other words, this detachment lets him live the character he plays, in total simplicity, and with all his being. Day after day, with confidence and enjoyment, he abandons himself to the adventure which is being played out and which, through his work, goes beyond the confines of cinema to become life itself.

Sitting in my Cinecittà office on certain listless, sleepy days, I sometimes feel bored. Lazily, I lean on my window sill, looking down at the various roadways and the building in front of mine where we have the make-up department. If, by chance, I know that Marcello Mastroianni is in there, I can't resist the temptation to go down and see him, to get in touch with his familiar, so vital friendship.

Getting downstairs toward the make-up department you can already hear snatches of music, snippets of songs, that increase in volume as you pass through the long corridor where the dressing-rooms fall in line, doors closed, owners' names tacked up on cards. Sometimes you read famous names, the international stars. I remember one hand-written name-card attached with scotch tape which said, "I'm not anybody at all."

The make-up rooms are different; their doors are always open, and you can hear voices muttering, people yelling calls, the metallic echo of the assistant directors' walkie-talkies as they confer with unseen figures, who knows where, swearing that the actor, the actress will be there in just five minutes or – no, as a matter or fact – they're already on their way, sure enough. There in that chaos, dressmakers and assistant hairdressers bustling back and forth, there under a steaming hairdrier that swallows his head, and covered down to his shoes by an enormous sheet-like affair, there I find Marcello. I recognize him by that dangling hand clutching a cigarette whose smoke drifts toward the ceiling.

And I know that even with all the hub-bub around him, underneath the sheet and the hairdrier, old Snaporaz is having himself a snooze. Finally he notices my reflection in the mirror and raises the hand with the cigarette to welcome me, hastily waving away cigarette smoke with his free hand because he knows it bothers me.

It's always strange for me to see him there, making a film for someone else. So that even when he's dressed as a corsair, or a nineteenth-century gentleman, or made-up with beard and sideburns like Abbot Faria, it's really hard for me not to stick my nose in and tell the make-up man to darken the eyebrows a little, adjust a wrinkle or a curl, or tone up the neck skin to camouflage his double-chin.

He gets up, stretching his legs, and gives me that resigned, faint smile you generally see on convalescents and life-term prisoners. He puts out the cigarette,

With Anita Ekberg in La Dolce Vita.

lights another, and we go out for a stroll in the corridor. There's nothing we actually want to talk about; it's just for the pleasure of being together, like two schoolboys, or a couple of soldiers on leave. When he talks he holds his mouth crookedly so he can exhale smoke away from me. Together we greet the dressmaker Jolandona as she comes by, holding a coat hanger high so that the wedding dress on it won't touch the ground; or we say hello to Giusy the hairdresser, that we both like so much, and she responds, flattered and arching her back with pleasure.

Marcello Mastroianni always reminds you of the school chum with whom you had that flash of mutual understanding which made you the most natural accomplices in the world.

For Marcello, friendship doesn't suggest anything ethical or obligatory; it just means being together, taking part in the same jokes, the same tricks, the same lies. You get the impression that this schoolboy approach to life continues right onto the film set, where even when Marcello is fully immersed in his actor's profession, he still maintains a psychological approach to his character and the author's vision of that character which I find ideal, that intelligent openness which is almost feminine in its gentleness. Before starting a film together we chat a bit, enough to establish our mutual awareness that we are starting yet another voyage together. I tell him what I know; and sometimes I don't know much at all. Marcello never asks embarrassing questions: he arrives on the set with the curiosity of someone who's just dropped by to see what's happening. And this attitude gives the author the stimulating feeling that the character really does not know what will happen to him in the next scene, that the character in hand has a kind of eternal virginity, the fresh newness of every dawn. Marcello has an instinctive ability to put things in pro-

portion and eliminate excess; he's far greater than he imagines, and his modesty protects him from all the dangers that beset an actor – vanity, exaggerated extroversion, proud peacocking and auto-exaltation.

It was Giulietta who first brought us together; she had acted with Marcello in the theatre, and it was she who first talked to me about him. But the character he played in *Dolce Vita* was created with someone else in mind. De Laurentiis was insisting on Paul Newman. Now he's a great star, but he wouldn't have been credible as a provincial reporter hanging around Via Veneto and trailed by his avid, free-lance photographer friends.

So how did I see him in my imagination, that sceptical, ambitious, treacherous, gabby journalist? I'd looked over so many different actors, considered different solutions; then I decided to see Marcello. We went for a ride in the car and started talking to each other as two kids do: we told each other things that you normally recount only to very old friends, and we discovered we had the same sly wiles in dealing with life situations and relationships. That was how our extraordinary complicity was born. I made him lose ten kilos (I always make him do that, before every film, and I did everything possible to make him seem a bit more nervously restless. We gave him false lashes, a yellowish complexion, dark circles under the eyes, had him put on a black suit, black tie ... touches that added a mournful quality.

It's not true that Marcello Mastroianni is really me, my cinematographic double, my *alter ego*. Fact is, Giulietta Masina is also my alter ego, as is Anita Ekberg: all the characters I put on the set are, even the rhinoceros in *E la nave va* (The Ship's Going). I don't put my hat on Marcello's head to identify him with me; I do it to leave him a trail, set up some clues, create a sort of magnetic field for transmitting

thoughts from one head to another, which is easier if the simulacrum is wearing something that helps him make contact. I think I make him resemble me because it's the most direct way for me to visualize a character and his story; and that's a very delicate operation, only made possible by a real friendship and an unabashed desire to put yourself on public display.

The evening I talked to him about *City of Women*, I didn't tell him that he was to be the lead. The truth is that the producer was insisting on Dustin Hoffman; and I have to confess that I, too, liked the idea of using this American actor and felt he was a very exciting choice. We were driving around, and as I was going on about the film, Marcello seemed to be only half-listening, as a person does for a story that doesn't concern him, but for which friendship and good manners force him to show a tepid curiosity. "It's the story" I was saying, "of a man who hangs around women a lot, looking them all over; but he ends up feeling bewitched and bewildered. It seems that he looks at a woman without the least desire to understand her, only hoping to get a pleasureable mix of sensations: amazement, admiration, enthusiasm, dismay, and a little tenderness. Maybe he's afraid because he thinks that possessing a woman means succumbing, disappearing, dying: So he'd rather keep up the chase, never making any real contact with her."

Talking about the film in that way had struck a chord in me, and I was moved as I spoke: I drove on in silence for awhile, and Marcello, too, was quiet. For a long while we avoided meeting each other's eyes. In that moment, almost without realising it, we had decided to work together on *City of Women*.

Am I going to make more films with old Snaporaz? I sincerely hope to. The sooner the better.

Federico Fellini

1

The Most Handsome Man in Europe

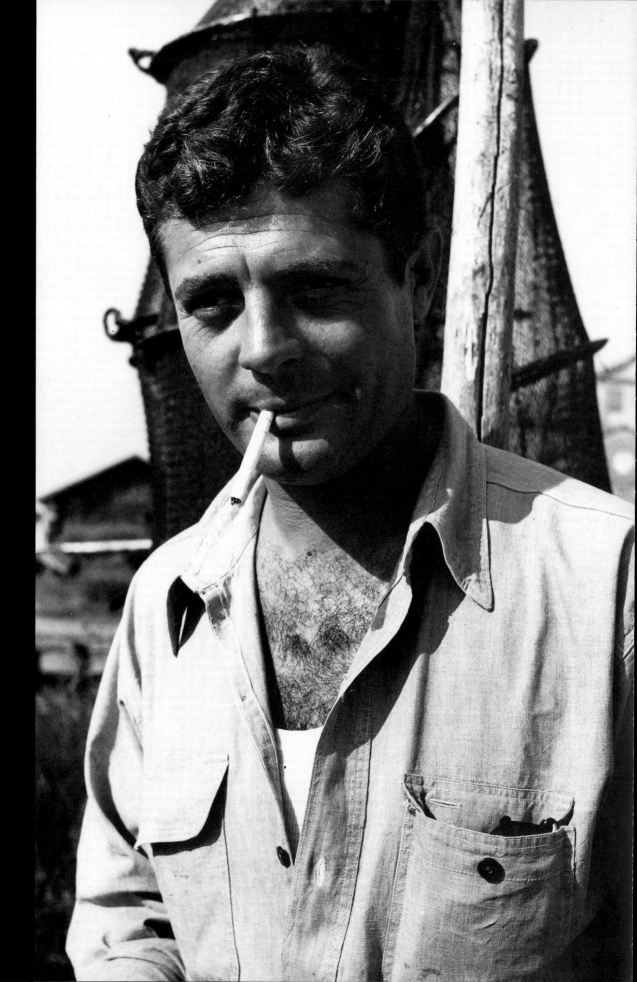

"**I** am one of the most handsome men in Europe," Marcello Mastroianni was once made to say by the screenwriters of the 1958 film *Un ettaro di cielo* (A Hectare of Sky) directed by Aglauco Casadio. This seems to sum up the deliberately limited type-casting to which Mastroianni was subjected in the first ten years of his career. The insistent references to his physical presence, so common in many of his films (one of them was even entitled *Il marito bello*, The Handsome Husband) seem to confirm the idea that Italian cinema has tried to contain Mastroianni's acting potential in roles where his physical presence is given greater importance than his rapidly growing acting ability. The cinema has tended to attempt to reduce his range to the narrow category of the working-class or middle-class hero and in its endless repetitions keep him constantly playing the same roles. So time and again we see the same characters moving from one film to the next: the good-natured if slightly dim-witted taxi-driver; the patient and resigned office-worker; the ingenuous but determined proletarian.

While we might define his relationship with the cinema at this stage of his career as largely 'physical', it was really in the theatre that he started to take shape as an actor. In fact it was in Luchino Visconti's theatre that he gained both the cultural preparation and the acting skills which were to provide him with a passport to the profession. "Cinema is holiday time. Theatre is school time. It is like a diet; afterwards we are slimmer, more refined." In reality Mastroianni's ambitions lay in the cinema which he had experienced as an extra since before the war. At that time it

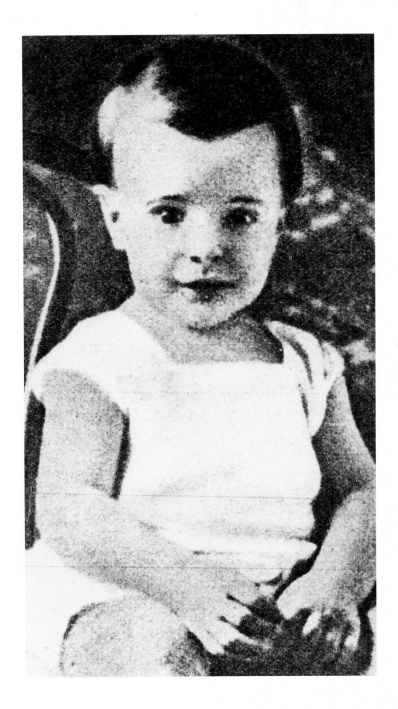

Marcello at eighteen months.

held a mythical quality for the masses; it not only meant the chance of work for those felt drawn to it, but also held the promise of the kind of riches that a working-class boy could not hope to earn in any other way. Only after his experience in the theatre, however, was he able to make his presence really felt. It was Visconti himself who gave Mastroianni the opportunity to make the first move towards the kind of cinema which allowed him to give depth to the roles he interpreted and freed him from the strait-jacket of former roles; a liberation which was to be his guarantee of international fame.

The turning point in Mastroianni's career came as a result of a process of personal maturation and a few chance acquaintances. It was thanks to the director Alessandro Blasetti, and the screenwriters Suso Cecchi d'Amico and Ennio Flaiano that the screen-couple Marcello Mastroianni-Sophia Loren was formed and the two successful 1950's comedies *Too Bad She's Bad* and *Lucky to Be a Woman* produced. It was due to the contacts he made in these two films that he went ahead to become a co-producer of the film *White Nights*. In fact he made this film in collaboration with Visconti and Suso Cecchi d'Amico. One result of this experience on the other side of the set was that it made him aware of a broadening of his expressive abilities. "*White Nights* was the first film in which the popular, honest, good-natured fellow began to take on a more intellectual aspect. It was the first step towards the presentation of more middle-class characters, a moving away from certain characters like the simple honest worker or driver towards an individual with a more middle class texture, the individual, in fact, that soon came into being in *La Dolce Vita*. For me as an actor it was an extremely positive experience for at least two reasons. It was the first time that I had worked with Visconti as a film director as opposed to a theatre director and as such it was useful for me to become aware of the different ways he had of working in film and in theatre. And then, perhaps this film showed that I was ready for the type of cinema which was to come shortly afterwards, and convinced other directors that I could be used in a different way. As a film director, Visconti was less coercive and left more space to the actor. On that occasion I really had the chance to appreciate his talent as a film director. In the theatre he was extremely demanding and really imposed his own personality on the actor, wanting him to

Twelve years old, and already an extra at Cinecittà.

16

act according to certain rules and formulas even to the precise reproduction of the intonation of a line; on the film set he was as precise as ever but he left more space to the actor because film-acting is a much more naturalistic thing than theatre-acting which is wholly artificial. He was fully aware of the differences in the two types of acting and it was a real pleasure for me to have my image of him as a great 'teacher'-director reconfirmed."

Born in Fontana Liri in the Ciociaria region around Rome, on the 28th of September 1924 to Ottorino Mastrojanni (the actor later changed the 'j' to an 'i') and Ida Irolle, Marcello immediately moves north with his parents, to Turin. On the 7th of November 1929 his brother, Ruggero, later to become a successful film editor, is born. When he is nine years old the family returns to Rome, where his father, a cabinet-maker, opens a furniture workshop. As a short-term measure they stay at the house of an aunt. Marcello had already started Primary School in Turin; he finishes his schooling in the Tuscolano quarter, a working-class area of Rome. During the school holidays he does small jobs to help the family: "I had my first job when I was thirteen. In the summer I worked in the Artillery headquarters in Rome, then I went back to school."

He comes from an artistic family. Richard Conte, the actor, is a distant relative. In fact his grandmother's name was Conte, a typical name in the Ciociaria region. His uncle Umberto Mastroianni is a sculptor, so too was his great-uncle, Domenico, whose work was very successful during the First World War. Domenico's son, Alberto, on the other hand, was a painter with an important studio in the Via Margutta, right in the centre of Rome; when he was a boy, Marcello often went to see him. Most of his grandfather's ten children either sculpted or painted, "all people who have always worked with artistic materials."

Marcello and his father Ottorino at Ruggero's first communion. "The family was important, possibly because it was the only thing there was. I feel quite nostalgic when I remember the gatherings that took place on public holidays. We would go down to our grandparents', and meet up with our aunts and uncles and cousins. And then there were the lunches, where we ate special dishes that were only made for those occasions. They used to become real feasts, which we looked forward to tremendously when we were small, but also when we were older. It was a very traditional, in fact almost patriarchal, close-knit family, where our grandfather laid down the law. Nowadays, we're all more like gypsies, and no longer have the same fortress mentality."

Marcello as a child, dressed in the Italian fascist uniform.

When he was a boy he wanted to be an architect. "But then somebody saw me act in a University production; they called me for an audition and I joined Visconti's company." Acting has always been his greatest love. His first acting experiences were in the parish drama group; he took part in amateur dramatics and during the war was part of a vocal quartet. The Tus-

colano quarter where he lived is the closest in Rome to Cinecittà, the Italian Fascist-built version of Hollywood, and while he was still a teenager he felt the draw of the set and got his first roles as a film-extra. When he was thirteen years old he appeared in *Marionette* (Puppets) by Carmine Gallone, with Beniamino Gigli and Carla Rust. "The scene I was in was a sort of grape harvest in a village. I was with I with a group group of children who listened to Gigli while he sang. My mother was in the scene too. They gave us ten lire for the evening's work. We ate masses of grapes; there were carts full of them. My best friends' parents ran the restaurants at Cinecittà. Their mother, who worked the cash till in the bar, used to get hold of the permit for me to work there in the summer when the schools closed. So I did a lot of work as a film-extra. I had my first experience of Cinecittà at an age when everything seems magical. I could see all the famous actors close-to: Beniamino Gigli, Nino Besozzi. For *I pirati della Malesia* (The Pirates of Malaysia) we had to go early in the morning at five o'clock. They smeared us with dye to make us seem like indians. We were dressed as thugs with loin cloths and daggers. I remember a scene with Massimo Girotti which took place in a tavern. He was playing Tremal-Naik and Camillo Pilotto was playing Cammammuri. He had to say a line, then leap athletically onto a table and escape. He couldn't manage to say the line. The director (I don't know who it was) said, 'Cut, hold it for a moment. Go and get some orange juice for Mr Girotti. Have a drink of orange juice; it'll loosen-up your tongue a little.' And I thought, 'What a jerk, a real softie; go and get some orange juice! Why don't you give him a kick up the backside; he can't even say a simple line. What an idiot!' That's what I was thinking. But he wasn't an actor. He was a beautiful athlete; then he learned. These were my big moments; every summer something hap-

"The cinema arrived slowly, thanks to the theatre, and thanks therefore to Giulietta Masina. Who knows where I'd be now, if it wasn't for her! In another profession, probably".

pened. I thought it was all great fun. I don't talk about it so that people will say 'Poor little thing; only thirteen years old and already working'. I enjoyed working because it seemed like an adult's game. I felt proud." He worked as an extra in Alessandro Blasetti's *The Iron Crown* and in Mario Camerini's *Una storia d'amore* (A Love Story). Here he met one of the film divas of the period. "I was in the lift in the warehouses in Via XX Settembre with some other extras. When the door opened and I stepped out, I found myself face to face with Assia Noris. I was deeply moved."

The boy who dreamed of becoming an actor has now become an eighteen-year old impatient to start working. He does the rounds of the production houses, leaving his photograph, hoping to be called; but he is still playing as an extra in *The Children Are Watching Us* by Vittorio De Sica. This time, however, he is not there by chance. De Sica's sister, Maria, had worked with Marcello's mother, Ida, and it is with her help that he manages to get close to the director. "I used to go and find him every time there was a break, wherever he was working. He used to tell me: 'Keep on studying and when you have finished then you can think about it.' I realise now that I really got on his nerves, poor man." De Sica's initial diffidence towards him, which Mastroianni could not ignore, was based on the conviction that he was not suited to becoming an actor because of his rather nasal voice.

Following the maestro's advice he carries on with his studies and in 1943 takes a diploma in construction design in one of Rome's technical colleges. As soon as he

finishes school he starts working almost immediately for Rome City Council as a technical drawing assistant. Thanks to his skill at his work he is sent by the army to work at the Geographical Military Institute in Florence. When Italy surrenders to the allies the Institute is taken over by the German authorities and transferred to Dobbiaco on the Austrian border. As soon as it seems certain that there will be a further transfer to Germany, Marcello flees to Venice with Remo Brindisi, a painter colleague of his who later becomes famous. In order to survive he helps Brindisi to sell his sketches and small paintings. He stays in Venice until the city is liberated and then leaves for Rome taking with him a suitcase

tied up with string containing all his belongings and a supply of beans and potatoes which he hopes will cater to the immediate needs of his family. On arriving, however, he discovers, that the presence of the American troops has finally rid the city of the nightmare of hunger. His brother, Ruggero, has found a job as a waiter in a bar where the American troops often go. With the help of a cousin, he manages to get taken on as a clerk for Eagle Lion Films, a distribution company which was part of the Sir Arthur Rank group.

Acting is still in his blood as much as ever and he enrols at the University in the Commerce and Economics department

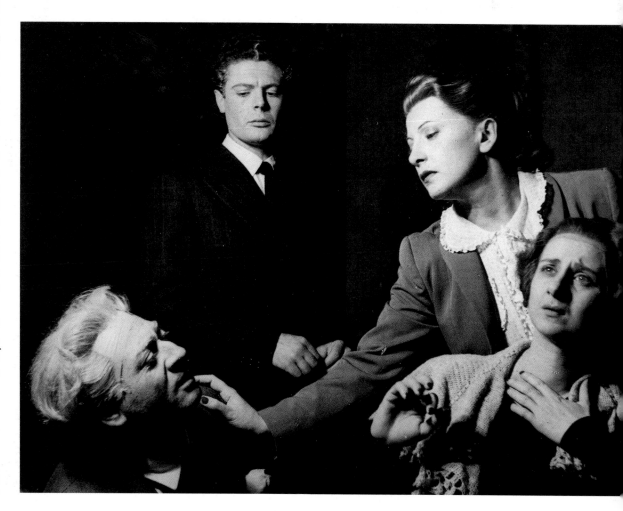

With Nino Besozzi, Isa Pola and Pina Cei, in April 1948.

21 January 1949, with Rina Morelli in A Streetcar Named Desire.

In a Ripafratta cavalier's costume, demonstrating his swordsmanship, beside Paolo Stoppa and Gianrico Tedeschi in La locandiera.

With Giorgio De Lullo e Franco Interlenghi, at the time of Death of a Salesman.

The following year, as Diomedes in Troilus and Cressida, *staged by Luchino Visconti.*

mainly so that he can join the CUT, the Centre for University Theatre. "At the CUT I acted in *Angelica*, an allegorical comedy by Leo Ferrero, an anti-fascist work written in the full bloom of Fascism. The characters were all hidden behind masks, but the comic roles were meant to parody the public offices they represented. I played Orlando. Giulietta Masina, Fellini's wife, was Angelica. Antonio Crast was the dictator. It was Giulietta Masina herself who got me into Besozzi's company.

They were doing *Time of Indifference* from the novel by Moravia. She did everything to get me in. I started out with an almost non-existent part; I had to say a line from the wings. I stayed with Besozzi all through the summer of '48. I remember I played a waiter in *The Importance of Being Ernest* by Oscar Wilde, a police commissioner in *Old Rascal* by Percy, and the father of Franco Scandurra in *Ex-alunno* (Ex-Pupil) by Mosca. Three small parts. While I was acting with the CUT I was spotted by Emilio Amendola, the uncle of Ferruccio Amendola who was the manager of Visconti's company. They were looking for a young man and he asked me if I wanted to become a professional. I told him that I had a job and couldn't leave it.

The day after he took me along to an interview with Visconti. Zeffirelli was there too. Visconti looked me straight in the eye and said: 'Mr Amendola says that you have got talent; we'll see'. I said: 'I'm afraid we won't see, Mr. Visconti; I have a job and responsibilities, I can't possibly leave them'. And he said, 'Three.' 'Three what?' 'Three thousand lire a day.' 'I'll sign'. I used to earn thirty-one thousand lire a month before taxes, and he was offering me three thousand a day, ninety-thousand a month. I still had to leave the house at seven-thirty in the morning, though; I could hardly tell my mother that I was going to the theatre to rehearse at two o'clock. I was the head of the family. My father had been seriously ill with diabetes for years and it would have

been a real worry to her. I used to hang around town until it was time to go to rehearsals. I only told her the day before the opening. Everything went fine." The company starts the new season in November 1948 with *As You Like It*; he is a noble in the court of the exiled Duke, played by Ruggero Ruggeri. For the first time he is acting alongside famous actors like Ruggero Ruggeri ("He never even replied when I said hello"), Rina Morelli, Vivi Gioi, Paolo Stoppa and many promising young actors like Vittorio Gassman, Gabriele Ferzetti, Luciano Salce.

His stubborn determination to work in film finally begins to bear fruit. In 1947 he gets a tiny role in Riccardo Freda's *Les Misérables*: "I had been haunting the production companies for two years by that time. They must have taken me out of desperation". At this time he is still living with his parents at the house of an uncle who worked for the railways, but when he starts to earn more money he rents an appartment for the whole family in the same Tuscolano quarter. Here he meets and has a brief love affair with a then unknown seventeen year old girl. The girl's name is Silvana Mangano and she later becomes one of the most famous and talented Italian actresses.

He stays in Visconti's theatre company until 1956 but does the majority of his theatre work in the first four years with the company. He plays Mitch in Tennessee Williams' *A Streetcar Named Desire*. The star part is played by Vittorio Gassman. The female roles are played by Vivi Gioi and Rina Morelli. A young actress called Flora Carabella plays the part of the nurse. It is the first time the two actors meet. In Alfieri's *Oreste* he plays Pylades. At first Visconti is unsure whether he can act in verse and thinks of replacing him with Giancarlo Sbragia. But he immediately changes his mind. Then he plays Diomedes in Shakespeare's *Troilus and Cressida*.

Not yet twenty-six, on the day of his marriage to Flora Carabella.

The young Mastroianni family, with little Barbara.

In Tragico ritorno *he performs for the first time along-side Doris Duranti. He will appear again in* The Divine Nymph *with this diva who was already famous in the 1940's.*

With Eleonora Rossi Drago in Sensualità *(Sensuality).*

On the 12th of August 1950 he marries Flora Carabella, daughter of the musician Ezio Carabella, composer of lyric operas, operettas, symphonic music and film music. In 1931 he was the composer of the music for Anton Giulio Bragaglia's film *Vele ammainate* (Down Sails). The witnesses at the wedding are the seasoned actors Tino Buazzelli and Paolo Panelli. In December his father dies. He carries on working in the theatre. In Arthur Miller's *Death of a Salesman* he plays the role of Joey. In the film *A Streetcar Named Desire* he plays the lead role of Stanley Kowalski. Flora Carabella plays the part of Eunice. On the 2nd of December 1951 their daughter, Barbara, is born.

On the 2nd of October 1952 Visconti's company presents the premiere of Carlo Goldoni's *La locandiera* (The Innkeeper's Wife), at the Venice Phoenix during the International Festival of Prose Theatre. Mastroianni plays the cavalier Ripafratta with Paolo Stoppa, Gianrico Tedeschi, Rina Morelli and Rossella Falk. Flora Carabella plays the part of Dejanira. On the 20th of December he plays the part of the captain Vasilij Vasilevic Solenji in Chekhov's *Three Sisters* at the Eliseo theatre in Rome. In 1955, while his wife joins the Compagnia dei Giovani (Young people's Theatre Company). He returns to the theatre with Morelli-Stoppa and, still under Visconti's direction, plays Michail Lvovic Astrov in Chekhov's *Uncle Vanja*. The theatrical phase of his career draws to a close in 1956 with three revivals. He plays Biff in *Death of a Salesman*, Michail Lvovic Astrov in *Uncle Vanja* and the cavalier Ripafratta in *La locandiera*. Early on, Visconti described Mastroianni as "the gawky lad who couldn't even say a line"; but after nine productions in ten years under Visconti, that boy has become an actor who is

beginning to make his presence felt in the cinema.

Film-acting has for some years now become his main activity. Quiet beginnings which bear the mark of the greater prestige of the theatre have snowballed and he now has dozens of titles to his name: *Passaporto per l'Oriente* (1949), *Una domenica d'agosto* (1950), *Vita da cani* (1950), *Cuori sul mare* (1950), *Contro la legge* (1950), *Atto d'accusa* (1951), *Parigi è sempre Parigi* (1951), *L'eterna catena* (1952), *Le ragazze di Piazza di Spagna* (1952), *Tragico ritorno* (1952), *Penne nere* (1952), *Sensualità* (1952), *Gli eroi della domenica* (1953), *Il viale della speranza* (1953), *Febbre di vivere* (1953), *Non è mai troppo tardi* (1953), *Lulù* (1953). These films represent that difficult period in Mastroianni's career when he was only starting in cinema. He could get parts because he was becoming known in the theatre but was never offered the leading role, as this was reserved, in most middle-of-the-road Italian cinema of this period, for those actors whose names were already well established. Aldo Fabrizi,

Amedeo Nazzari, Raf Vallone, Massimo Serato, Paolo Stoppa: these were the big box-office successes of the time, and the young Mastroianni could only manage to get the most marginal of roles. Very often actresses whose names were already better-known than his like Delia Scala, Tamara Lees, Ave Ninchi, Lea Padovani, Gianna Maria Canale, Lucia Bosè, Eleonora Rossi-Drago and Valentina Cortese take precedence in the scenes in which he appears, even in group stories where co-stars proliferate and events become intertwined.

Of all the characters he played in those years, perhaps the only one that Mastroianni really remembers is the character of Daniele in *Febbre di vivere* (Life Fever).

Another 'good' character but one determined to succeed against the odds. "I have always felt a profound sense of affection for Claudio Gora's film. For me it was a film very much before its time in that it dealt with certain themes which Italian cinema only later began to take an interest in. You could say paradoxically that it was almost a *Dolce vita* ante litteram. It started to move in a certain sphere, not as grandiose or as rich in images and situations as Fellini's film but it introduced a particular world, certain types of character which might seem rather extravagant, the rich middle class, who had rather fleeting relationships with others, with the masses. A curious little world of characters which contained a certain ambiguity, something which we were not yet familiar with. For me it was something new, to play these characters who had a certain dose of cynicism, a dark side which wasn't common to everyone."

Films over-lap and the images become confused. "I worked in the theatre in the evening and in the cinema during the day. They were films I took part in between plays. This explains the enormous number of films I did in those few years. I would often be in a film for just four or five days. I used to appear, hang around working for a few days and then leave again. It's not surprising I have a very vague memory of those occasions, though I wouldn't want to seem ungrateful to the people who gave me work. And anyhow, let's be honest, lots of films were made then just to make a bit of money; they were just bits of things that you forget about and more important things take their place, things you spend more time on."

With Nita Dover, Novella Parigini and Paola Mori in Febbre di vivere, *a sort of* Dolce Vita *ante litteram.*

One of the characters he has probably forgotten is his Carlo Danesi in *Vita da cani* (It's a Dog's Life) by Mario Monicelli and Steno. He makes his appearance in the film on a bicycle wearing a black leather bomber-jacket like those worn by American airmen. He goes to collect his girlfriend (Tamara Lees), who is just finishing her shift at a factory in Milan. They go back to his house in the working-class district, Bovisa. The girl is tired of the miserable life she leads and has decided to leave him a few days before they are due to be married and go off to seek her fortune. But first she wants to make love to him. Carlo doesn't understand her; he is so sure that the invention he is working on, designed to reduce the energy consumption of a mechanical loom, will make them rich one day. But Franca is impatient and wants to find someone who can give her the comfortable life she so desires. When he realises what her intentions are he responds by

slapping her. The young man's face, sweet, good-natured, so sure that sooner or later he will make it, is the face of a patient man. Still very stiff, his reaction to a declaration which is supposed to ruin his life is almost imperceptible. He only makes one other brief appearance in the film when the old industrial baron whom Franca has married and who is unaware of their past relationship, presents him to his wife as a talented young man, the right arm of his business: "He's going places this young man".

A prophetic film *Vita da cani* and one which takes its place in Mastroianni's filmography alongside the other films he has made with the director Luciano Emmer.

Sunday in August, *Parigi è sempre Parigi* (Paris Is Always Paris), *Girls of the Spanish Street*, and a bit later *The Bigamist* and *The Most Wonderful Moment* in which he finally has a fine leading role, are all so many stages in a process as Mastroianni develops within Italian cinema and in his character-type which is gradually evolving from the proletarian towards the middle-class. Inevitably this process is itself a reflection of post-war Italian society in evolution during the difficult period of reconstruction. The cinema begins to abandon images of a reality of the kind presented in the films of neo-realism and starts to present images of the middle-class in recovery. While actors like Tognazzi and Sordi use

In Sunday in August, *a film that enjoyed considerable success in France, he played a policeman. "He was delightful as the cop with his pregnant girlfriend." On this occasion, Mastroianni was dubbed by Alberto Sordi. Was this due to the cinema's mistrust of his voice at that time, or to theatre engagements elsewhere?*

Paris Is Always Paris: he begins mass tourism.

comedy to directly represent the country's more immediate problems and preoccupations, Mastroianni, whose talents lie more in light comedy and drama, is left to interpret the more personal dramas, love stories, jealousies, betrayals, lovers' tiffs. In short the history of man's relationship with the opposite sex including the existential *malheur* of the films of Fellini and Antonioni.

Modest traffic-cop in the deserted streets of the city in the stifling heat of the summer when everyone has gone off to the seaside; office-worker who speaks a little French and quarrels with his fiancée while on a trip to Paris; extrovert and generous taxi-driver who helps to sort out the problems of the young workers in Rome's Piazza di Spagna; in reality they mark the end of a season. That time of life in youth when family responsibilities still seem a long way off. Then all of a sudden the honest, good-natured young man in search of a wife finds himself up in Court for having not one but two in *The Bigamist*. Now the moral, upstanding individual, that mainly dramatic character of the early films, gives way to a travelling salesman who flirts with the wives and daughters of absent businessmen, giving each the same perfume so he can palm off his other goods on them. He even manages to make up to his own wife, overcoming her jealousy by smothering her with kisses. Much acclaimed the year before for his light comedy roles with Sophia Loren in Blasetti's productions, Mastroianni is only really convincing in the film's initial lighter phase. In the second half of the film, when he finds himself in prison on a charge of bigamy, the characterization requires a certain amount of ambiguity to create the right measure of suspense. Instead he appears weak and unconvincing. His lawyer, played by De Sica, who has agreed to defend him only if he is guilty, is a powerful and imposing presence and it is he who really dominates the scene.

The almost psychoanalytical line taken

by his defence lawyer leaves him perplexed: "Bigamy, bigamy. The last case of bigamy I undertook was in 1946. Just after the end of the war. A really brilliant case, in Trapano. I based the whole line of defence on the desire to escape, which is tied to the very essence of the individual. Man, the human being, gentlemen, tends to forget facts, places, events, people, things which are distasteful to him. A sort of vacuum forms in his psyche, a wall is constructed, blocking off his memory. And inside this space he builds isolated compartments, tombs in which he buries all the dross, the filth, all the bad things he has done and as a result he feels free, liberated. Free to start again, free to start over doing the same things he has done before, as in the case of Mr. De Santis, here." In his cell, Mastroianni-De Santis bites his nails and chews over the story about the wall: "The lawyer says that we have a wall in here and behind it are all the memories. What if I had forgotten? Sure, you can forget something if you want to, that's easy." He alludes to his wife, played by Franca Valeri, who in the film is made to appear grotesque and distasteful.

His last encounter with Emmer is in 1957. "*The Most Wonderful Moment* wasn't one of his best. His best work was in the films where he dealt with the mundane things of everyday life. When we were in Paris making *Parigi è sempre Parigi* (It's Still Paris After All), they were showing *Sunday in August*, the first film I did with him, and he was really well-known. In fact *Sunday in August* was a big success; it had something new and different about it and was a sort of forerunner of Italian-style comedy which dealt with the little problems or big moments that even ordinary people have. Emmer managed to apply the same formula of neo-realism to the everyday problems of the Italians. In the first films I made there was an almost Manichean distinction between good and bad; and it was more difficult to find characters which were a bit

less two-dimensional. I always ended up playing the part of the good guy who takes all the raps even if everything usually turned out fine in the end. After a while my characters started to evolve a little, moving away from the one-sided good characters of the initial period towards a more complicated individual with a few grey areas. In other words they started to become more ambiguous, more hypocritical. They followed the same path that each of us follows in life, and then again perhaps the kind of youth I interpreted was not so far from the truth. Young men today are much more complicated than I was."

In *The Most Wonderful Moment* Doctor Valeri runs a painless childbirth course.

Embracing the lawyer De Sica in The Bigamist.

Elevated to doctor, Mastroianni addresses the issue of painless childbirth, at the height of its topicality in the 1950's.

Promoted to the role of doctor, Mastroianni dedicates himself to the difficult question that was the topic of the day in 1950's Italy. In fact only the most illuminated doctors and religious men of the time thought that the most wonderful moment in a woman's life, when she gives birth to a child, could really become the most wonderful moment if freed from pain. Most people used the biblical quote "you shall give birth in pain" to support the idea of pain as a moral necessity. "If you take away from a woman the joy of pain, you leave her humiliated, mortified; you will have taken away her glory, the halo of martyrdom. Martyrdom is the triumph of motherhood." The words of a respected profes-

sor in the film, unconsciously inspired by a long tradition of sado-masochistic relationships between men and women.

Emmer's film contains some intense moments which chronicle the epoch, but it doesn't manage to find the right balance between the development of its theme and the treatment of the relationships between the film's characters. The love story between Mastroianni and Giovanna Ralli, doctor and nurse in the film, who carry on an affair in secret, leave each other and then reunite, remains a superficial pretext for the intellectual argument of the film which is closer to the director's heart. It is a fault of the film which neverthless highlights the director's continued interest in

the social problems of his day, an interest which Mastroianni shares.

It is no coincidence that the treatment of *The Most Wonderful Moment* is by Vasco Pratolini, author of the novel *Cronache di poveri amanti* (Chronicles of Poor Lovers), which Carlo Lizzani based a film on in 1954. In both cases one of the screenwriters is Carlo Amidei, an author who distinguishes himself among cinema writers for his dedication in representing a certain Italian social reality. Set in Florence during the early years of the Fascist regime, it recounts the lives of a group of young people who are opposed to the regime and who end up paying for their ideals of liberty with their lives. *Cronache di poveri amanti* was to be Mastroianni's first experience of producing a film with a cooperative. His ideals being very much the same as the film-director's, Mastroianni agrees to work on the film for no immediate recompense in order to work on a project that he believes in. There had already been numerous attempts to adapt Pratolini's novel to the big screen; Visconti himself had wanted to produce a large-scale work ever since the book's publication.

In Lizzani's film the main characters are reduced to a handful and the events are given a stronger political interpretation. Mastroianni plays the part of Ugo, a travelling fruit and vegetable vendor, lighthearted and amiable. "The love, the love that makes my heart beat," he sings while stripped to the waist to perform his morning toilette. Then he approaches the lady of the house, his mistress, and kisses her on the neck, just as her husband happens to enter. Apparently superficial and unconcerned about the consequences of his actions he is accused by his anti-fascist friend, Maciste, of having only two ideas in his head: women and gambling. But he retorts: "Whenever there has been anything real to do I've always been the first in line. I prefer to do things, not stand around thinking about them." Always

With Anna Maria Ferrero in Cronache di poveri amanti (Diary of Poor Lovers), *which evokes a particulary grim moment in Italian history.*

29

In Anatomy of Love, *on the steps of the church, where Marcello and Lea Padovani intend to abandon their baby son.*

ready for action, he taunts the others with cowardice and carries on as before until the time comes when action is needed.

In the intimate world of Via del Corno, where all the characters live, the joys and pains of each become everybody's concern. *Cronache* carries the impact of a choral work and in its compact construction becomes a detailed fresco of a moment in Italy's history, that time of violence and repression in the mid-1920's. At the same time, with historical perspective, events are seen in the light of the moral climate of the Resistance. The moral heroes of the film are therefore conscious of the situation they are living in and act with lucid awareness. In one scene in a brothel, Ugo, with characteristic impulsiveness, expresses his disgust for the uselessness of political action to a fascist who is badly treated by his comrades: "With politics you always have to throw something on the pack. You lose your friends; your business starts to go badly; all so as you don't have to give up on your ideas. Of course my ideas aren't exactly the same as yours but I can give you one piece of good advice: stuff 'em'."

But as soon as he is told by the same person that the anti-fascist activists are going to be caught and punished, he doesn't hesitate to put his own life in danger by going and warning them. In the night raid Maciste is killed by the fascists. Ugo is wounded but is saved by Gesuina, the maid of the Signora, who herself plays the double role of street guardian angel and usurer. Hidden in the girl's room, Ugo undergoes a transformation. Rejected by Gesuina whom he tries to make love to, he explains his transformation to her: "You're right to treat me like this. If I stop to think that until yesterday I lived like a... But a night like tonight is enough to last for a hundred years. An experience like this can change a man's life completely. You can't understand, can you Gesuina? What right have I to expect you to understand?"

The cruel injustices of *Cronache* seem to

follow Mastroianni into the next film he makes with Alessandro Blasetti, *Anatomy of Love* in the episode *Il pupo* (The Kid). Here he is content to back up Lea Padovani, who plays a mother resplendent in her instinctive, maternal love. They are two paupers, parents to a horde of children who decide to abandon the latest arrival because they are unable to provide for it. It is he who sets in motion the mechanism and who would like to carry it through but in the end, incapable of the cynicism and desperation required by such an act, he finally gives up on the idea. Long-bearded and down-at-heel, Macilento, in some way epit-

omizes the 'defeated' character type so typical of post-war Italian cinema. But his resignation has another side to it: a fatalistic hope of good luck, in which he has a sort of fundamental belief. A belief in the ability to survive which is so common among poor people; a sense of hope for the future reconstruction of the country which was just getting under way in the early fifties.

"I really must say how much Blasetti has always believed in me. He saw me in the theatre in *Orestes* and in a way became my talent scout. He was immediately convinced that I could make it in the cinema, took me on as a protégé and gave me this

role to do in *Il pupo*, a really nice piece. For the first time I felt I had it in me to play a character with dramatic aspects, a really human character. The brief episode was pervaded with a sense of melancholy, the melancholy of poverty. Then he gave me roles in *Too Bad She's Bad* and *Lucky to Be a Woman*, both with Sophia Loren, whom I had met some years before as an extra while I was making *Cuori sul mare* (Hearts on the Sea). I met up with Blasetti again many years later in *Io, io, io... e gli altri* (Me, Me, Me... and the Others), which I took part in largely in homage to the old maestro."

His appearance in 1966 in Io, io, io... e gli altri *alongside Walter Chiari is merely a tribute to the old maestro of Italian cinema, Alessandro Blasetti.*

2

He's Not Dangerous, He's Good

A moment of abandonment for Mario and Natalia.

In spite of many years of patient work, Mastroianni is not yet a famous actor. He has not yet found a director capable of exploiting his acting talents to the full and above all capable of helping him to develop the kind of character which audiences can really identify with. He might be defined as the good but luckless actor. None of the roles he has interpreted so far have produced the popularity he deserves or the acclaim which could put him on a level with Raf Vallone and Gabriele Ferzetti. Could *Too Bad She's Bad* be the chance he is looking for?

A deserted summer Sunday afternoon in Rome. Paolo cleans and polishes his taxi and Lina and her two friends get themselves a lift to the seaside. She gaily sings "Bingo, bango bongo you're only fine in the Congo, I'm not going nowhere, oh no". They get to the seaside and while she allows Paolo to flirt with her, her two friends set about trying to steal his taxi. These are the opening scenes of *Too Bad She's Bad*, a fast-moving hilarious comedy which also stars Vittorio De Sica playing a thief specialised in stealing suitcases at Rome's central station, Termini. His specialist tool is a bottomless suitcase which he places over the suitcase he intends to steal, holding it in place with a large spring. Marcello and Vittorio meet in a workshop; one is there looking for the thieves and the other is there getting his spring repaired.

When the mechanic warns De Sica that an outsider has come in, the thief replies with a look which says: "Don't worry. He's harmless". The stamp of innocence is to stay with Mastroianni for a few years yet, even though the films where he appears more cynical and urbane are beginning to alternate with those in which he is all good. The story written by the screenwriters Suso Cecchi d'Amico, Alessandro Continenza and Ennio Flaiano reduces the characters to types. There is the fanatically honest taxi-driver who bears the marks of the war; all that remains in memory of his family, lost in a bombing raid during the war, is his mother's wedding ring which he wears on his right, ring finger. Then there is the two-faced thief: De Sica plies his trade in all seriousness, according to certain rules, not like "young people today, a lost generation. They don't respect their work, they don't want to try hard; they still believe in the black market, in adventure. I know that life isn't like that; it's hard, hard work, day after day." The art of getting by has come to be a sort of regular job for him. He doesn't make a distinction between honesty and dishonesty and, instinctively, he carries on a Catholic tradition of the double truth: at one and the same time the unrepenting thief and the caring father who brings his daughter up to be a perfect housewife. And of course he must have assurances about the financial possibilities of the young man who is courting her: "In his own way, you could say that a driver has a certain standing. Of course, on principle, I wouldn't have been

From Too Bad She's Bad *onwards, Mastroianni and Loren become one of the longest-lasting partnerships in Italian cinema.*

in favour. What are you up to, marrying into the middle class? Nowadays they don't do anything exept read write and think. They think and others get on and do".

There is also the girl who makes use of her looks with the same ease and naturalness as she picks pockets. Talkative, easygoing, dishonest, strictly logical, she so takes the taxi-driver in with her inexorable

Blasetti discusses a scene from Too Bad She's Bad *with Marcello and Sophia. "I won a 'Nastro d'argento' and a 'Grolla d'oro' for this film, which my mother pawned immediately at Monte di Pietà, the government pawnshop. I went there too, and the pawn-broker said to me quite kindly: 'Look Mr Mastroianni', (I had already made a number of films by then, and was quite popular with the public) 'there's no need to feel embarrassed - I won't name names, but you wouldn't believe who's been here'. They gave me 120 000 lira."*

assault that all he can do is give in. In vain he tries to prepare himself in advance for their meetings, producing monologues in which he manages to become a little aggressive; but he never succeeds in overcoming the girl's irrepressible self confidence. Aware of his excessive amenabilty, he castigates himself: "imbecile, cretin, idiot, fool". Whatever happens he ends up somehow the loser; he is the legal face of a society which is showing the strain after the conflict. The others, small-time profiteers, react in precisely the opposite way to the same problems.

De Sica's children, Lina's brothers, who get on and steal the taxi-drivers' tyres, are straight out of *Shoe-Shine*, an exposé of post-war ills.

Mastroianni's career does not seem to be moving in the direction of greater quality and he carries on with minor films like *La principessa delle Canarie* (The Princess of the Canaries) by Paolo Moffa. It is a costume role in which he plays a Spanish Cap-

With Memmo Carotenuto and Giacomo Furia, two well-known comic faces.

With the native princess Silvana Pampanini.

tain who falls in love with a native princess, and with it he makes the first of what are destined to become many transfers abroad. "It is a film that I would like to see again because I have always felt that I made a ridiculous Spanish Captain, in doublet and hose; I don't even know how to ride a horse or fence. It was stiflingly hot in the Canary islands during the summer and I had to wear two or even three pairs of tights to make my legs seem more muscular, so I felt extremely ridiculous and unhappy. I would

like to see that film again, perhaps one evening with friends so that I can laugh at myself. It happens sometimes, my goodness how often it happens that you find yourself laughing at old films. Yes, but look at what a ridiculous face I had, and I expected to do goodness knows what. At that time I used to complain that they didn't give me enough satisfaction, enough space. How could they? I was ridiculous with my beardless chin and my expressionless face. When we are older there is more intensity, apart

from the experience we have gained which is also important. When I was young and I had this sacred, burning desire to perform, I felt that I was misunderstood. But now, many years later, when I see myself again, I find myself saying: on the contrary they were all too generous to give me any work at all."

Tam-tam Mayumbe by Gian Gaspare Napolitano "was another absurd adventure, this time in Africa, as we ended up in the French Congo, an amazing, incredible thing, but as far as I can see completely senseless. It was a very expensive film. We were isoloated up there, exposed even, exposed to the risk of snake bites and goodness knows what else. Half the team went down with malaria. It was hellish, it seemed like war-time. Then I made *La ragazza della salina* (The Girl of the Salt-Works), a Yugoslav-German adventure which then became an Italian co-production as well. It was the first time that I had worked with foreigners. It was with Bavaria Film, a German production company. The story was set in a salt-works near Trieste and I played a fisherman."

In *The Miller's Beautiful Wife*, a remake by Mario Camerini of his previous film *The Three-Cornered Hat* featuring Peppino and Eduardo De Filippo, he appears again with Sophia Loren. The next year the same group that made *Too Bad She's Bad*, with the exception of De Sica who is replaced by Charles Boyer, gets together for another film. *Lucky to Be a Woman* is in fact to be a general screen-test for *La Dolce Vita*. Not yet a journalist, he plays a paparazzo who moves in the worlds of cinema and fashion, rubbing shoulders with divas and models. He is part of the same artificial world made up of the camera's flash and the glare of the spotlight.

The diva's flight arrives. A bunch of photographers rushes to get the first shot of her. Corrado, clinging to the aeroplane steps, is the most audacious of them all: "Marilina, Marilina" he shouts, with an explicit allusion to the film star of the period. As she turns round, he snaps a shot of her. Unashamed paparazzo to the core, he feels no remorse at stealing a shot of Antonietta as she lifts up her skirt to check a run in her tights. The photo ends up on the cover of a weekly girlie magazine and sets the film's mechanism in motion. The girl demands damages. He replies by suggesting that this could be the start of a brilliant career, and with a swagger gives her the number of a top designer. The number, of course, is false. When they next meet he invites her to pose for him in her swimming costume. When she protests at his lack of gallantry, he replies that on the contrary there are certain tricks that he would not stoop to to get what he wanted.

An active male character, he has a seductive rather than audacious approach to sex; with much tact and constant denials, he nevertheless tries it on. His attitude towards women is more confident. This time it is he who takes the initiative, even if he continues to claim to be a 'fool'. In reality he seems all too cynical about the cinema world, about his profession, about women. He plays the anti-hero. "The important thing in life is getting on. Five years ago I studied day and night. I wanted to get a degree; a load of balls. God knows what got into me. I could have ended up in the nut house. Who's driving me to it, I ask you? But here I just snatch a photo of a big man with his girlfriend, or a film star pulling faces and bingo !" "And are you happier?" "It keeps the money coming in." Just a scripted line or a piece of self-irony on his own history, the fact that he has given up his studies for the cinema? While lacking the pace of *Too Bad She's Bad*, the film is very good at wittily satirizing some of the conventions of the period. The female characters, whether they are chaste

The Mastroianni-Loren partnership continues with The Miller's Beautiful Wife.

upper-middle-class young ladies or working-class girls with a racier lifestyle, all have one ambition in life: marriage. A good one, naturally. Their first concern is always to find out if the man in question is available: "Are you married?"

For their part, the men are into more concrete concerns and believe that the girls say no, in obedience to the morals of the day, but in fact mean yes. Corrado in true male-chauvinist mould slaps his girl on the backside as he adjusts his belt. For him sex, naturally seen from the male point of view, is what makes the world go round: "If only I had your luck." "What's that?" "The luck of being a woman. I'd have them all falling for me one after the other". A touch of cinephilia creeps into the film when he paraphrases a quote from *Miracolo a Milano* (Miracle in Milan): "Who knows where these legs will take you!"

The constant references to the previous film emphasize the film's already strong characteristics of a sequel. When Corrado addresses her familiarly, Antonietta replies: "What's all this chumminess? Have we been out stealing together sometime?" The two actors are playing on a level and both have an equal share of one-liners and close-ups. They also have to play up to the satirical comments the screenwriters have written into the script at their expense. The sharp jibes against Sophia Loren are countless: "You certainly find some real brainless people" the butcher whom she has mistaken for the famous designer comments

With Sophia Loren, who plays the aspiring model in Lucky to be a Woman.

The photographer he plays in Lucky to be a Woman *anticipates the tabloid journalist of* La Dolce Vita.

when she telephones him. She asks Boyer, the most important casting director of the city, "What's Archaeology ?", and he replies, "Nothing to worry about, my dear." "I want you to teach me how to be a lady." "Believe me, my dear, it would take too long."

Open to change as an actor and curious by nature, Mastroianni loves to constantly vary his characters. He seems to enjoy surprising audiences with the widely differing role-choices he makes as he works together with directors who choose him partly because he has already chosen them. In the case of Luchino Visconti the collaboration is a long-standing one. In *White Nights* Visconti is expert in drawing out of Mastroianni many of his hidden capacities. Intimidated and lost in the face of what is happening, he is the lower middle class character of low-key comedy having to face up to life's big decisions. Affairs of the heart, the birth of passion, a meeting with destiny. In reality the director chooses him for what he is and for the experience he has gained in his previous roles. But for the

The couple face their destiny in Livorno (which has been totally re-created in the studio).

With Luchino Visconti and Maria Schell, during the filming of White Nights, *one of the films he also helped produce.*

actor it is an important event to find himself on the set with Visconti. Finally the director, who knows him so well, is able to give him an opportunity which he could not give him in the theatre. Under Visconti's demanding eye Mastroianni searches earnestly for the right tone to express the confusion of someone who feels unequal to the task set before him, but he manages at the same time to express the fragility and tenderness of his manhood. At this difficult margin between fragility and tenderness the character is born. It is a flash, an intuition, something which takes shape during the course of the film and never becomes concrete for very long but for the young actor it is a conquest and a promise of things to come.

He shares the set with Maria Schell, an actress who is better known than he is and who can help make a commercial success of the film. But in spite of being awarded the "Leone d'argento" at the 18th Venice Film Festival, the film is not a box-office success. It ends up incurring heavy losses for those involved in its making; having set out with the object of small budget production, they instead found themselves caught up in an expensive project. The town where the action is set, Livorno, was reconstructed at Cinecittà because the director wanted everything to appear false, like a theatre backdrop. Instead of using the usual cinema smoke, the effect of mist was created by using yards and yards of tulle which produced a more immobile atmosphere.

In a small seaside town, groups of workers move through the mist, taking a stroll before turning in for the night: barflies, delinquent youths, tramps who sleep under the bridges, sad-looking prostitutes. But Natalia and Mario, the two leading characters, are nearly always alone. He finds her weeping on a bridge and in spite of his declared timidity asks to walk her home. The following night the girl tells him her story. She lives alone with her grandmother who is virtually blind and to earn some money, in addition to repairing old carpets, they also rent one of their rooms. Natalia has fallen in love with the latest lodger who promised to return for her when he left a year ago. And so from that day she has waited for him every night on the bridge.

For Mario it is the discovery of an exceptional capacity to love: "Perhaps I'm foolish but I didn't think that girls like you existed any more. You see, for me, its like believing in fairytales again." When Natalia asks his advice, even though he already knows what he is going to do, he gives a common-sense answer: "You have to get things clear." But when the girl gives him a letter to deliver to the lodger he is unable to believe that it is his own younger brother.

In the film Mastroianni plays the messenger of love, low-voiced and mournful; a real change from his roles as the handsome good guy, the one all the women are in love with. He is tempted to burn the letter, then he tears it up. Like Natalia, he too wants to deny the evidence. He takes her to a night club and tries to seduce her. He performs a solo surrounded by applauding onlookers. His jerky movements give him a puppet-like appearance and his suit and tie set him apart from the rest in their black pullovers. He expresses his lack of well-being, his not-belonging, his sense of being different,which manifests itself in his awkwardness and hesitancy.

It is in some senses too a sort of initiation ceremony. "Now, I too can say I have been dancing" says Natalia. And he says: "Now, I too can say I have been happy." He allows himself to be seduced by the idea of being in love but in the end he can only manage to love the idea. "Listen, Natalia, look, I, I really feel something for you, I love you. I'm in love." But Natalia refuses to give up on her dream. For a moment she seems to waver but she immediately repents: "I've betrayed him".

Mario (perhaps Visconti's *alter-ego*?), lets

He discovers fatherhood in The Tailor's Maid. *"This film tells the story of a boy who is brought to live with me. At first I don't accept him, but then, when his mother comes to take him back again, I realize how lonely it had been before he arrived, so much so, that my wife and I decide to adopt a child."*

himself go in a moment of exasperation: "If they're not tarts, they're off their heads." Later he confesses to tearing up the letter: "I was only thinking about myself. I told you I didn't believe in fairytales, and I myself was starting to believe in mine." When he thinks that the lodger will never show up, the unimportant office worker with his little grey life believes for a moment that he has been given one more chance, and he again makes his declaration of love: "I am such an ordinary man, so insignificant." At that moment, in the distance, the lodger appears.

As the two characters come to grips during the course of the film, Mario grows in credibility and wins the audience's sympathy. Natalia on the other hand seems false and irritating. She is a decisive woman who knows what she wants but manifests in a rather puppet-like manner a sort of adolescent uncertainty, the appearance of trepida-

tion, whereas in fact she is merely marking time. The two levels of existence place heavy demands on the actress, and she is in the end unable to give credibility to the sense of pleasure in being with Mario while at the same time not wanting to give up on her dream. The fragility is entirely external, since the truth is that she has already made her decision and her only fear is that her dream might not coincide with reality.

Houses still in ruins after the bombings,

mist, rain, wet streets, stones shining in the rain, canals, stagnant water; the external scenario of internal solitude, of a labyrinth of unresolved emotions, of the elemental relationship with the great water-mother. The beauty of the film lies in the way it puts each character on the spot and places him or her before the most frightening thing that each of us must face: ourselves. It is a typically Russian attitude which Visconti has successfully managed to translate. The artificial mists of a recreated Livorno carry the stamp of Dostoevsky.

Only a few months before, Mastroianni had played two roles of a less demanding nature but which reflected in full a certain Italian social reality. *The Tailor's Maid* of 1957 and *Il medico e lo stregone* (The Doctor and the Magician) are linked in various ways. They both share the same director, Mario Monicelli, the same producer, and the same actors. The casts in both are large, and the stories intertwine. *The Tailor's Maid* is in fact made up of a series of sketches joined together to make a film. Mastroianni stars with Franco di Trocchio, a little boy whom Monicelli had discovered in a slum quarter of Rome. The piece, by Leo Benvenuti, centers around a couple who are unable to have children and must have been written from experience as Benvenuti himself was childless. Appropriately, the film's Italian title is *Padri e figli* (Fathers and Sons).

One of the children in a large family falls ill with the measles. In order to avoid infection the parents decide to send the other children to stay with various friends and relations. Alvaruccio goes to the house of uncle Cesare. "In *The Tailor's Maid* I did a beautiful piece with a little boy. There were lots of parallel stories about the relationships between parents and children. I was the only childless relation and I suddenly found myself with a little nephew running around the house whom I consequently became very attached to because I led a lonely existence. My relationship with my wife had become tired and sour, probably because we had no children."

Initially cool, the uncle little by little grows to love his nephew to the point that he really suffers when the child has to return to his family. As a result, he and his wife decide to adopt a child. At the orphanage, however, he is unable to choose: "You can't choose children as if they were artichokes. I like them all. You see, I don't want to hurt any of them." He wants a child to be chosen for him instead. This film adds to Mastroianni's range of lower-middle-class characters and is a role played in undertones on a rather solitary note. The film is a great success and is awarded a prize at the Berlin Film Festival.

After the success of *The Tailor's Maid* the producer decides to do another film with Monicelli. But *Il medico e lo stregone* in spite of its prize at Karlovy Vary is a run-of-the-mill production. "*Il medico e lo stregone* was nice but not the most interesting of films, I would say." Mastroianni plays a doctor, the first real medical practitioner to arrive in a small village which up until that time had been cured by the healer, Don Antonio. His antagonist is played by De Sica. In the scenes where both characters appear, Marcello appears hesitant and overwhelmed by the other's overbearing self-confidence. Almost like a pupil before a demanding and rather condescending master. The film does have the great merit, on the other hand, of making the actor aware of this impotence; this brings out his violence in those moments when he is alone. He blames not only the charlatan who is willing to use whatever means are necessary to maintain his leadership, but also the peasants who listen to him: "Bastards, wretches, pigs, pigs, pigs," he yells as he wrecks the furniture in his clinic. It is the same meek character's violence that we have seen break out in other films, and seems to express the impotence of the Latin male who becomes aggressive because of his weakness in in the face of matriarchal power.

In the little world of Pianetta near Naples where the film is supposedly set, the women are assigned only subordinate roles. In the peasant society all of them can be identified through family or social ties with a male character, a co-protagonist. Clamide is Don Antonio's grandaughter, Mafalda is the Mayor's sister, Pasqua the doctor's maid and assistant.

During the fifties, Mastroianni is in films based both in the country and in the town. From the sixties onwards, apart from a few brief excursions, these definitely become town-based. As does Italian cinema for that matter. His award-winning and well received films alternate between the two territories. *Days of Love* by Giuseppe De Santis won him his first 'Nastro d'argento'. "I enjoyed playing this charming peasant in De Santis' film; of course there was an element of returning to my roots, as the action took place in Ciociaria and I am from those parts. It was a little sentimental trip to my home ground. I have fond memories of the film."

His next transfer to the Italian countryside, a setting which has never been exploited enough by Italian cinema, comes about when he makes a film with the French director Jules Dassin. "I have never felt that *Where the Hot Wind Blows* was a successful film, even though parts of it were really good. It is always difficult for a foreign director to deal with aspects of a country which he does not know in real depth. And then the film started out badly for Dassin; he encountered real trouble getting it edited, and I think he had to accept all sorts of compromises. I'm saying this without knowing exactly all the details of the affair, just going on what I could understand through his occasional outbursts. The most interesting thing in the whole situation was the discovery of Dassin, a really talented director whom I had not had the chance to get to know close-to. He really is extraordinary in the way he deals with actors, having been an

In Days of Love, *Marina Vlady and Mastroianni play two peasants in love, who have to overcome many obstacles before they are able to marry.*

actor himself. It is just a pity that I happened to meet him in an unfortunate film. It was made in Rodi Garganico in the Gargano, not in Corsica, as the Italian dubbing would have one believe."

He won the "Grolla d'oro" for his role in *Too Bad She's Bad* and his second "Nastro d'argento" for *White Nights*. In the same year, 1958, he is invited to appear on *Musichiere*, a popular television quiz programme of the time. A return to the stage with Valentina Cortese seems imminent but nothing comes of it. In the meantime, Mastroianni returns to the country, to the valleys of Comacchio in Casadio's Film *Un ettaro di cielo*. (A Hectare of Sky). He travels around in his van marked "Great Representations" to the fairs of the lower Po Valley. Generous, good looking and jovial, he is also something of a lady-killer, and there is much of his earlier role as the travelling salesman in *The Bigamist* in his characterization. A seductive braggart, he gives free rein to his fantasy. "I am sentimentally attached to this film, as one often is with works which have had less popular success. It was the work of a new director, Aglauco Casadio, who had already produced some very interesting documentaries, and it was also virtually the first film for Tonino Guerra, who at that time was just starting out in cinema, but afterwards became one of the best Italian screenwriters. He had left his home town in the Romagna and made his first moves towards the cinema as a poet and a writer with this story for Casadio. The film was a curious fairytale, which I liked tremendously. I put a lot of enthusiasm into its making and I think it was a good film; in fact it had very good critical reviews. It was a story about those groups of people who travel around the provinces, especially of the lower Po, in their vans. This travelling salesman of words, who managed to enchant people with his talk, used to sell hectares of sky to the ingenuous old inhabitants of the valleys where they raised eels; really off the beaten track. The film was interesting but perhaps lacking in credibility for a public used to much more realistic stories and not accustomed to tales of fantasy in cinema."

Severino arrives in the marshlands of the Po amid the joyous greetings of three old people who get him to give them a lift in his Balilla. At the hostelry he meets up again with Marina (Rosanna Schiaffino), whom he greets by asking, on his knees, what she has been eating to turn out like she has. In the village square he plies his trade, showing the peasants a marmot which has survived the H-Bomb thanks to a miraculous powder of which he is the only dealer. He goes to eat fish with some of the old peasants and fascinates them with an amazing proposal made to him by a friend from Rome. "But that's an entirely different thing, really big business, the kind few of us ever do in our lives, not for money, though; more for the thing itself. You'll never guess what in a million years. It's the sky. They're selling it off in lots, like pieces of cake." He does not have any trouble convincing them that it is an opportunity not to be missed. "Just think of the no-access you could put up and stop the aeroplanes from passing. If they come on my territory I'll stop them. This is my property; if you want to go through you'll have to pay. And woe betide anyone who doesn't stop; they'll have to pay a fine. Let's just say for the sake of argument that a comet arrives in your space. It's just priceless; a spectacle that you give the whole world. The least you can do is put a tax on their binoculars." Back in the village, he finds Marina again, but with her his silken words are useless and he has to give up. "After all, I have given up all the things I love. I used to love football, travel, the Cote d'Azur, old aeroplanes. Life is all about giving things up and now I don't enjoy myself any more. I know too many things."

While the old people are making up their minds to commit suicide in order to get to their hectare of sky as soon as possi-

Theatrical gestures and fast talking are the hallmarks of Severino Balestra, the unusual itinerant of Un ettaro di cielo.

ble, having scraped together their savings to buy it, Severino is courting Marina on a boat. The boat is shaded by a big umbrella, and Severino imagines that he is setting off around the world. The girl, who is a realist, remarks that at the most they will arrive at Goro: "Look here, Marina, if we are going to get on, you mustn't contradict me when I invent something. If we can't enjoy our-selves like this it is all over." They meet Germinal, one of the old people, who tells them that the others have all gone to drown themselves. Severino doesn't believe it. "And you come and tell me about it. Why I'm the man who taught the chickens to ride a bicycle." And he sings: "The chicken that on a bicycle goes, keeps going fast and never slows."

Day-dreaming or half-asleep in a boat with Rosanna Schiaffino.

When he realises that the old people really are in danger, he rushes desperately to their aid but finds them safe and sound. After an initial outburst of joy he turns on them in rage: "You're worse than children; people can't say anything to you. You shouldn't have done it to me, you shouldn't have done it to me". And he bursts into tears.

It is the discomfiture of someone who is caught out lying and sees his own defects amplified in others, of someone who realises that imagination, that very excess of imagination which is his livelihood, can also be a dangerous thing. The principal of his own pleasure is at odds with other people's reality and it leads to death. In an interpretation which centres on the naïve, the actor manages to express perfectly the immaturity of the man and the misconduct of the child. Here too we are given a glimpse of Mastroianni's self-irony: "I may have my faults, but where can you find a more serious man than I am?". The film's other screenwriters, together with the director and Tonino Guerra, are Elio Petri and Ennio Flaiano. It is a powerful mix which manages to create dialogues which contain some acute truths about Mastroianni. The actor himself takes part in the game and is expert in playing up to the screenwriters' satire.

Mastroianni has by this time become a sure thing. He co-stars with Gassman, Totò and Salvatori in Mario Monicelli's *The Big Deal on Madonna Street*, a cult-movie of the time. Secondary roles are played by Tiberio Murgia, Carla Gravina, Carlo Piasacane, Memmo Carotenuto and, for the first time on the big screen, a very young Claudia Cardinale. The origins of the film are rather complicated. In some ways it is born from the ruins of *White Nights*. The co-producers of Visconti's film, reunited under the title CIAS, decided to re-use the extremely expensive reproduction of Livorno which they had built at Cinecittà. They were thinking of a low-budget film to be produced using the same back-drop. In the end they dismantled the set but the film itself, based on the story of some small time thieves who might have

The spare arm of the artist/photographer of The Big Deal on Madonna Street.

Marcello plans the grand-slam with Tiberio Murgia, Carlo Pisacane, and Renato Salvatori.

operated in that kind of down-town setting, began to take shape.

Age, Scarpelli, Monicelli and Suso Cecchi d'Amico had all thought of a sort of parody of *Rififi*. Drawing their inspiration from newspaper articles which talked about "the usual nobodies", house-breakers and burglars, they built up a story about a group of inept thieves who try to pull off a job which is bigger than they are. Naturally they fail. Monicelli really had to fight in order to use Gassman in a comic role. Until then he had been best known in the cinema for his 'bad guy' roles. Neither Cristaldi nor the distributors could be convinced and it was only by surrounding him with big name actors that the film got off the ground.

"In *Big Deal on Madonna Street* I played a character that I had already played, for example, in *Too Bad She's Bad*, the good-natured ingenuous type who isn't exactly comic but occasionally has reactions which make you smile; in short, he belonged to the same family."

If it is true that Mastroianni's character is again a 'good' character it is also true that this time the character takes on the function of a reflection on the nature of goodness. It is a character who thinks, is more refined, who belongs to a different civilization; what we might call the urbanized second generation of his rather simpleminded heroes. He has already undergone a process of disenchantment. He is the most refined of the group of thieves. Cosimo, their leader, tries to steal a car but ends up in prison. When he learns of the possibility of an important job his friends and accomplices look for a pawn who will accept the guilt and take his place in prison. Mario and Ferribotte think of Tiberio, the photographer: "He's the unluckiest bloke I know; they've put his wife inside for selling black-market cigarettes." But it is precisely because of this that he refuses. He needs to take care of their young baby and doesn't want to leave him in prison with his mother: "The kid will go to prison when he's grown-up, if that's what he wants to do." They decide on Peppe, a crazy boxer, instead. But no one believes his story and they release him immediately; not, however, before he has made Cosimo tell him the plan of the robbery.

With his bow-tie, his french beret, his well-fed appearance and his profession as a photographer, Mastroianni represents the artistic-intellectual element in the group of thieves. Even the arm-and-mind trick, in which he uses a fake arm in plaster so that with his free hand he can steal a cine-camera from a market stall, is accompanied by an improvised lesson in art-appreciation: "Well sir, I can assure you that if you give this as a present to your cousin you really will make a good impression. Don't you think so? There is a certain depth; this tree, it certainly is a tasteful gift. Yes, really, a refined aristocratic present. This cypress tree silhouetted against the sky, the gentle countryside, the ducks, the peasant-woman."

He takes up position on the terrace in front of the savings bank they are intending to rob. His job is to film the clerk as he opens the safe, "the godmother", so that they can reconstruct the combination code. But the film shows only unfocused images: his child crying, washing on a line which hides the safe while the clerk is opening it. They can't see a thing. He defends himself: "Look here lads, the camera's old, the lens is old, it's not as though we're in Hollywood." At the crucial moment, the film runs out. Totò (Dante Cruciani), called on as a master safe-breaker, is there at the showing of the film and gives his opinion: "The film's an absolute mess. However what I have seen is better than nothing. The safe is a Commodore model 50, and it isn't one of the toughest."

During Dante's 'training sessions', he is the only one who asks any intelligent questions. When he takes the child to its mother the night before the job, he arouses the admiration of her fellow prisoners: "He's a fine figure of a man, the husband!". He gets to the meeting this time with his arm really in plaster. He has run into the stall owner from whom he stole the cine-camera, had his arm broken and the camera taken back. At the end, in pain and in a bad way, he becomes more and more like the other poor unfortunates. He day dreams about what he will do with his cut: "I'm not like all those other blokes who

The punch-drunk boxer, played by Vittorio Gassman, completes the gang.

Thief and policeman during a romantic interlude (with Michèle Morgan).

once they get the money, spend and spend until their money burns a hole in their pocket. I'll go for a nice little four-roomed appartment and a bank account made out in the boy's name so that he will remember the sacrifices his old dad has made."

He has no illusions about their chances of success: "We'll never manage it, you know. Stealing is a demanding business; you need serious people, not people like you. At best you lot could go out to work." And he treats Peppe with a harsh realism: "Look, listen to me. Just don't bother thinking, that's the best thing. You are strong, a big, man. You use a bit of muscle, that's your thing." He eats pasta and chick-peas with the others in the kitchen of the ruined appartment. It is dawn when they leave. Tiberio goes back to the prison to collect his son from his wife.

In one short step he moves from being a thief to being a policeman. In *Love on the Riviera* Marcello is travelling on a train towards the French border, where he has to hand over a lovely thief (Michèle Morgan) to the local police. But the train they are travelling on is a local one and they stop in the seaside town of Rapallo. There is a two-hour wait before the train is due to start off again. The heat is unbearable and the policeman suggests to the prisoner that they go down to the beach for a swim. They miss the train and in an atmosphere of growing intimacy they end up spending the night in a hotel. Mastroianni is trans-formed from policeman to lover, ready to wait for the thief until she is released from prison.

This episode is only one of a whole series featuring a host of actors (Alberto Sordi, Sylva Koscina, Gabriele Ferzetti, Franco Fabrizi, Lorella De Luca, Franca

As a football referee, getting rough treatment from the fans, in Il marito bello, *which he made with Giovanna Ralli.*

Marzi); yet the Marcello Mastroianni-Michèle Morgan duet remains the most self-contained. It portrays the story of two lonely people and its strength rests entirely on the sincerity of their feelings for one another. In this pre-Fellini stage of his career, Mastroianni again finds himself playing the 'good guy': the meek individual who is perhaps a bit lacking in personality and who allows himself to be ruled by circumstance. The on-screen meeting of the young Italian actor with perhaps the most mature of the French divas sets up an atmosphere of slightly melancholic nutual admiration.

Two other films which come immediately before *La Dolce Vita* are *Ferdinand of Naples* and *Il marito bello* (The Handsome Husband). In the latter he plays a football referee. All that we see of his chosen occupation, however, is the state he has been reduced to by angry fans who have vented their frustration on him. Forced by a shrewish wife who hates football to live in a house filled to bursting with mechanical objects of all descriptions (buttons, levers, record players, fridges, food mixers), he occasionally gives way to outbursts of rage. He throws things on the floor and cleans his shoes with the expensive American ties

his wife has bought for him. Italian-style comedy on the theme of difficult conjugal relationships, the film does not provide Mastroianni with the opportunity to really show his talent.

He remains relegated to the role of the lower middle-class-husband who is fundamentally under his wife's thumb. She is the bread-winner in the family and as a consequence treats him with the contempt she feels is his due. He is more of a dreamer than a realist and gives expression to his feelings of oppression through violence, in an attempt to re-assert his masculine superiority.

3

The Extraordinary Experience of *La Dolce Vita*

"You are mother, sister, lover, friend, angel, devil, earth, home."

On February 4, 1960 *La Dolce Vita* arrives on the screen as a film-event. Its premiere is at the cinema Fiamma in Rome, and there is warm applause interrupted by some whistling. With all the film's actresses in the audience, the photographers have a field day. But on February 5th the film has its Milan premiere at the Capital cinema, and now the real controversy starts. Fellini is insulted and even spat upon. Mastroianni is greeted with shouts of "Vagabond, communist, scoundrel".

Discussion becomes increasingly heated. In Parliament Senator Turchi calls for the film to be condemned: "Initiatives of this kind should be crushed immediately because they are highly corrosive and mark the lives of today's young people with the stain of an easy materialist life without ideals, and contribute to the destructive power of subversive political elements." On the other hand, Pietro Ingrao, perhaps the most hard-line of the Italian communists, claims that it is a pillar of democracy in the face of clerical-fascist oppression. Even the Catholic world is divided on the issue. Most clerics and bishops condemn the film but the Jesuits at the San Fedele centre in Milan greatly applaud it. Those in favour and those against go to great lengths to make their feelings known. Left-wing intellectuals hurry to organize debates while right-wing activists favour sabotaging the showings.

Begun on the 16th of March 1959, the filming of *La Dolce Vita* carries on until the beginning of September. Mastroianni appears in every scene. At the start he seems a bit stiff, but as the film progresses, he gradually loosens up. His role as a chronicler of society takes him into a world of ceaseless agitation, which draws him in and makes him part of events dreamt up to fill a void, an existential nothingness. His disenchanted sense of irony makes his natural role that of the independent observer, but it is a role he is ready to abandon when the desire to be part of a better social class takes hold of him or when he becomes involved with a woman. It is always a woman who mediates between Marcello-Federico and the world of 'la dolce vita' (the sweet life) or simply of life.

"Who are you, Silvia? You are everything, everything, do you know that? Eh? You are the first woman of the first morning of creation. You are mother, sister, lover, friend, angel, devil, earth, home. That's it, that's what you are: home." Fellini, Flaiano, Pinelli and Rondi, the film's story and screenwriters, produce this speech, a sort of summary of femininity, for Mastroianni to address to the astonishingly beautiful Anita Ekberg. But inevitably present in this endless and awestruck admiration is the principle of inequality. The woman as home, welcoming, ready to receive the lover, forms part of a commonly accepted fantasy, and yet its usage has assumed a purely negative aspect. Man has always exploited and made use of it to exorcise his fear of being absorbed and overwhelmed. Mastroianni's attachment to Fellini, begun with *La Dolce Vita*, continues throughout his career. But the relationship is not as all-inclusive as one could be led to believe. In reality what draws them together above all is their mutual vision of woman as maternal, mediterranean, the inheritor of an ancient matriarchal civilization.

When Fellini began to think about the film, he knew that he wanted an Italian actor to take the leading role. In reality he was simply looking for a face to assume the role of his own ideal autobiography. This itself was the cause of an early break-up with the producer De Laurentiis who had initially wanted a big foreign name in order to ensure the film's international success. "When he called me I went to see him in Fregene. He was sitting on the beach under a huge umbrella. He told me that the producer had wanted Paul Newman in the leading role. But Paul Newman was not right for him. He was too important, too exceptional. What he wanted was just an ordinary face. In saying this I think there was just a little touch of malice in hurting me. But I didn't feel hurt because I had never felt that I had an exceptional face or personality."

In the end the film is produced by Rizzoli and takes six months to make during 1959. It is an experience which in some way changes Mastroianni. He is no longer simply an actor playing a part but a man, moving in an environment until then unknown to him, who has to come to terms with himself, his father, mother, friends, and with the women in his life. The total absorbtion in the role that the part demands in some way changes his personality; it is an event which leaves a mark on his life which goes beyond the effects of the film's success.

Marcello Rubini teases a carnation between his fingers. Dark glasses shade his eyes and serve perhaps to mask his insecurity and sense of insignificance as he makes rapid notes on the famous and talked about guests of a fashionable night

Anita Ekberg's irreverent apparel in La Dolce Vita *was one of the many 'scandalous' aspects over which the film was criticized.*

club. He defends his work as a scandal-mongering journalist with the argument: "I've got to keep the public informed; it's my job." He moves through the night with an agile feline ease; the streets of Rome are his territory: "It is a sort of jungle, warm, peaceful, where you can hide yourself easily."

While he follows up chance encounters, dissatisfaction is his constant companion and he defends it like a cause: "It's not a misfortune really, there are so few of us left who are really dissatisfied with ourselves." He is perfectly at his ease when adventure calls, scenting the trail, giving in to curiosity. He hardens only when threatened with responsibility, which he always rejects, pushes away or puts to one side.

A sort of open baroque creation, cumulatively constructed, *La Dolce Vita* is a film about excess. Two helicopters fly over Rome. From one of them hangs a statue of Christ. From the other Marcello waves to four girls in bikinis who are sunning themselves on a terrace. At night he rides in the enormous American limousine of the exceptionally rich Maddalena and they make love in the flooded basement of a prostitute who calls him Gregory Peck. When he goes back the next morning to his unfurnished white appartment, he finds his girlfriend, Emma, who has tried to commit suicide. He takes her to casualty then goes to meet the diva's aeroplane. Anita Ekberg, a monumental beauty resplendently curvaceous, with a marble complexion, is like a "great doll". He follows her to the press conference, onto the cupola of St Peter's, to the night club and to the Trevi Fountain, but he doesn't manage to find anywhere to make love to her. The following morning in a church he

meets his friend Steiner, an ascetic thinker, who praises one of his articles.

"It was good, very good. Lucid, impassioned, I could see the best of you in it, those qualities which you try to hide and which in spite of yourself you can't help having." "No, I really can't write you know," he replies. In spite of his talent, or perhaps because of it, Mastroianni is not a credible writer or journalist. He is still too ingenuous, too naïve. He doesn't let the depth show through. He has not yet constructed his image. He is blessed with a sense of youthful vitality which leads him to produce his best moments in the viscissitudes of courtship rather than in the greyer tones of desperation.

With Emma (Yvonne Fourneaux), who is neurotic, possessive and maternal, he is the impassioned and irritated boyfriend-husband. With Maddalena (Anouk Aimée), who lives only for love, he is allusive and sensual, and with Silvia, who in

Mastroianni has become a star inspite of himself, but at the time he doesn't realize it. "Many years later, someone told me: 'We all wanted to know where we could get those striped shirts, that white suit and those sunglasses you wore in La Dolce Vita. *The same was true of the car you drove, the Triumph Spider, which came back into fashion.' In* La Dolce Vita, *the image of the anti-hero was almost transformed into one of a hero. For that reason, I couldn't understand why I never had any fans waiting for me in hotel lobbies, or outside cinemas."*

her effusive carnality represents the very essence of woman, he is fascinated and frightened.

On the miracle field, where two children say they have seen the Madonna, Marcello, from the vantage point of a small tower, follows the movement of the crowd with a sceptical eye. Beneath him we see the rites of an outmoded religion being performed, a religion which mixes superstitious mysticism with infantile play, and serves only to take advantage of the hopes of the poor who have nothing more to lose. In Steiner's living room, once the height of fashion but now outdated, Marcello expresses his cultural beliefs, warmly advocating an art of the future: "It will be an art of precision, clarity, without rhetoric, without lies, without adulation."

In the sometimes insufferable chat of the intellectual salon we see the typical inferiority complex of cinema in relation to culture, a constant element in the more serious Italian films of the 1960's. The

The orgy scene outrages the orthodox.

characters are images and prototypes of a certain kind of rich middle class individual who will become an ever-more-familiar figure in the cinema as the years pass. Even in Steiner's living room Rubini-Mas-

troianni has some of his best moments when he is talking about women. He tells his friend that he would like to "know women of all races and have children of all the colours of the rainbow: red, yellow, like a bunch of wild flowers".

The following day he is in a restaurant at the seaside. He is trying to write but is distracted by a waitress, Paola (Valeria Ciangottini), who is singing while she prepares the tables. That evening, in Via Veneto, he meets his father who has come up from the country with a letter from his mother. He takes him to a night club and discovers that he has unsuspected talent with the ladies. Later, at a dancer's house, his father feels bad and he decides to return home immediately. The story of a continually deferred and perhaps never to be accomplished meeting. The next evening Marcello joins a group of nobles who take him to an old castle. Here he finds Maddalena again who seduces him while talking to him from another room. But when he goes to her he finds her with another man. The following evening he has an argument with Emma. He is afraid: "of you, of your egotism; can't you see that what you are suggesting would be the life of an earthworm? You never talk about anything except kitchens and bedrooms. Don't you realise that a man who decides to live like that has had it? He really would be a worm. I don't believe in this aggressive, cloying maternal love of yours. I don't want it, I don't need it. This isn't love, it's brutishness. How can I tell you that I can't live like this, that I don't want to be with you any more, that I want to be on my own". He goes off, but then he comes back for her.

The scene with Emma is one of Mastroianni's virtuoso pieces. Aggressive, lucid and malicious he manages to bring out unsuspected grit in his passion; something which he had rarely been asked to show. He is in bed with Emma when he receives a telephone call. Steiner has killed his two children and committed suicide. Yet another exasperated episode which makes *La Dolce Vita* a case placed at the extremes of experience, a sort of paradigm of a humanity which exists without hope.

It is night time again. A motor caravan drives towards a villa. Marcello is celebrating the annullment of Nadia's marriage with a group of friends. An extraordinary event at a time when divorce laws had yet to be passed and separation was looked on as a desperate measure. The spur-of-the-moment party lacks swing and it culminates in a strip-tease by Nadia and in a girl being covered with the feathers from a cushion which Marcello, in his drunkenness, has torn. He has changed his job. Now he is a publicity agent and for three hundred thousand lire would be willing to launch a modest actor as another Marlon Brando or for four hundred thousand as a second John Barrymore.

On the beach at dawn, while the fishermen are bringing in an enormous monster of a fish, he meets Paola again, without recognising her, and she talks to him from far off. But her voice does not reach him, just as his own voice at the beginning of the film, drowned out by the noise of the helicopter, had not reached the four girls sunbathing. *La Dolce Vita*, which begins and ends with a loss of speech, marks one of the most significant turning points in the actor's career. It is the end of his rather eclectic efforts in various directions and the start of the mature period of his acting career.

"For me it meant that I achieved greater weight in the international field, even if other films I had made had already been released internationally. It was an event: to use a big word, a sort of consecration, so much so that after *La Dolce Vita* I received offers of contracts in America which I didn't take up, firstly because I didn't yet speak any English, and secondly because I had good offers in Italy and so had no need to go to America. It was an

exceptional experience, incredible, six months of thoroughly enjoyable work. It didn't even seem as though we were making a film. It is almost as though we really did live that "sweet life", which until then

On the beach at dawn.

57

I knew nothing about. I wasn't a part of that world; I didn't belong to Via Veneto. So it was really a somewhat sensational experience which brought about a real change in roles for me. *La Dolce Vita* really was a cornerstone, the true start of a new direction after years of work in the cinema and the theatre, a turning-point after which came all the films with the great Italian film directors; Germi, Antonioni, Petri, Bolognini. It was really after

La Dolce Vita that I started to receive offers to play different characters, and there was an increase in my box-office success, because, having achieved a certain international recognition, there were more offers coming in and I had a better choice. That was also the start of my friendship with Fellini, which was very important to me. While he was making the film Fellini used an image which was full of colour and imagination: he used to say that we

were like shipwrecked people on a raft being carried where the wind took us in total abandonment; a really beautiful image, terribly exciting. It was an experience that went beyond an actor's ordinary professional activity; it was something that

With Claudia Cardinale in a particularly intense scene from Il bell'Antonio.

I lived more as a person than as an actor."

While the concept of the 'dolce vita' achieves its own significance as a way of living life on a grand scale, Mastroianni in a flourish of articles, photographs and scandals, hits the international scene and becomes the actor of the moment. Having received a "Nastro d'argento" for his role in *La Dolce Vita*, he wants to make an immediate break from the too limiting role of the latin lover. The fact that he plays an impotent man in his next film *Il bell'Antonio* (The Beautiful Antonio) is therefore no coincidence. "I got the part on the rebound. It should have gone to Jaques Charrier, who at that time was married to Brigitte Bardot, but, for what motives I don't know, at the last moment he changed his mind. Who knows? Perhaps he was worried that the impotence label would stick. Sometimes actors get confused and think that they need to preserve an on-screen image of virility which has nothing whatever to do with the profession of the actor. Apart from all this, I loved the book and was pleased to be offered the part, even though it arrived only a few days before they began to shoot. When an actor makes a successful film, people try to stick a label on him straight away. The offers I was getting after *La Dolce Vita* were all lovers and seducers who roam the local night spots. I immediately wanted to destroy this image. I refused to be type-cast, so I deliberately went to the opposite extreme and took on the role of an impotent man. This was why I decided to accept the offer of *Il bell'Antonio*, really, because I wanted to escape from the fear of being trapped in a role. My origins as a theatre actor made

The Latin lover destroys his own myth, in a role that other actors might have considered embarrassing.

With Simone Signoret. The cowardly racketeer of Love
À La Carte *is one of the least attractive characters
played by Mastroianni.*

me reject the label, I wouldn't accept it. I enjoy being an actor when I have the chance to broaden my experience, to renew my role, to change it, to "put on make-up", as we say in theatre jargon."

This time he "makes-up" as a loser. In the film his inability to feel like a man with women assumes the aspect of adolescent immaturity which seems to make him vascillate between masculine and feminine. He spends his time reading poetry and lying on his bed smoking, frowning and solitary. In the screenplay written by Pier Paolo Pasolini and Gino Visentini from the novel by Vitaliano Brancati (1949), the whole story of his impotence is pre-announced in his resounding shout of "mother" as he gets off the train at Catania, in their prolonged embrace and in the kisses she gives him as they descend the station steps. The mother is played by Rina Morelli, an actress whom he knew from his years in Visconti's theatre.

Antonio's latent homosexuality, the more obvious signs of which are his excessive beauty, his long eyelashes, his face assuming the expression of contained melancholy, is a current which runs all through the film. Again Mastroianni shows his exceptional ability to absorb himself in the part, to bring the character to life, to make it really credible. A young man with high hopes, after several years in Rome trying to enter the diplomatic service so dear to his father's heart he eventually returns to Sicily where his parents have arranged a good marriage for him. But his chosen bride-to-be, Barbara Puglisi (Claudia Cardinale) turns out to be a surprise for him. She is beautiful, kind, innocent and he falls madly in love with her. He hopes to succeed with her where he has failed with other women. But after a year of chastity the girl eventually confesses to her parents that she is still a virgin. The marriage is annulled. Antonio's father, who is proud of his own virility, will not accept his son's impotence: "Do you know why they made me party secretary of Catania? Because I went with nine women in one night". He dies in the arms of a prostitute, giving final proof of his sexual prowess. Antonio's public image is greatly improved when the housemaid gets pregnant and he is pointed-out as the probable father. But he is the only one who suffers for the fact. In his exacerbated sensitivity he sheds tears for Barbara, imagining the suffering it will cause her.

In Sicily, where marriage is simply a business contract between two families, non-consumation is regarded as an anti-social action. In a society where the male, precisely because he is more insecure, is more than ever in evidence, to be impotent is to upset the whole of that society's foundations. "Beautiful" Antonio is a sort of anti-conformist in spite of himself, and he is made to pay for being different through his own suffering. He has to suffer the pain of a man who has never been able to have what everybody else has. But perhaps it is Antonio's moral impotence which remains incomprehensible to us. Completely lacking in irony, he is mastered by his obscure sense of shame and does nothing. Guilty, like the rest of them.

In *Love a La Carte*, directed by Antonio Pietrangeli, the character Piero Salvani is completely different from the role of Antonio Magnano. A wily used-car salesman with a cheeky manner and easy banter, Piero gets Adua's attention by playing on her sympathy. He is fundamentally immature and not even able to take care of himself, still less his four friends, ex-prostitutes who want to set up on their own. As a front for their activity, they open up a restaurant, but their plans are cut short by an avaricious pimp who forces them back onto the streets. When Adua asks him for help, Piero turns scornful: "What can I do about it?". He feels persecuted and victimised by the women: "They've all got something against me; what do you want

from me?". A poor fellow, but with a dishonest streak: Piero's open, good natured face is illuminated by a serpent's eyes, the serpent that hypnotises and is ready to turn on you and betray you in the age-old Italian tradition of "getting by".

This film sees the birth of a *leitmotif* which is to accompany Mastroianni throughout the rest of his career in his public as well as his private life. Adua scolds him for smoking too much: "You

never stop. What's the matter? Are you trying to save matches?". "Look; I've heard it all before: if I smoke at night, too, if one box of matches would do me for life, if I stop when I'm making love." "And do you?" "No." Thirty years later, on the 8th of December 1991, when Bernard Pivot asks him on "Boullion de Culture" what his favourite drug is, he taps his packet of cigarettes and replies: "Do I need to say it?".

Marcello and Jeanne Moreau, the algid stars of The Night. *"I would have preferred this writer to have been a bit angrier, a bit more cynical. But then, even if he had been, I wouldn't have been able to play him. I had a writer friend, Ennio Flaiano as a model – who knows why, but this writer seemed to me to resemble him. This evidently wasn't something Antonioni intended, however."*

Giovanni Pontano, the writer of Antonioni's film *The Night*, was not a satisfactory writer for Mastroianni. There is something that does not quite work between them. Both Mastroianni and Jeanne Moreau, who plays his wife in the film, seem held back, their emotions smothered in some of their best moments. Both were subjected to a process of de-dramatisation in order to conform to the director's poetic of non-communication, which seems inspired by Moravia's "noia" (boredom).

"I was a little bit disappointed because I felt that the character, this writer suffering a crisis, was a little bit conventional.

Perhaps I would have preferred him to be more angry, more cynical, but then I probably wouldn't have been able to play him anyway. I suppose I felt that I had an example of a writer before me: my friend, Ennio Flaiano. And somehow or other, I don't know why, I felt that this writer should be like him, which obviously wasn't what Antonioni intended. So there was a sort of incomprehension between me and the director. As I went along I lost some of that joy, that enthusiasm I had felt which had made me want to do the film. This was the state of mind I was in while I was making the film. I would have liked to be closer to Antonioni but it

wasn't possible. I don't know if it was my fault or whether it was because he (and it is something he has always said) prefers not to to have much interaction with the actors. He uses them rather like silhouettes; I don't mean objects, because that wouldn't be true. He tells his stories through atmospheres, through images, in which the actor's interpretation is less important. That was probably where the

The writer doesn't know how to extract himself from a nymphomaniac's embrace.

problem lay. Then again I'm not a very insistent person by nature; if I see from the start – to use a boxing term – that the distances aren't right, then I just retire into my corner."

The result of this lack of comprehension is evident in the film. *The Night* is very similar to *La Dolce Vita* in structure; it is a journey rather than a story. A journey which Giovanni and his wife Lidia make from a clinic where they visit a dying friend, to the publisher's where Giovanni's latest book *La stagione* (The Season) is being promoted, to Sesto San Giovanni, in the suburbs of Milan, where Lidia returns to the field where they first used to meet, to a night club, to a millionaire's villa.

In all this wandering, the most significant encounter in the film is the encounter with culture. Naturally so, considering that the main character is a writer. But culture remains something which is overlaid on the the story; it is exhibited, named, displayed like something to be exorcised. Mastroianni is merely propped up from the outside by the books on display, the magazines he mentions, the people he meets. He tells his friend in the clinic: "I have brought you a copy of *Literary Europe* with your article about Adorno. It was very interesting. I had to read it in a hurry. I'll have to get back to it later, but it was very interesting." At the launch of his book, attended by intellectuals and members of 'Society' he is welcomed by Count Valentino Bompiani. There also seems to be a very young Umberto Eco in the crowd, not yet thirty with a roundish face and no beard but wearing his distinctive dark-rimmed spectacles. Then we see Giovanni returning home with a copy of the Bompiani Literary Almanac tucked under his arm and well in view of the camera. At this point one begins to wonder if the film has been sponsored by Bompiani.

Why was Italian cinema of the early

After Michèle Morgan, Simone Signoret and Jeanne Moreau, it's Micheline Presle's turn, in The Lady Killer From Rome.

1960's suffering from a culture-complex? Naturally the middle class has the right to seek an entry into high society, to become part of the nobility. But in this case culture remains a sad, lugubrious thing. The economic boom (which was also the title of a film by De Sica) was not a happy affair. The cinema, like society's unquiet conscience, acutely perceives it and its best authors represent it. The newly born aristocracy needs the intellectual to give brilliance to its court. But the new-style jester is depressed, lost in a personal crisis: "I know I can't even write any more. Not what, but how"; lost too in his personal relationships with his wife, and with his girlfriend.

An industrialist draws him into conversation: "What keeps a writer going is certainly not a desire to make money but more a sense of necessity. You write because you know it is necessary both to yourself and to others. Life is what we know we can create for ourselves with our own works. What would you do, Pontano, if you didn't write?" "I wonder how many times a writer asks himself if writing is some sort of ancient and irrepressible art. This solitary, craftsman-like activity, this process of painstakingly putting one

word after another, this art which it is impossible to mechanise. But you industrialists have the advantage of being able to make your stories with real people, with real things; life's time and rhythms are in your hands. I suppose that the future is in your hands." Replies slide obliquely past the questions like the paradoxical geometry of nonsense.

In 1960 Mastroianni stars in three films. Three very different roles which emphasise, yet again, the supreme versatility of the actor. In *The Lady Killer From Rome* by Elio Petri, he plays an antiques dealer suspected of murder. "Petri, who was a friend of mine, made me read the script of *The Lady Killer From Rome*. I liked it and accepted the part. This also helped the debut of a very talented young man who until then hadn't managed to make a name for himself. It was his directing debut, even though Petri, whom I greatly respected, had already assisted in other productions I had worked in and it was easy to see that he had great talent. I wasn't disappointed that he got me into doing this film as *The Lady Killer From Rome* turned out to be a very well-made and successful film." The critics are unanimous in their praise of Mastroianni, his

*Baron Cefalù of is one of
the best performances of
the actor's career.*

The ambiguous fascination of transvestitism in Phantoms of Rome.

measured and secure performance being on a par with his previous role in *La Dolce Vita*. Another important aspect of the film is that it presents a character of a certain psychological complexity, a melancholy even slightly repulsive individual. Mastroianni is awarded a prize by the German film critics for his performance.

In *Phantoms of Rome* he actually plays two roles: Reginald, the frivolous ghost of an eighteenth-century dandy, and Federico his direct descendent who makes use of the family name and fortune but wants to sell the ancestral home because he is short of money. The suavely satirical fairytale written by Antonio Pietrangeli from an idea by Sergio Amidei, is adapted for the screen by Ennio Flaiano, Ruggero Maccari, and Ettore Scola, authors who have been directly responsible for the development of Mastroianni's screen persona.

Baron Cefalù of *Divorce Italian Style*, with his dark glasses, slicked-back hair and long cigarette holder, comments in his voice-over on the crime of honour he has organised and carried out with cold determination. It is precisely this veiled voice which, like a subjective thread, carries us inside Sicilian reality, a reality entirely closed in upon itself. It is a character entirely unlike any that he has been asked to play before; the first really individual character.

"The history of my involvement in *Divorce Italian Style* is not exactly exceptional but it is at least rather unusual. I was in fact the last of a long list of actors to be offered the part, including an American actor whose name I can't remember. Germi's image of me as an actor was strictly limited to my image in *La Dolce Vita* and perhaps he also felt I belonged to

the same social class. He was a reserved man, almost rude, a misanthropist who seemed almost to despise anyone who had anything to do with the frivolous world of cinema. He didn't know me personally and the only image he had of me was the one he had perceived in Fellini's film; he certainly had no idea that I might be the

right actor for his film. When, for various reasons, a long list of actors turned down the offer of the film, and in addition, according to the usual laws of cinema, they needed a big-name actor, a box-office success, to star in the film, he followed up a suggestion of one of the film's production organizers who had mentioned my

The game of deception gets underway, during a walk in the city centre with Daniela Rocca.

name. I took him some photographs, some images that had been produced while I was making *Phantoms of Rome*. I had my hair curled then straightened, moustaches applied and so on. In other words I did the kind of audition you do when you are first starting out in cinema. When he had seen the photographs and the audition he changed his mind and I went ahead with the film, which was a big success all over the world; in fact it was a big personal success. My performance came as a bit of a surprise, especially to the Americans who couldn't understand how the young lady-killer of *La Dolce Vita* could turn round and do the kind of role I did in *Divorce Italian Style*. In American cinema the actors suffer from a system of categorization. In fact they are forced into a sort of role-specialisation where they are not asked to play a particular role but to always be a cowboy or a gangster or some such; that's why they were amazed at such a radical change. They were so amazed in fact that I was actually nominated for an Oscar for my part in this film. In the re-creation of certain rigid movements I had Monicelli's instructions to Tiberio Murgia while we were making *The Big Deal on Madonna Street* in mind, when he used to say, 'Be haughty Murgia, be haughty.' The only person who noticed was an American critic who asked me in an interview if I had had Ferribotte in mind while I was working on the character."

He even adopts a physical twitch, a sort of sucking in of the mouth which he actually copies from Germi himself. Germi is at first annoyed but later amused by the actor's gentle satire. Another example of the grotesque characterisation which helps to make the character of Fefé more believable. In the village of Agromonte, in Sicily, the principle subject of conversation is women. It seems to be an inexhaustible source of inspiration and verges on myth-making. Married for many years to a licentious and mawkish woman (Daniela

A new look and new companions for the acquitted Baron. With Stefania Sandrelli.

Rocca) whom he can no longer stand, Baron Cefalù has fallen in love with a young cousin, Angela (Stefania Sandrelli) who returns his love and whom he wants to marry. His only way of ridding himself of his wife is to take advantage of article 587 of the Italian penal code which refers to a 'crime of honour': "Homicide and bodily harm in the cause of honour. Whoever causes the death of wife, daughter or sister in the act of discovering her in an

illegitimate carnal relationship and in the state of rage at the dishonour caused to him and his family, is to be punished by a period of imprisonment from three to seven years".

He skilfully arranges for his wife to meet up with an old flame and sets things up for the act of adultery which he times to occur the night when they are showing *La Dolce Vita* at the local cinema. In an outbreak of scandal and to the echoes of

polemic and protests, anathema and praise, a sensationalist film had arrived in the village. The parish of San Firmino had hurled its condemnation against the licentious film and adjured its parishoners to boycott it, but to little effect. And here Mastroianni plays his very downfall like a victory. He is doubly the hero both of the film he is playing in and of the film which is being talked about. The absolute hero, he is almost always alone in the scenes and appears in a series of memorable poses which have entered his own anthology of film images. He is again awarded a prize by the German film critics for his performance. Germi's amusing satire is instrumental in exposing some of the gross underlying contradictions of Italian society which, in spite of its progress towards an economic well-being equal to that of some of the leading world powers, still remained far behind as regards the laws and customs of a modern state.

For director Louis Malle's *A Very Private Affair* Mastroianni manages to live and work in three places at once: Geneva, Paris and Spoleto. Made in 1962, the film is basically the director's homage to Brigitte Bardot, and Mastroianni, who plays a rather colourless Italian lover, is himself sacrificed to this cause. "It was fundamentally a commercial enterprise. Bardot was then famous, I was famous, so we got together. Malle, who had come from a fantastic film like *The Lovers* which had been really successful everywhere, put this film together but it wasn't anything special. When we started out, the idea was to make a film about a couple with all their problems and emotional crises, but then somehow it turned into what one might imagine the biography of someone like Bardot to be, someone who is

Marcello goes west, on his first trip to the U.S.A.

obsessed with the press, with photographers; it turned into something else and wasn't a great success. Well made, of course, but it didn't get good reviews, even the New York critics were pretty damning."

Family Diaries by Valerio Zurlini divides the critics. Some say that it is a work which creates a particular feeling by presenting a serene contemplation of suffering without taking recourse to the simple expedient of direct emotion. Others find it a colourless production which manages to wipe out those rare occasional of bitterness, lyrical passages and protests against fortune which are the most precious aspects of Vasco Pratolini's book. Mastroianni receives good reviews all round. He brings a touching humanity to the role of the journalist who learns that his younger brother has died after a long illness and recalls their life together with all its joys and problems. The actor manages to manipulate all his acting talents to get right to the heart of the character and make him really credible.

His television work is rare and only very occasionally is he drawn into making brief appearances. One such appearance is on the successful television programme *Studio Uno*, hosted by Lelio Luttazzi. He takes part in the fifth show and sings a song he has composed himself, "Sera di

With A Very Private Affair, *Mastroianni and Brigitte Bardot both rise to stardom.*

novembre" (November Evening). In October, 1962, the American magazine *Time* publishes an article about him. An unprecedented phenomenon is taking root in the United States: foreign stars are beginning to receive the same kind of adulation that American stars had previously received throughout the world. And, naturally, Mastroianni is foremost among those stars. While he is visiting the United States, staying as a guest at Joseph H. Levine's house, he meets Greta Garbo.

"After the success of *La Dolce Vita*, I went to New York for the first time. Guidarino Guidi came with me and acted as my interpreter. A gentleman we met told us that Greta Garbo wanted to meet me, but when I met her I had to pretend that we had met by chance. 'What is all this rubbish?' I remember asking Guido. I wasn't very impressed because she wasn't an actress that did anything for me in particular. She always reminded me of Snow White's stepmother in the films I had seen her in. I preferred Ginger Rogers, Lana Turner and Barbara Stanwyck. At five o'clock in the afternoon a limousine arrived to pick us up and we were taken to a very elegant street on the East Side. We went into an antiques shop and were welcomed by a gentleman who looked like Jean Gabin. He showed us up to the second floor where we found three ladies in a small sitting room: the owner of a cosmetics company, an important Hollywood hostess and, sitting behind them, Greta Garbo. According to the script I had been told to play, I pretended to be amazed and said the only thing I knew how to say in English: 'How do you do?' She was still very beautiful, dressed with great simplicity: a pleated skirt, a cashmere pullover; with that wolfish, seductive face. The first thing she did was to look at my shoes and exclaim: 'Nice shoes, Italian shoes!' Actually they were English but I slyly said, 'Yes'. Then she added: 'Italy is beautiful, Rome, the Pope.' Then she stood up and

started to dance the Cha-cha-cha. While she was dancing, the owner of the cosmetics company said: 'I've seen *Camille* again; how beautiful you were then!'. Without saying a word the actress left the room. We felt extremely embarrassed by that abrupt and unexplained exit. We made our excuses and left to go to a cocktail party at the Lee Strasberg Actor's Studio. I met lots of famous actors, pupils and ex-pupils and among them Paul Newman. At a certain point someone said: 'Greta Garbo on the telephone for Marcello Mastroianni'. Guidarino went to take the call for me and he told me that the diva had said: 'I really must apologise, but I can't stand stupid women'. I have often wondered what we would have talked about if things had been different."

His next film is Federico Fellini's *8 1/2*.

"Doing this film was like looking into a mirror, observing, getting to know oneself. It was like a psychoanalysis session, or rather a form of self-psychoanalysis, because Guido was a man of my own generation, a sensitive, intelligent man, a very particular kind of anti-hero. He was the prototype of that generation which is now entering its forties, with all their fragility and confusion; the kind of man who is useless now. Today they need men who are much more sure of themselves. It was an effective X-ray." Working with Fellini means being able to receive his very precise instructions, to trust him, to collabo-

With his Mercedes coupé, one of the many cars Mastroianni owned. For years, he and Fellini shared a real passion for them, to the extent that they would change models almost weekly, in a contest that lined the pocket of a notable Roman car dealer. Jaguars, Triumphs, Porsches, BMW's, Alfa Romeo 1900's and Lancia Flaminia's are just some of the cars they competed with.

rate in producing the kind of character he has in mind. "Above all you have to really make an effort to understand the spirit, the world that the director, if he is the author, wants to represent. You need to be on the same wavelength, only then can you really collaborate. If only I had had the qualities to have been able to construct *8½* with Fellini. I collaborated, I adapted myself, I tried to respond well, and like a musical instrument, to play well in Fellini's hands, nothing more."

A film about making a film. In *8½* Mastroianni plays the part of a director suffering a crisis. Trapped in a bottle-neck in an underpass he suffers an attack of claustrophobia and only manages to free

himself by 'flying' out. Guido's nightmare is perhaps to be explained by the passion for motor cars that Fellini and Mastroianni both share. In an infantile spirit of competition they both manage to change their car every week. They make a rich man of a car salesman, a certain Borniggia, who takes advantage of Fellini's exhibitionism by tempting him with a selection of showy cars: Jaguars, Mercedes, Flaminias, Cisitalias. He would drive one round to Fellini's house then ring the director and tell him to look out of the window. Fellini could not resist the temptation to try out the new car even if it was a matter of just driving it round to Mastroianni's house to show him.

Guido is known affectionately as old Snaporaz, a nickname Fellini used for Mastroianni, and the protagonist's name in *City of Women*. He has more than enough qualities and defects which could belong to both of them. In a large hat and dark-rimmed spectacles Mastroianni becomes Fellini's alter-ego. And for a time he is willing to play the game. Guido has retired to a spa town to have a rest and at the same time to continue his latest film. He is joined there by his mistress, Carla (Sandra Milo); he dreams of Paola (Claudia Cardinale), an innocent and unaffected young girl ; and he calls his wife, Luisa (Anouk Aimée), to join him. Narcissistically looking at his own reflection in the mirror while hiding the fact behind dark glasses, he divides his time between the three of them. He sees his father and mother in psychological flash-backs, relives a moment when in the company of some school-friends he secretly goes down to the beach to see the enormous and diabolic Saraghina, a monstrous vagrant prostitute. He is caught by his priest-teachers and punished for his crime by being made to wear a ridiculous dunce-cap and to kneel on some crushed nut-shells. He afterwards makes his confession in a gigantic grotesquely-shaped confessional.

Playing the clown, he tries to avoid speaking to the production inspector who is questioning him about the film. He kneels down like a moslem facing Mecca, then approaches him offering a watch as a gift. After this he moves away with small furtive steps, to the poor man's general frustration.

An image that symbolizes a film that is fundamental to the history of cinema

The director having a crisis amidst the crowd at the thermal baths.

of his wife who after a quarrel asks him, "Why have you brought me here, how can I be useful to you, what do you want from me, what do you want?". The only thing he gets an answer to is his desperate confession: "Eminence, I am not a happy man". And the answer is: "What makes you think we should be happy? That is not our purpose. Whoever said that we came into this world to be happy?"

With his wife's jealousy on the one hand and his mistress's frivolous egotism on the other he takes refuge in his harem. Here all the women in his life with his wife chief among them, are united harmoniously together to pamper and take care of him, preparing his bath in an enormous tub: "My dears, happiness is being able to say the truth without ever hurting anyone". But as soon as he starts to question himself, he undermines the whole foundations of his world. "A crisis of inspiration. But what if it wasn't merely a passing phase, my dear Sir? What if, instead of that, it was the final downfall of an old liar with no more ideas and no more talent? Gulp." The artistic crisis is echoed by an existential crisis. "Would you be capable of leaving everything and starting life all over again? Of choosing something, just one thing and being faithful to that? Of making it your reason for living? Something which includes everything, which becomes everything, because your belief in it makes it infinite? Would you be capable of doing that?" he asks Claudia. The film ends with his acceptance of the crisis, in confusion, because Guido is as he is and not as he would like to be. Once the fear is over, the scene ends with a big party.

Mastroianni leaves Fellini's cinema and,

Mastroianni's interpretation is sparkling, ironic, amusing. He moves with complete ease, with true self-assurance; he really is in control of the scene. He is masterly in putting all his acting talents into motion. And it is really he who, physiologically in tune with the story, helps to create the atmosphere of lightness by not giving replies to serious questions like, "Is Italy a fundamentally Catholic country or not?", or to grave critical assertions such as, "The Catholic conscience, just think for a moment about Suetonious at the time of the Caesars. No, you start out with the desire to denounce and end up by favouring an accomplice", or to the supplications

The ingenuous and idealistic Professor of The Organizers *is a hero in his own way, even if Mastroianni claims: "I have never played the part of a hero in any film. I never did when I was young and I can't do so now, as heros are almost never old."*

heedless of any sense of continuity, goes over to Monicelli's. An ingenuous dreamer by nature but above all prompted by an altruistic sense of justice, professor Sinigaglia of *The Organizers* is the guiding element in the action. Mastroianni plays the part with the necessary candour, but also manages to show the confusion of a man who sees the justice of opposing and fighting against an overwhelming power but who does not know how to go about it and tends to send others to their defeat. The main thing is to win a victory of ideals. The life of the individual human being is not that important to him, even when that human being is himself. And so he willingly puts his own life at risk. A film which documents the beginning of the labour protests in Turin, the first of Italy's industrialized cities, *The Organizers* is a rigorous black and white account with a choral treatment in which there is a large cast of characters whose stories intertwine.

Mastroianni flees from Genova and arrives in Turin where the discontent of the factory workers who are having to work a fourteen-hour day is beginning to turn into rebellion. He becomes their leader and encourages them to strike. With his little metal-rimmed spectacles, his alert eyes, badly shaven chin and thin moustache he is the image of the poor, proletarian left-wing intellectual. He has nothing to eat and nowhere to sleep. In the room which serves both as a night school and as a meeting room for the factory workers his mouth starts to water

when he notices a sandwich left behind by one of the workers. He is about to take a bite but then changes his mind and gives it back to the worker who has returned for it. He very carefully puts it in the newspaper, wraps it up and gives it back with the resigned desperation of someone who can not even ask for charity.

His only possessions are a small clarinet and a wooden egg which he uses to darn his socks, biting the thread with his teeth. During the workers' meetings he is courteous and kind but he is also decisive. Nor does he hold back when things turn nasty and he ends up being attacked. He defends himself with a cudgel yet at the same time exhorts his attackers to accept more rational means of coming to terms: let's reason this out, lets talk about it. He does not give up even when it seems that the battle is lost, and points out to the workers that he is much worse off than they are: "I'm not like all of you. I haven't got a house. I have nothing and nobody". He is ironic when he says that he has chosen this life because he has a head full of foolish ideas.

He tries to scrape together a bit of money by playing his clarinet in a cafe. And he meets Niobe (Annie Girardot), a worker's daughter who has become a prostitute. "Why have you got yourself into all this trouble ?" she asks him. And he replies: "Out of egotism, because I like it, and when you like something it's not a sacrifice any more. And also because I hope one day that a girl like you will not have to do what you have had to do". In the end the workers, worn down by hunger and desperation, decide to go back to work. He is the one who makes a stand and tries to stop them: "It isn't true that we have lost. The man who lasts another hour wins the battle". The factory owner calls in the army against the crowd of men who march on the factory. They fire on the crowd and a young boy is killed. "It's all your fault, you bastard; you killed him. Now I'm going to kill you; I'll kill you" the boy's distraught girlfriend shouts at him. Professor Sinigaglia says nothing to defend himself. He looks for his glasses which have fallen to the ground and allows the guards to take him away. Even in prison he continues to work for others. He remains unvanquished on his release and looks set to win the elections.

The film, which in looking at past events makes an acute comment on the present, is a few years ahead of the great social upheavals of 1968 and in this shows that real quality of foresight, typical of some of the best artistic creations. "*The Organizers* was a brilliant film. When it was released nobody went to see it perhaps because the title , which was entirely ironic, was taken seriously and many people thought it was a 'red' film and didn't go to see it. When it was shown on television everybody went mad about it. Abroad, where they don't have the same predjudices, it was considered one of the best Italian films made after the war. And even today, people still talk to me about *The Organizers* or *Les camarades* with awe. Many people consider it to be a classic."

After the rather serious Professor Sinigaglia, Mastroianni, with his almost proverbial need for change, is more than ever ready to take on different types of characters. By now he has become famous and between 1963 and 1969 he makes four films with a member of the cinema world who was already famous before Mastroianni even started: Vittorio De Sica. In all four films he shares the set with Sophia Loren, a return to an already well established partnership which had begun in the 1950's.

"For a number of years, Sophia Loren, De Sica and I came to be a sort of inseparable trio. For example De Sica was with me in *The Miller's Beautiful Wife* and he was in various films I made with Ralli, like *The Bigamist* and *Il medico e lo stregone*. I had worked with De Sica many times, before acting in a film under his direction. I always had a very affectionate relationship with him, something which went beyond the sphere of our profession. He seemed like an uncle to me and I never managed to talk to him without being conscious of this, and he seemed to react in the same way. I feel like it was almost a sort of family relationship which probably has something to do with the fact that we were both from the Ciociara area; so he was a person I felt attached to. I felt a lot of affection for him. Apart from the admiration I felt for the director, there was this attachment which did not have anything to do with cinema, which was related to almost adolescent feelings; and then there was his personal presence, like that of an impressive almost legendary relative, an important uncle. But the films I made with him are a bit lacking in story-line. *Yesterday, Today and Tomorrow*, is a jokey film, nice and amusing; it was well received. *Marriage Italian Style*, no comment really, a good film. *A Place for Lovers* was a purely commercial operation and was not a successful film. Even De Sica knew that, but we were both in debt and that was one of the film's major motivations. In *Sunflowers* I even had to act a whole scene in Russian when I didn't know a word of the language but I had to give the cues to a Russian actress so there was no getting round it."

The trio is in reality a quartet since all four films are produced by Carlo Ponti. *Yesterday Today and Tomorrow* is Mastroianni's first experience of De Sica as a director. It is also the occasion of the re-establishment of his partnership with Sophia Loren after an eight-year separation. The film is actually constructed around Sophia Loren who plays the leading characters Adelina, Anna and Mara in the three episodes. Mastroianni serves mainly to provide the backing for her in the full bloom of her beauty. In *Adelina*, written by Eduardo De Filippo, he rather unconvincingly plays the part of an ignorant but good hearted working class character; an obviously caricatural role. He is married to Adelina who earns their living by selling black market cigarettes. Forced into the role of the kept man, it is he who brings up the children which he regularly has to collaborate in producing in order to keep her out of prison. But when they get to the seventh child, Carmelo starts to experience some difficulty. He is worn down, with dark rings under his eyes, and his wife takes him to the doctor's. The doctor diagnoses a nervous breakdown. The break in production is fatal and

With his wealthy lover Anna, in Yesterday, Today and Tomorrow.

"Sophia Loren, De Sica and I form a kind of indivisible threesome."

A wanton dance with the call-girl Sophia.

77

Adelina, who has not managed to get pregnant, has to go to prison. Fortunately the generosity of the inhabitants of Forcella, a working-class area of Naples, saves the day.

In *Anna*, adapted by Cesare Zavattini from a short story by Moravia, he plays an anonymous-looking middle-class man with short hair and an English-style overcoat. He feels ill-at-ease as the lover of a very rich woman who drives him around in a flashy car and almost as an act of revenge he insists on driving the car himself. He ends up crashing into a road digger with various consequences for the car and for their rather dull relationship. *Mara*, whose story and screenplay is by Zavattini, is the best of the trio of films. Mastroianni plays the part of the son of a small time industrialist from Bologna who goes to Rome on business. He makes use of the occasion to visit Mara, a call girl who is his habitual lover. His lively interpretation of a virile, easy-going, fun loving young man, gives proof of his true qualities as a light comedy actor and he is well matched by an equally exuberant Sophia Loren. While the girl performs a striptease he yells: "Gnaghh!", holding her face between his hands, almost as if he wants

Domenico Soriano in Marriage Italian Style *has the same moustache and lady-killing instinct as Baron Cefalù in* Divorce Italian Style.

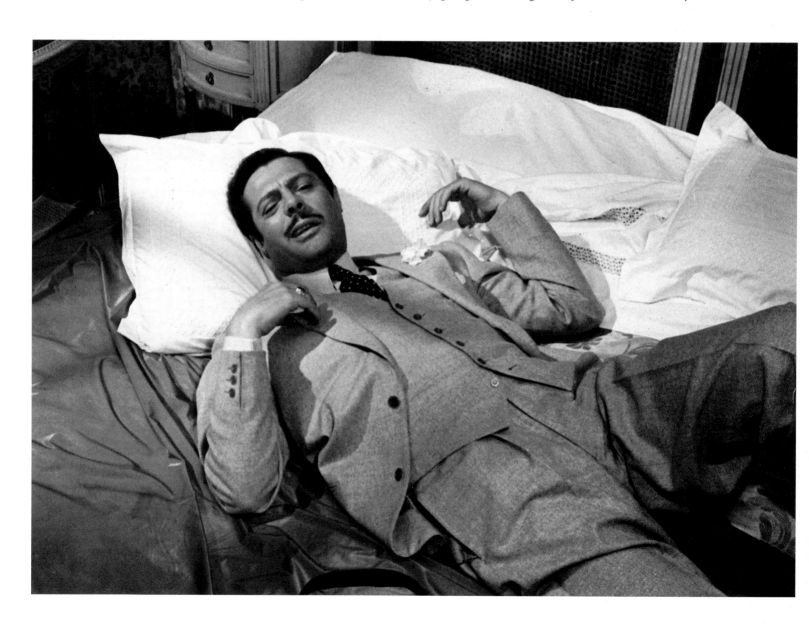

to eat her. He yells and shouts, wiping his face with the paper tissues his father manufactures, and leans his head back against the headboard of the bed. He is like an excited child at a circus. The strip-tease receives a comic treatment and is anyhow interrupted at the last moment, but it serves to emphasise the radical change in customs that has come about since the controversy caused by *La Dolce Vita*. Nonetheless, the reaction of the Catholic Centre for Cinema remains condemnatory. "The entirely exhibitionist strip-tease of the leading actress" signs the fate of the film and it receives a negative classification: it is banned.

On the 3rd of April 1964, he receives the British Film Academy award for the best foreign actor for his role in *Divorce Italian Style*. The French magazine *Paris Jour* publishes a survey in which fourteen world famous actresses are asked to say which actor they would most like to make a film with. Sophia Loren, Claudia Cardinale, Joanne Woodward, Annie Girardot, and Anouk Aimée all choose Mastroianni and he is classified first on the list. Catherine Deneuve, who Mastroianni has not yet worked with, chooses Samy Frey instead.

In the meantime he continues to work with De Sica. The title of *Marriage Italian Style* seems to indicate a parody of the earlier film by Germi and suggests a sort of family tie between the protagonists of the two films, Domenico Soriano and Baron Ferdinando Cefalù. Both are Southern males and are consequently cast in the role of lords and masters whose cynicism leads them to get rid of their women like getting rid of old clothes. Their affinity shows through too in their physical likeness and in the habits they have in common. In addition to the cigarette-holder and sunglasses, he now has a moustache and slicked-back hair. The film is based on the play *Filumena Marturano*, by Eduardo De Filippo, and owes a lot to the

film which De Filippo had adapted from the stage play.

Filumena is unexpectedly struck by a serious disease. Domenico is in one of the cake shops he owns, parading up and down in front of the mirror and showing the young shop assistant he wants to marry some hats he has bought for her. He is about to sign a cheque when he receives the news. Annoyed and disappointed, he throws the cheque-book into the air but has to rush home all the same.

When confronted with Filumena's death, which now seems inevitable, Domenico reluctantly agrees to marry her on her death-bed, in 'articulo mortis'. After a close-up of Mastroianni, whose face expresses astonishment rather than pain, the film moves into a long flash-back and

The deadly-serious game with Filumena is one that Domenico loses.

we see the first meeting with Filumena, then a seventeen-year-old girl, in a brothel during a bombing raid.

Two years later, when the war is over, they meet again and he takes her into a gate-keeper's lodge, where they make love. They continue to see one another. But the girl keeps working in the brothel and receives other clients . It is on her insistence that he sets her up in an appartment he owns and only when he needs her to act as a maid and nurse to his mother does he take her to his house. Filumena sleeps with him but remains in the role of servant and general assistant in his shops. The situation continues until she finds out about the imminent marriage with the shop girl.

The priest leaves the room and suddenly she is better. It was all a trick, not so much to tie him to her as to be able to give a name to the three children she has always hidden from him. In an outburst of rage Domenico overturns a coffer and feels ill. But "someboby who hasn't got a heart can't have a heart-attack", Filumena comments. Another flash-back shows the past years, this time through Filumena's eyes: having to bring up her children alone with nursemaids and in various institutions, always having to keep her activities secret. The marriage she has won through trickery is not valid but she wants at least to reunite her three children so that they can meet one another. "This isn't a detective film; it is a Russian tragedy because you are all my children," she tells them. Then she prepares to leave Soriano's house. But before she goes, she plants the seed of doubt in his mind; one of the three children, she tells him, is his.

The task of discovering the truth about his paternity gives a new meaning to Domenico's life. It makes him sharper. He tries to reconstruct his own past movements, studies old photographs, investigates the birth dates and personal characteristics of the three children. This research into the start of a life makes him realise that his relationship with Filumena was not as superficial as he had thought. He decides to marry her. But right up until the last, while he is waiting for the wedding ceremony to begin, he continues to try to find out which of the three possesses his own characteristics.

"When I was young I used to love singing It was my favourite thing. Which of you likes singing ?" he asks the three children. But they are a very rare strain of Neapolitan; they are all tone-deaf. Only at the end is he emotionally moved for a moment, when he hears himself greeted "Goodmorning, papà."

Never was a marriage so procrastinated and celebrated with such delay. This is precisely because the entire film moves around the central question, "Will he

A Place for Lovers *is another De Sica film. The love-affair between Marcello and Faye Dunaway has no future.*

marry her or not ?", a question dictated by the social mores of the day, which delimit the space within which the characters move. The woman of easy virtue who redeems herself is one of the perennial themes of light romantic literature. Cinderella finds her handsome prince. But even if the theme is dated, the mechanisms which are working in the male consciousness and the subsequent effect on the way the woman behaves remains perfectly topical.

Mastroianni gives Domenico Soriano the necessary superficiality and egotism for him to be convincing as a person interested only in women, horses, clothes, English shoes and enjoying himself. He remembers the clothes he was wearing on a particular occasion but can not remember the date of a romantic meeting. In his relationships with women he makes a clear distinction between the roles of wife and mistress. His relationship with his mistress, which is seen as an alternative to marriage, is based principally on sexuality, which here implies certain social conventions of exclusion. A marriage relationship, on the other hand, is based on the combined principles of sexuality, affection and family. And family relationships absorb everything, are the cover element for sex, and so social relationships come to the fore. Filumena, with her marginalised social role, can not be a wife even though she performs all the duties of a wife. She represents the alternative, the mistress who, because she plays the social game, is herself prepared to be identified with sexuality and can only take minimal recourse to sentiment. Because of this, Domenico can rightly say that he has never seen her cry but only because he has mistaken her dedication to her role for a lack of love.

Marcello and Vittorio De Sica's last meeting

Marcello and Sophia are tourists in Moscow.
Inside the stadium.

Mastroianni, suspended between cynicism and erotic instinct, occasionally appears opaque in his characterisation, almost as if he felt that the character was too schematic. More of a caricature than a psychologically complex character. He shows the embarrassment that is evident in all the films he has made with De Sica. Always caught between two women, he does not have the schizophrenic disposition necessary to easily mediate between two realities. It is a role which De Sica himself, on the other hand, played to perfection as actor.

In *A Place for Lovers*, Mastroianni plays an engineer who invents a guard-rail made out of water-filled plastic sacks. He tests it on the track himself in a racing car. "Driving doesn't tire me, I'm used to it." Yet another link between screen life and real life. Giulia, played by Faye Dunaway, is a rich American woman he has already seen

Antonio and Giovanna's
marriage
in Sunflowers.

With Ljndmila Savaleyeva, his Russian wife.

at an airport and been attracted to; she invites him to spend a few days together. He is a married man but even so accepts her offer with enthusiasm.

Their relationship, which started as a light affair in the mountains around Cortina, starts to become something deeper. But the girl, who is suffering from an incurable disease, decides to go back to the United States and leave him free to get on with his life. The story draws its inspiration from former greats: a late nineteenth century play by Maurice Donnay and the 1938 film *Joy of Living* by Tay Garnett, with Kay Francis and William

Powell. But De Sica's film is itself a mediocre production. Certain sociological elements allow him to set the film in the permissive climate of that period. It is the woman, because she is independent and American, who takes the lead. It is she who steals a suitcase from the villa where they are staying and a razor and some shaving cream from a department store.

Sunflowers (1970) is the last film he makes with De Sica and sees him again in partnership with Sophia Loren. The film, shot in Italy and in Russia, is the occasion of the actor's first transfer to Russia. As in *Marriage Italian Style*, De Sica makes use of a great many flash-backs, a very common technique in those years, but they tend to hinder the film's fluidity and make it appear dated. Giovanna remembers her

fiancé, a northener from Bellosguardo, leaving for Africa. She suggests that they get married so that he can avoid going to war and he replies: "I'd rather have the scorpions." In the end they get married. But marriage is not enough to escape conscription; so Antonio pretends to be mad and to suffer from murderous feelings towards his wife. His duplicity is discovered and he is forced to leave for Russia after all.

When the war is over and Antonio does not return and nobody can give her any news of him, Giovanna sets off to find him or at least to see his grave. When she finds him she discovers that he has re-married and has a young daughter. So she goes back home, determined to forget him. This time it is Antonio who can not

forget the past. He meets up with her again in Italy but now it is Giovanna's turn to pretend to have started a new life. In fact she has simply had a child from a casual relationship. The Mastroianni-Loren partnership is by now so well established that it works in spite of the film. Mastroianni has put on weight; his face is much more rounded than it usually is, something which even De Sica remarks upon in a letter to his daughter Emi: "Mastroianni has turned up fatter than usual. He can't stop eating. His face is all puffed up like a cushion. he has promised me that he will lose two kilos in the two days left before we start filming." But he does not seem to have kept his word if the enormous meals De Sica continues to refer to in his letters are anything to go by. Caviar, sturgeon, Georgian hors d'oeuvres, liver and onions, devilled chicken, and naturally gallons of vodka end up disturbing everybody's sleep. In the film Mastroianni is even forced to speak Russian. But an affectionately malicious comment by De Sica suggests that his Russian is more like Arabic than anything else.

In the years 1963 to 1969, between one film and the next with De Sica, Mastroianni meets up again with Mario Monicelli in *Casanova '70*, with Elio Petri in *The Tenth Victim* and with Luchino Visconti in *The Stranger*. He works for the first time under the direction of Marco Ferreri and Eduardo De Filippo. He appears in the theatre in *Ciao Rudy*. He even goes to England where he manages to act in English even though he still does not know the language well: a real shot in the dark. This amazing surge of activity seems to be pre-announced in *Casanova '70*. Major Andrea Rossi Colombetti, a NATO official, only manages to feel sexually excited when he is in danger. One of his lovers accuses him of being impotent. A visit to the psychoanalyst reveals that his particular perversion could become dangerous. But he decides to ignore the voice

In Moscow, at the circus with his daughter Barbara and his wife.

of caution. He writes in his diary: "Professor's prophecy found true. Demon broken loose in me. Resist? Why? Decide to go ahead and cross the Rubicon, General's wife first objective".

"*Casanova '70* is an amusing film which is built around the attempt, close to my heart, to destroy the image of the Italian 'Latin lover' stud, a label which is far from flattering. In my trips round the world I have noticed that the Italian male is invariably regarded as a stud or something like that, which is fine if that is the way someone is, but it would be nice if this physiological quality was coupled with perhaps a certain sensitivity, which is something which foreigners don't often think about. For this reason I have always wanted to do films in which the amorous fragility of the Italians is emphasised, which show that they are not freaks, that they are like everybody else; perhaps they are more in love with love than others, but in an imaginative sort of way, not like animals. So *Casanova '70* grew out of this desire to destroy this image of the Italians, by showing a man who, on the contrary, could never manage to make love and actually needed a fantasy-related situation, in fact a dangerous situation in order to become excited sexually."

Mastroianni creates a caricature of himself; he does not hesitate to parody the harem of *8½* and to make fun of his own image as a latin lover. He enjoys making fun of himself in an acrobatic, circus-like sort of love. But when he falls in love he discovers that "the most marvellous adventure of all is the conquest of the woman you love," which unites fantasy, surprise and mystery. It is the happy ending that softens the film's sharpness with its unexpected encounters and its unusual comical-humoristic veneer. True to his motto "A woman who is easy to get is not worth getting," he launches his assault on the wife of a crafty and insanely jealous old Venetian count who pretends to be

deaf in order to keep an eye on her. Marco Ferreri, the baddie in thick glasses, ends up suffering the fate he had intended for Andrea: he is squashed beneath a huge boulder which falls from the top of his villa.

He works with Ferreri-actor immediately before working with Ferreri-director. But *The Man With the Balloons*, their first film together as director and actor, did not meet with much luck. "With Ferreri there is the pleasure, the real joy of collaboration because he gives the actors space. He is the one in control; but if the actors enter into his world in a way he likes there is the chance to invent, the chance to really have fun. The first film I made with Ferreri was *The Man With the Five Balloons* or *The Man With the Balloons*. Ponti was not convinced of the validity of the

His encounter with Ferreri is one that is to be repeated several times during the actor's career. "Working with Ferreri is a pleasure, because he gives actors space. He controls them, but if they succeed in entering into his mental world, they can enjoy themselves and invent."

film and he cut it down, or rather mutilated it, and inserted it into *Kiss the Other Sheik* together with two other episodes. It was not a good idea. I remember fighting with him over it for a while, saying: 'If you have cut the film down because you are not convinced of its commercial viability, since it's about a suicide, the story of a suicide, why not do two other sketches on the same theme?' I had even managed, I must say without any difficulty, to persuade Pasolini to consider doing one of the episodes. He told me that he would like to make a film about Petronio Arbitro's suicide because it seemed like it had been a joyful thing. When I suggested it to Ponti he asked me if I was mad, wanting to put three episodes of suicide together. Actually I thought it was a very modern idea and that it would have been very interesting. A year later, Ponti allowed the film to be re-constructed. But by the time it was released it was too late. It is Ferreri's most interesting film because it already contains all the elements which were to come out in the films he made after that: food, solitude, misogyny, the inability to establish a relationship with a woman; it was all condensed in there, a sort of sketch or study from which he then drew one of the themes to develop in each of his subsequent films. One could almost say that each of those five balloons became a film."

Receiving a stern look from Catherine Spaak, the businessman of The Man With the Balloons *finds himself in difficulty.*

Life is an empty balloon. It is useless and dangerous to fill-up on air. Everything could end in a big bang, the screenwriters and authors, Marco Ferreri and Rafael Azcona, seem to joke in the apologue, which moves around the two central figures Mastroianni and his girlfriend, Giovanna (Catherine Spaak). It is Christmas and Mario Fugetta, a confectionary manufacturer, is giving away balloons as gifts in order to advertise his products. He blows them up until they burst. He is assailed by a doubt and tries to find an answer to it by questioning an engineer friend of his. "I want to see just how much I can blow up this balloon, because if I stop blowing it up, and there is still some space left inside then I have failed. Can you see why I have failed? The problem is simple yet at the same time very serious because if I don't manage it, inside I am a moral failure. And what about you?

Haven't you got any moral problems inside? You are all idiots. Do you understand?" He is talking to his friend, but the question comes just as we see a close-up of Ferreri gorging himself on a sandwich.

Food and sex seem to be the only answers to Mario's desperate demands. The woman he makes love to, in whose lap he seeks protection, the womb as refuge, puts up with him until his neurosis becomes intolerable and irreversible. When the moment comes she bursts his balloon with her lighted cigarette. Mario has a fit of hysterics and wants to kill her. Instead he throws her out. He identifies himself with the balloon and realises how fragile and exposed he is to the woman's unimaginative but positive action. The woman saves herself. He is the one to throw her out but it is she who provides the excuse to escape from him. At that point he decides to eat the enormous amount of food he has bought all by himself. But even this is a false solution. The male crisis has by now taken hold and the only solution is to throw himself out of the window.

Is it the man who is first to realise the crisis of consumerism in society and denies it by taking his own life, or is it the woman who, in her practical way, accepts it and goes beyond it? In *The Man With the Balloons*, Mastroianni is also the child who plays with the balloons. Or rather, the adult regressing to the infant stage in the oedipal attempt to return to the maternal womb. The image of the balloon which arrives at breaking point and then bursts, symbolizes the temptation of a man who returns to the moment of birth when he dies.

Mastroianni's interpretation is sharp and of a rare intelligence. The neurosis of the modern male touches and assails him. He feels it to be part of himself. He plays the part surrealistically, drawing out the character's contradictions. He is capricious and methodical, lively and oppressive, maniacal and depressive. The film passes virtually unnoticed in Italy. It fares better on the continent where it is distributed under the title *Break-Up*. Reduced to a short episode and given the title *The Man With the Balloons*, the film is included in *Kiss the Other Sheik* together with *Rush Hour*, written by Eduardo De Filippo and *The Blonde Wife* by Luciano Salce, in both of which Mastroianni also plays the lead role. Mastroianni's presence in all three films was intended to provide a sense of unity, but the film still remains rather unbalanced. In all three episodes there is a futuristic quality which takes the edge off the provocation.

In *Rush Hour* he plays a scientist who receives a Nobel prize nomination and returns to Italy after a twelve-year absence for a brief period of rest. He has suffered from a nervous break-down which has left him with various nervous tics and a phobia about noise. He is unlucky however, as the couple of friends he stays with have the habit of settling their quarrels by firing a round of shots with a pistol. To be precise the husband terrorises the wife by shooting at her. Michele, who carries over his rather child-like qualities from Ferreri's film, wants to join in the fun and hopes to settle the affair by inventing a happiness-bullet which would make the wife gentle, meek and understanding. The fear of not maintaining his dominance over a woman is carried over from the manufacturer, Mario Fugetta. But the shots which are fired in houses all over the city, mainly blanks but occasionally real bullets, are only a sign of the cinema's impotence and inability to confront, even metaphorically, the social upheavals which are taking place.

In *The Blonde Wife* he plays a cashier whose wife is far too beautiful and far too expensive. In order to get rid of Pepita who is like a gas-guzzling American car, Michele decides to sell her into the harem of a prince he has met at the bank. But

the emir already has more than enough of her type and instead recommends approaching a friend of his. It is Michele who ends up in the desert, however, dressed as an odalisque, in the rather original harem of the emir, who prefers young men. His wife has caught on straight away and, in a reversal of fortunes, sells him off at a nice profit. And so the final scene shows him in flowing veils, make-up and jewels trying to catch up with her car as it disappears into the desert.

A lesson in aggression for Pamela Tiffin, the wife for sale in Kiss the Other Sheik.

4

I'm Not Rudolf Valentino

The Stranger is one of the films that Mastroianni most wanted to do. The screen adaptation of Camus's novel came about due to the actor's desire to produce as well as appear in the film.

For some years now he has been the best paid, most photographed, most talked about actor in Italy, second only to Sophia Loren. He is one of a small group of highly paid international stars, including Albert Finney, who earns a little less than he does, Peter O'Toole and Richard Burton, who earn a little more, Omar Sharif and a few others. Mastroianni's price to do a film at this time is one hundred and fifty million lire. But when he makes *Ciao Rudy*, a musical about the life of Rudolf Valentino written by Sandro Garinei, Pietro Giovannini and Luigi Magni and directed by Magni, he accepts a lot less. One hundred thousand lire a day and fifty per cent of the takings. He is keen to get back on the stage and in spite of his claims of laziness accepts spending two hours and forty minutes on stage singing and dancing. And no sacrifice is too great to achieve his objective; he gives up parts in several films and even takes singing and dancing lessons.

He starts rehearsals punctually on the first of October 1965 at the Teatro Sistina. Every evening, feeling dizzy and with aching legs, he practises the steps laid down for him in the script and tries out the songs written by Armando Trovaioli, including the theme tune "Quattro palmi di terra in California" (Four Plots of Land in California). Among the many offers he receives during this period, one is from Tony Richardson to play the lead in *The Sailor From Gibraltar*. But he has little desire to work abroad and turns down the offer. In the end the film features Jan Bannen and Trevor Howard, with Jeanne Moreau and Vanessa Redgrave.

He appears on the Italian television show *Studio Uno* hosted by the popular 1960's pop singer, Mina. He sings a song with her "The Man For Me" and does a sketch with a dog: an affectionate parody of Bobby Solo. Ever since the start of his career he had been asked to sing and he has always enjoyed it. Developing his voice is one of the many aspects of acting that has always appealed to him and yet again we see his natural talents making up for a lack of formal training, with excellent results.

Between his mother and his wife, made-up as Rudolf Valentino.

In 1965 he plays the leading role in *The Tenth Victim*, directed by Elio Petri, an interesting experiment in introducing science fiction into Italian cinema. "The American story which inspired the film was rather dramatic, not to say tragic. In a world where war no longer exists, people continue to invent games where thay can kill one another. Many years later, Petri told me that he would like to re-make the film's ending because the happy ending in the film had been forced on him by the distributors. These are the limitations of cinema when it becomes an industry; it forces the film maker to abide by certain rules which have nothing to do with the truer dictates of his creativity."

Inspired by Robert Sheckley's short story *The Seventh Victim* it tells the story of "The Big Hunt", a lethal game in which a hunter and a victim are chosen by an electronic brain in Geneva. The important thing is that they do not know one another or suspect anything. It is a battle of wits to the death. The American, Caroline Meredith (Ursula Andress) is the hunter. Marcello Poletti, a clean-shaven Italian with highlighted hair and glasses, the victim. The film is treated in a humoristic fashion made still more amusing by the continual references to contemporary Italian society and to Mastroianni himself.

When interviewed he is asked: "Do you believe in God?" "Of course." "Do you believe in the family?" "Not as much." Caroline, who is observing him on a monitor, says: "I've always been wary of lazy types; you never know which way to take them". About marriage in Italy, he says: "In Italy hardly anyone gets married. It's not worth it; we co-habit; we are very religious". On sexuality: "You're ticklish. That means you're very sensual"; "A real cyclone. Shall we go through with it?". On

With a peroxided crew-cut, he gives a stylized recital in an interesting Italian experiment with science-fiction.

the cinema character: "Poor Marcello caught up in his problems with women, wife, mistress, prey, hunters; and I who looked on you as the symbol of savage man in all his glory". On lies, Caroline: "You need truth in a relationship". Marcello: "Who needs truth? Nobody likes the truth. It's much better like this with lies and complications. Even though I am ashamed to say it". The actor plays along, making fun of himself and of the myth of well-being in a rather stylised interpreta-

A new Mastroianni in The Tenth Victim, *with Ursula Andress.*

After a ten-year absence, he returns to the theatre. In Ciao, Rudy *he acts alongside the eternal Paola Borboni, amongst others.*

tion which is, however, well-suited to the role of a futuristic male, more robot than man.

On the 7th of January, 1966, *Ciao, Rudy* opens at the Teatro Sistina in Rome. Mastroianni has given-up smoking, he has lost ten kilos and he makes his debut a little worn-out but also moved. His eye shines with that rare enthusiasm which an actor only gets from the theatre, with its emotion and anticipation. He is surrounded by a host of actresses who play the various women in Valentino's life. Olga Villi (Tatiana Nimova, his second wife), Paola Borboni (Cecilia Patterson), Giusy Raspani Dandolo (Rosy), Ilaria Occhini (Annie, his first wife), Giuliana Lojodice (Betty Green), Paola Pitagora (the president of his fan-club), Tina Lattanzi (his mother), Raffaella Carrà (Margie), Angela Pagano (Teodolina, his Italian fiancée), Virginia Minoprio (Bonita, his dance partner), Nina da Padova (Mamma Caruso), Simona Sorlisi (Mabel Thomas), Eleonora Mura (the secretary). They all move around him, the only male character. It is not a complete critical success, but the public love it. It draws people and interest. Some illustrious colleagues come to see it, like Barbra Streisand and Gloria Swanson. But after three tiring months, Mastroianni decides to pay a penalty of one hundred million lire instead of continuing with the show which is scheduled to run a tour in Italy and a four-month American tour. His decision comes as a big disappointment to his American female fans who feel the same about him as their mothers and

Dancing the tango from Rudolf Valentino's film The Four Horsemen of the Apocalypse *with Virginia Minoprio in* Ciao, Rudy.

Made-up as Mandrake for a Vogue *photo-session. He will appear many years later in the same disguise in* Intervista.

One of the screen-tests for Il viaggio di G. Mastorna, *Fellini's project that never became a film.*

grandmothers felt about Rudolf Valentino. Like Valentino, Mastroianni too had left his hand print in the cement of the famous Chinese Theatre in Hollywood.

That same year Fellini's project to make a film with the title *Il viaggio di G. Mastorna* (G. Mastorna's Journey) is again on the cards but once again comes to nothing. On the 12th of March he takes part again in the television show *Studio Uno*, hosted by Sandra Milo. He appears in various sketches in which he plays the trumpet, sings and dances, all the time protesting his reluctance. As a finale he joins in a tango from *Ciao, Rudy* with the whole of the show's cast. During the year he moves house to a villa near the baths of Caracalla, one of the prime sites in Rome; his old friend Franco Bartoccini is in charge of the restructuring, and the famous set designer who worked on *Ciao, Rudy*, Giulio Coltellacci, does the furnishings. He acts in *Io,*

io, io...e gli altri (Me, Me, Me... and the Others) by Alessandro Blasetti, *The Poppy Is Also a Flower*, by Terence Young and in *Shoot Loud, Louder... I Don't Understand* by Eduardo De Filippo. It is the result of a long-awaited collaboration which is finally decided when De Filippo goes to congratulate Mastroianni at the first night of *Ciao Rudy*. This was the first of the two films produced by Master Films, a production company set up by Mastroianni and Joseph H. Levine, an energetic American who had made his money by establishing a company to distribute famous Italian films in America. In order to launch De Filippo's film in America, Levine organizes a large-scale promotion tour in America with an enormous number of press conferences.

After the experiment in production with *White Nights* and *Contro la legge* (Against the Law), Mastroianni tries on

the producer's hat again and decides on a very special director, Eduardo De Filippo, who was one of Italy's great theatre talents. But *Shoot Loud, Louder... I Don't Understand* is not a success. "Mainly because Levine was depending on me for the organization without knowing that I had never been able to organize anything, not even myself. Precisely because I was the film's producer, I preferred to leave the directing to Eduardo. I greatly admired him as an artist but felt that if I didn't suggest it myself nobody else would have got round to suggesting that he direct me. Perhaps this wasn't such a good idea, however, because, in spite of his undisputed talent in the theatre, Eduardo hadn't had much experience as a cinema director. I don't know why, perhaps producers preferred to use a different director and only use him as an actor or perhaps he himself had not really taken the cinema that seriously. But

On the set of Shoot Loud, Louder…
I Don't Understand, *with Eduardo De Filippo.*

I wanted to be directed by him so I organized it with this production. The film wasn't a complete success because we had to give way to certain market forces. The American distributor, who was financing the film, insisted on having Raquel Welch in one of the roles, because this was important for the American market. Eduardo's excellent play *Le voci di dentro* (The Voices Inside), on which the film was based, suffered the consequences, was violated and thrown out of balance, and as a result the film was not convincing. Still, I have no regrets about doing it. As the years pass it isn't the takings that count but memories and experience, and for me it was a great honour and a real privilege to be directed by Eduardo."

Alberto Saporito, sculptor and assembler of carnival lights, with his dyed red hair, long side-burns which extend into a halo all round his face, thin moustaches and a single earring in his left ear, lives in an antiques warehouse. His uncle Nicola, who lives on the ground floor, communicates with his nephew by letting off firecrackers in a complicated and noisy Morse code. Alberto often dreams and sometimes he confuses dreams with reality. One night he dreams that he has seen a murder and goes to the police to report it. But the murder, which hasn't happened yet, gets him involved in a plot by some shady characters who even try to drown him. The Neapolitan comedy which is full of confusion due to an excess of imaginative input, turns out to be muddled and chaotic. Mastroianni tries to keep the film going with his own interpretation, which moves from madness to agitation to sentiment to farce. The film ends in a great explosion which destroys all the furniture, apart from the chairs, which fly up in the air and then fall back to the ground unharmed. Alberto leaves Naples in the sidecar of a motorbike ridden by Raquel Welch, an unlikely prostitute who has been forced to return north with an obligatory "exit visa." Uncle Nicola has gone up in smoke together with the rest of the warehouse but Alberto still seems to hear him throwing fire-crackers as if he wanted to communicate with his nephew as before.

In March 1967, on the invitation of the theatre critic and director of the *Accademia di Arte Drammatica*, Renzo Tian, he gives a talk to the students of the drama school

With Tecla Scarano in Shoot Loud, Louder… I Don't Understand.

about his occupation. His direct and sceptical way of presenting his profession and his lack of the typical actor's self-glorification make a big impression on the students. He starts working on Visconti's *The Stranger* which is presented at the Venice Film Festival on the 6th of September.

"It was the second film I made as a producer; I made it for de Laurentiis with Master Films. Visconti was asked to direct it, partly, too, because Camus' widow would not give the rights for a cinematographic treatment to anyone else. The film was not an immediate success; at the time it was said that Visconti had produced too literal a treatment of the book, that he should have given it a more personal interpretation. But he had had to respect the wishes of Mme. Camus, who didn't want anything changed and wanted everything in the film to remain faithful to the author's intentions. In spite of all this I still think that it is an excellent film, and know that many people agree with me, because when it was first shown on television, it was re-discovered, in spite of the rather luke-warm reaction of the critics. There are often changes in the way a film is received, even by the public."

The film is long overdue in being made, since Visconti had wanted to make a film based on Camus' novel back in 1962, straight after Algerian independence. In the end it comes into being principally thanks to Mastroianni's intervention. Only with his name and his capital, which convince the distributors, does De Laurentiis decide to go ahead and produce it. Tired of comedies and stagey acting, Mastroianni, like the book's principal character, Meursault, wants to try himself *jusqu'au bout* (to the limit). "If an actor does not take risks, he becomes a commercial product, like a bottle of Coca-Cola. An actor's choices are important, often crucial; they are the thing that really counts. There is the risk of making a bad choice, the worry about remaining popular. It rarely happens

that you get a role like this one, so complete and so perfectly sculpted in every detail. And here stands the risk. You have no leeway, and everything is expected of you. How to convince the public that your face, your way of moving and seeming are his and not the ones each of them has given him in their imagination?"

The character of Meursault had already proved a fascinating one for such actors as Montgomery Clift, James Dean, and Alain Delon, but none of them had been successful in interpreting him. For Mastroianni, who is perhaps ten years older than the book's protagonist is supposed to be, the character becomes a real challenge. He immerses himself in the character to the point of eradicating all useless gestures, in an attempt to represent, through the immobility which is broken only by a half smile, in a tired movement which is immediately repressed, the psychological (or moral?) apathy of the ambitionless French office worker, a *pied noir* who is thoroughly oppressed by the relentless African climate.

Arthur Meursault, accused of the murder of an Arab, is taken, handcuffed, before the public prosecutor. A long flashback recounts the events of the days immediately before the murder. It is accompanied by a voice-over commentary by Mastroianni-Meursault; a narrative device which restores the subjective viewpoint and provides us with direct access to the psychology of the protagonist. When his mother dies, Meursault travels to a village some distance from Algiers to attend the funeral. "It was very hot, I slept most of the way." Right from the start we are given proof of this purely physical way of reacting which guides his behaviour. Phys-

With Visconti, during filming in Algiers.

97

ical and biological needs and behaviour and an ever-present sensual awareness are the elements which dominate. The day after his mother's funeral he meets Marie, an ex-colleague, on the beach and they begin a sexual relationship. A neighbour of his, Raymond, gets him to help write a letter to his Arab mistress. As a result of his collaboration, Raymond regards him as a friend. Meursault gives evidence in his favour when he beats his mistress up. One Sunday Raymond invites Meursault and Maria to the beach. He is uneasy because they are followed by his mistress's brother and some other young Arabs. While they are walking along the beach, the young Arabs accost them and Raymond receives a knife injury. Meursault stops him from retaliating and takes the pistol off him. Later, he goes back to the beach alone and meets one of the young Arabs, who draws his knife. He takes out Raymond's gun and fires one shot. Then, blinded by the sun, fires another four shots into the corpse.

At the trial he defends his action: "It was the sun". He is accused of insensitivity towards his mother because the day after her funeral he started a relationship and went to the cinema; and he is found guilty not so much for the murder he has committed but for being different from other people. "I accuse this man of burying his mother with a criminal's heart," the public prosecutor concludes. Only after being sentenced to death does the stranger realise what an absurd world it is, this world from which he has now been excluded. Meursault's consciousness awakes to realise that the only reality is death. Mastroianni's interpretation gives Meursault the mediterranean lethargy, the gestual sensuality, the vitality of appetite and the inertia

On the beach with Anna Karina, before tragedy strikes.

of sentiment which make him live as film character as he had lived as a book character.

This second and final production by Master Films is again not very successful. But it seems that the role of producer is appealing to Mastroianni, since during this period he contemplates producing a screen version of *Ciao Rudy* and financing a Lina Wertmuller production, a thriller set in a dance club. In December, Gastone Guidotti, the Italian ambassador in England, presents him with a British Film Academy Award for *Yesterday, Today and Tomorrow*. Mastroianni happens to be in London because he is working on *Diamonds for Breakfast*, by Christopher Morahan. It is the first film he agrees to make in English and the fact that he does not know the language means that he has to learn his lines parrot-fashion. He has accepted the offer, having turned-down many other similar offers, because the failure of the Master Films experiment means that he now needs the money.

Lots of projects have to be abandoned. *Mafia Business* by Mario Monicelli, which should have been made in the United States, *Yes, Sir* by Dino Risi, *Christopher Columbus* by Edward Dmytryk and even two films by Visconti: a version of *Macbeth* and a film about the life of Puccini. On the 27th of December he is decorated by the President of the Republic with the honour of a Knight of the Order "To the Merit of the Italian Republic".

In England he plays the descendant of a Russian noble family exiled in the Bolshevik revolution. Nicky the grand-duke plays a double role. On the one hand he is the pleasure-loving and vulgar modern youth: "there are certain parts of the female anatomy that I never forget to observe particularly well," he asserts, looking at a woman's backside. On the other he is the grotesque, austere prince, made-up like Eisenstein's Ivan, one of his ancestors. At all events he is determined to take back the

The Russian grand duke of Diamonds for Breakfast *plots the 'reappropriation' of the jewels of the Czar with Rita Tushingham.*

family jewels, on display in a gallery.

In a strange confusion between noble Russian and Italian lover, he creates his own harem like Guido in *8½*. But this time the sexual revolution of the 1960s has left its mark (it is 1969) and he finds himself with seven live-in lovers. Nicola, an easy-going lover who doesn't suffer from any form of guilt complex in his relationships, feels completely at ease with his seven girlfriends who for their part keep him constantly active sexually. But in midst of his euphoria over his successes in sex and banditry, Nemesis appears in the form of his old aunt, and he ends up the loser. She manages to take the jewels off him and loses them gambling. The revolutionary atmosphere of the film lends a certain edge to the characters. For instance Bridget, the leader of the group of women, has collaborated with the others in getting round the Soviet commissar responsible for the jewels, but refuses to join-in the toast to private property, being both a Marxist and a thief. Mastroianni, surrounded by beautiful women, moves from the sharp and snappy to the slow and sensual in his interpretation.

"*Diamonds for Breakfast* was an amusing piece. I went to England partly, too, because I wanted to get away from Italy. I felt that I had been wrong to refuse all those offers of work abroad, and so I set out without knowing even a word of English and managed to do it by learning my lines parrot-fashion. I enjoyed myself: London was beautiful at that time, with its hippies and the Beatles; it was an enjoyable experience." One of the promotion slogans invented for Mastroianni by Paramount to launch the film ran as follows: "Take the soft skin of seven sexy elusive jewel thieves and add a grand-duke, Nicky; shake vigorously in an ice-bucket and leave over-night. What you will get is a rich profusion of *Diamonds for Breakfast*. This cocktail of mine will give you a kick. And no kidding! Take it from me, Marcello Mastroianni."

He makes two other films in England but they pass with little notice. In *Giochi particolari* (Strange Games), he plays a sort of voyeur who uses his cine-camera to capture an image of a world that he feels increasingly distant from. It has been compared to a sort of *Blow Up* in reverse. In Antonioni's film the image framed by the camera is a rival version of life, something which emulates real life. In Franco Indovina's film, whose screenwriter was Tonino Guerra, it is more like the first stage of death.

Leo the Last (1970) was another film which met with little success. "I made *Leo the Last* because John Boorman, who had seen me in *The Organizers*, asked me to do it. I was happy to return to London, having enjoyed myself there the last time. The film won the Cannes Film Festival award for the best director. It is a very beautiful film, but it has had virtually no popular success; hardly anyone has seen it. Nobody even went to the cinema. Every now and then I bump into someone who says, '*Leo the Last*, beautiful film.' Especially foreigners. And I say: 'You're right; and you're the fourteenth person who has seen it. There are only fourteen of you, but you all thought it was beautiful'. Why on earth no one ever went to see this film is a mystery. I think the distribution was badly handled, even though right from the first day nobody went to see it; it's a strange thing."

Again cast as an impoverished Eastern prince, this time he combines characteristics of the two previous roles in one. A voyeur who spies on the movements of the pigeons on his roof and people in the neighbouring houses through his binoculars, and at the same time an anarchist ready to shout out in protest against the injustices he sees around him. He is at his most convincing when he speaks out against privilege at his window; but when he turns to action, he loses credibility. Boorman's political allegory is based on Leo's "disillusioned passivity" which itself lends a grotesque angle to the fairytale. Mastroianni's interpretation, in which he presents a character who allows himself to be carried away by events and by compassion and who doesn't understand the political significance of his actions, has been misinterpreted by Italian criticism and, as a consequence, undervalued.

During one of his visits to London he is approached by Sam Peckinpah, who offers him the lead in a film about a man who hides in Harrods in London because he is being chased by himself and then disappears. Mastroianni, who only knows Peckinpah as the director of violent films, and whose English is still not very good, does not manage to understand what the director is talking about. So the film is never

Leo the Last, *which won a prize at Cannes, gives the actor the opportunity to play another eccentric nobleman.*

101

made, even though Peckinpah tries to repeat his offer when he goes to Rome in 1978 to do a part in an Italian film.

Capitalizing on his 'classy' image, English directors dress him up as a member of the nobility, even if he is a rather shabby representative. Ettore Scola, on the

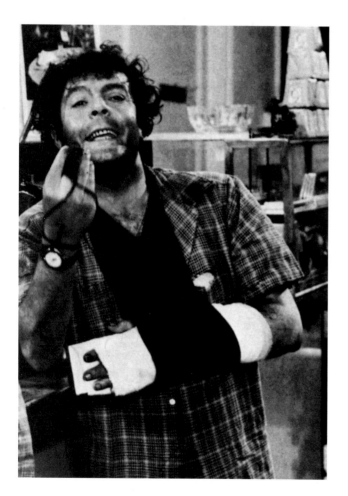

In this first encounter with Ettore Scola, the actor returns to playing vaudeville-type roles.

other hand, in the first two stories he asks him to play in, offers him working-class roles. The intentions of both are, however, the same: to make Mastroianni's face, which has become part of the collective imagination, the face which epitomises and reflects a sense of social discontent which they can recognise as their own.

"*The Pizza Triangle* is a film I am very attached to; for me it is a real masterpiece. A return to popular characters, who were at the same time transformed by a new kind of language, in a more fantastic atmosphere which was highlighted by an interesting strain of irony. I had a lot of fun playing this ingenuous, retarded Communist which also won me a prize for the best actor at the Cannes Film Festival."

The film makes frequent references to the politics of the day, and is written by the Age-Scarpelli duo, together with Scola. It recounts, in a style both ironic and grotesque, the loves and betrayals of three lower-working-class people. The story is reconstructed by the voice-over comments of the three leading characters during the trial and by the characters' dialogues. The first scenes show Mastroianni-Oreste being accompanied by the police to the fruit-market to re-construct the crime. The end of a Communist Party rally is the meeting place for a bricklayer, Oreste, who is married to a woman much older than he, and a young flower-seller, Adelaide. The urban landscape is dominated by rubbish; the first sign of a society suffocated by its own excessive consumerism. The lovers look for a place on the sand to make love; but the beach is covered with debris. In a moment of passion Adelaide offers herself to Oreste like a heroine in one of the light fiction novels she enjoys reading: "Do what you want with me, ask what you want of me." "Vote Communist next Sunday," he replies.

But the passion between them starts to

wane on the arrival of Nello, a Tuscan pizza chef whom Mastroianni has met in a demonstration in which they were both beaten up by the police. Mastroianni's ingenuously progressive politics are accompanied by an equally straight-forward sentimental rigidity based on the simple possession of the beloved. "The worker has one and only one possession, his woman. So what if someone tries to take that one thing off him? If someone tried to take my woman away from me, I'd kill him." Abandoned by Adelaide and reduced to the level of a tramp, Oreste is true to his word. In the moment in which Adelaide is about to marry Nello, Oreste leaps on his rival with the intention of killing him. He ends up killing Adelaide instead. When he is released from the prison asylum, he wanders around the streets of Rome, talking to an absent Adelaide. "I mean, instead of asking other nations to be more humane, why don't we start with our own? Look here: we have changed the heart of a historic city into an infernal merry-go-round for Gianni Agnelli's Fiats."

It is a comment which is more topical than ever and what must originally have been said in a subversive key now reads like a statement of what is the unfortunate and irreversible truth. With his curly hair and heavy eye-brows Mastroianni finds himself in a Roman comedy mask and in his agitated representation of an obtuse proletarian is very close to Dino Risi's gallery of horrors. "Oreste is a really naive, coarse, ingenuous bricklayer but he has a truly amazing relationship with a sense of the ideal. He confuses his Communist beliefs with his passion for a girl who in the meantime has fallen in love with a pizza chef. There is a gem of a scene where there is a Communist Party meeting in Piazza San Giovanni, and while the meeting is being addressed, Oreste carries on talking to his group leader about his sentimental problems," Mastroianni recalls. He places *The Pizza Triangle* among the most

My Name Is Rocco Papaleo *is an adventure set in America, where the Italian art of "getting by" is put to a hard test. The main character is very like Oreste in* The Pizza Triangle. *"Rocco Papaleo is practically Oreste's brother. They're both workmen, though Rocco has emigrated to America. They're ingenuous, puzzled by events. Not because they're stupid; they aren't at all shrewd and can't really figure what's going in their lives. They're very modest characters and so very similar."*

important moments in his career. In fact his performance wins him the "Palme d'Or" at the 1970 Cannes Film Festival.

When we see them again today, the characters Oreste and Rocco Papaleo, two pariahs of very low intellectual and social pretensions, seem rather predictable. Perhaps an indication of the bias of certain assumptions. "The adventure of *My Name Is Rocco Papaleo* was not a complete success. But we are all fond of this film partly, too, because we made it for free, asking

only a share of the profits if there ever were any. But there never were. So we spent three months in Chicago and it was okay; it was a valid experience. Sometimes it has happened that I have made films without being paid. If you like a story, if you like working with a particular director, if it is something you really believe in, then you just go for it. If there are profits, all well and good. If there aren't, too bad. It's not something you can do all the time, naturally; it has to be a special kind of relationship. Someone to whom you can say: 'Let's do it, whatever it costs us; we like working together and we'll see how things go.' Rocco Papaleo is really Orestes' brother. He is the same ingenuous guy who has emigrated to America and works as a labourer. One stayed in Italy to work and the other went to America. He has the same confusions; he doesn't understand, like Oreste. They neither of them understand, not because they are stupid; they are not shrewd; they just don't know how the world works. Being the extremely modest characters that they are, they are very similar."

A busby on his head and wearing a red and black checked jacket, Rocco, who works the lift of an Alaskan mine, goes to Chicago to see a boxing match. He arrived in America hoping to become a famous boxer but he has only become a dozy ex-boxer. His former profession has left him with a tic: he frequently touches his lips with his thumb and fore finger as though he were licking them to count some money. He is run-over by a car driven by a beautiful girl and although she only takes care of him out of civic duty, he falls in love with her and follows her, hoping to be loved in return. But, in order to get rid of him once and for all, Jenny (Lauren Hutton), the top model whose image smiles from bill-boards all over town, points out how he allows himself to be walked all over: "Look what they have done to you; you lost in the ring and you'll go on losing all your life". Brought brusquely back to reality, Rocco moves towards a group of carnival floats, carrying the bomb given to him by Gengis Khan, a tramp friend of his who has been run over by a lorry.

The television-style flashbacks and situation replays recreate the flux of experience and of memory in which before and after are not always easy to distinguish. It is an entirely subjective vision which is a product of Rocco's mental confusion but also of his dreams. Scola's fairytale realism presents an image of marginalization in the two films by inventing an eccentric language which gives the impression that the characters are even more estranged, that they live in a parallel reality. Rocco's speech, for instance, is rich in adverbial phrases: "I have never distantly seen someone like that"; "We hardly know one another at all". In *The Pizza Triangle* it is Adelaide who talks like the light fiction novels she reads. In both films, Mastroianni makes a timid attempt to sing. With Adelaide, he sings for joy in a dream. As Rocco he sings a song by Domenico Modugno, "Piove", to the jeers of a group of American spectators. Another of the film's social comments worth mentioning is the scene in which a young black boxer reveals to Rocco some of the activities of the American Nazi Party. He puts a coin in the phone, dials a number and they hear a repeated message: "There is only one efficient way of resolving the problem of the negroes: kill them all."

From confronting the problems of social injustice, used as an element in presenting his own personal existential crisis, Mastroianni moves to the apparent calm of the character Mario Carlisi. In *The Priest's Wife* by Dino Risi, he seems hardly touched by the effusive ardour of Valeria (Sophia Loren), who wants to marry him. The understanding voice on the end of the phone, he takes a help-line call from a woman who has attempted to commit suicide for love. But for Valeria, a voice is not enough. She wants to meet him. Her disappointment at his priest's robes makes him comment: "What did you expect to find in a community centre, a film actor?". Joking about his role, he brings to life a character who seems to develop psychologically, but in reality remains static. This time he speaks in a cultured way: "To commiserate with oneself is akin to making a myth of oneself." He quotes from the classics: "Baudelaire said that the priest is magnificent because he makes people believe a whole load of incredible things."

The film is shot in Padua, traditionally one of the strongholds of reactionary ecclesiasticism, and is built around the controversy of marriage in the priesthood. Don Mario seems the only one within the Church who understands their difficulty, who is willing to put forward any proposals and who wants to change the status quo. But he knows even while he speaks that it is all lies. There is more truth in his friend who has been thrown out of the priesthood and leads a difficult life. He is prudishly embarrassed in the first part when he is the disarmingly untrustworthy voice on the help-line and hypocritically efficient in the second part when he is called to the Vatican and all his falsehood is revealed.

The film opens with Mastroianni wearing the beret and little round glasses of the poor priest. It closes with him dressed up as the elegant and urbane monsignor, when he proposes not marriage but a discreet co-habitation to Valeria. In both aspects it remains one of the minor performances of his career. Sophia Loren is not in top form either, and her fuller figure does not quite manage to get away with the fashionable mini-skirts of the period. The sharper edge of Risi's vision is made to bear, as ever, on all the characters; but this time it leaves little impression. What the film does do, however, is to highlight a still unresolved problem in the Catholic priesthood. Twenty years later the phenomenon of married ex-priests has become much more widespread. There are now around eighty thousand. On the 18th of September, 1991 a newspaper uses a photograph from Risi's film showing Mastroianni as a priest together with his 'girl-friend' Sophia Loren, to illustrate the news of the marriage of a young German monsignor, a brilliant diplomat of the Holy Seat, to a young German woman.

Scipione detto anche l'Africano (Scipio the African) by Luigi Magni is a curious adventure. The director, an expert in Roman History, casts Ruggero Mastroianni with his brother Marcello: "The only time that we have managed to act together was in *Scipio*. 'Gigi' Magni had to persuade my brother, who was a little reluctant, to play my brother in the film too. It was fun. I was completely bald; I had shaved my head to make it, I enjoyed myself." Accused of extortion, Scipio shows his moral superiority by renouncing

With Sophia Loren and Dino Risi, in 1970,
Mastroianni plays The Priest's Wife.

Scipione detto anche l'Africano: *Marcello gets a chance to act with his brother, Ruggero, who, their mother says, is even better than Marcello.*

all his offices on discovering that his brother is the guilty one.

From the Rome of the Caesars he moves to the Rome of the late-19th-century Popes in a television film made by Alfredo Giannetti. In *Correva l'anno di grazia 1870* (1870, Year of Grace) he acts alongside Anna Magnani. "It was the first time that I had acted with Magnani and it was a moment of high emotion. Without wishing to insult anybody else, I have to say that the emotion I felt working with Magnani was unique. Her intelligence and greatness as an actress are beyond words. I remember there was a really long speech that she had to make, commenting on some political events in the film but she wouldn't have any of it and said: "What is this ridiculous spiel that I have to say while Mastroianni stands around waiting; first I say a bit, then he says a bit.' What I mean is that all those stories about Magnani being hell to work with just aren't true. And then, I think when someone is that good they ought to be given some leeway. So many really stupid actresses play the prima donna and she is so intelligent, so generous. Perhaps there was also an element of respect for me in her attitude, I don't know. Afterwards, we tried to make another film together, based on a French play called *Cin-cin* about a couple who end up as alcoholics, but we didn't manage it. The cinema is cruel when it puts aside an actress or an actor while at the same time recognizing their qualities, because it has decided, nobody knows why, that they are no longer fashionable. A real disgrace. Perhaps these are the things that the public loves most. When an actor has gone through a rough patch and then makes a come-back the public is very generous; it likes to see someone making their way to the top of the pile again, someone who refuses to be kept down. But it is difficult here. Everyone wants to see the latest star. Here everyone thinks that boobs and bum are an actress's most important assets; they reduce everything to its crudest level, and then often it doesn't work anyhow. American cinema, which for me is the true model, is not concerned with these things. It takes into account an actor's or an actress's true qualities, not his or her physical beauty. If they've got it, all well and good but it only counts if they have real artistic talent."

The idea of making a film with Magnani based on the François Billetdoux play comes to nothing. But *Cin-cin*, which is presented at the Spoleto Festival with Daniel Gélin and Betsy Blair, still interests Mastroianni and he eventually manages to make a stage and a film version of it many years later.

Correva l'anno di grazia 1870, tells the story of Italy's unification seen through the eyes of a typical Italian family. The role of Augusto (husband of Teresa Parenti) a conspirator who lies gravely ill in the papal prisons and dies right at the moment that the city is liberated, is only a small one for Mastroianni. It is part of *Storie Italiane* (Italian Stories), a series written for Anna Magnani by Alfredo Giannetti. Her co-stars from time to time include Massimo Ranieri, Enrico Maria Salerno

and Vittorio Caprioli. The stories are set in particular periods which mark some of the fundamental turning-points in Italy's history. *La sciantosa* (The Singer), tells the story of a failed singer who enjoys a brief moment of fame singing to the soldiers at the front. *1943: un incontro* (1943: A Meeting), is a Second World War love-story. *L'automobile* (The Automobile), set in an Italy which has left behind the hardship of the post war years, is the symbol of

a time of well-being which even touches the life of a prostitute. *Correva l'anno di grazia 1870* remains tragically linked to the name of Anna Magnani. It is the last film she makes, if we except a tiny part she plays in Fellini's *Roma*, and is released, almost unnoticed, at the cinema in January 1972. It is shown only on the 26th of September 1973 on Channel Two television, to commemorate the actress's death on that day.

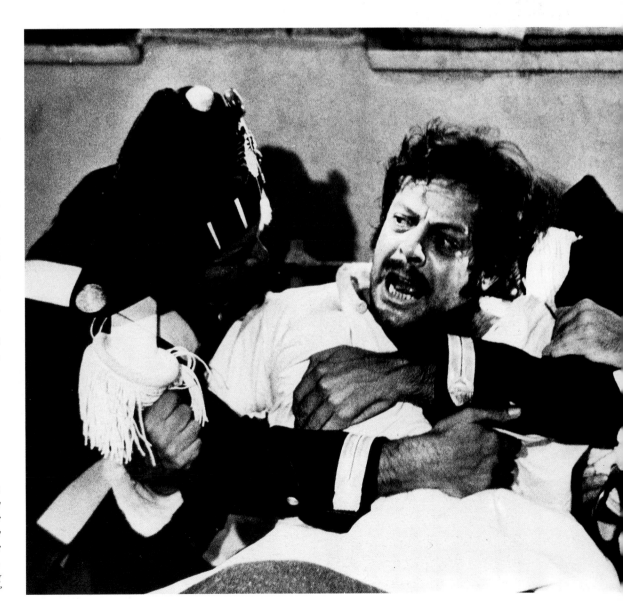

The bearded conspirator of Correva l'anno di grazia 1870 *struggles to get free of the police. This was the only time Marcello acted with Anna Magnani. "It was the first time I'd acted with Magnani, and I was very excited. In all respect to my other leading-ladies, I have to say that the experience with Magnani was unique. There's no way to describe her extraordinary acting abilities."*

5

The French
Adventure

*With Catherine Deneuve
again, this time in Liza, a
bitter view of the male-
female relationship.*

In 1971, Mastroianni's French adventure starts. Italy begins to seem too small to him. He has already spent time abroad, but only for the brief duration of a film. By now an international name, he needs to go further afield and gain wider experience in order to develop as an actor. He moves to Paris, to an appartment in Avenue Georges Mandel. His film activity and private life intertwine. His first film is with Catherine Deneuve, *It Only Happens to Others*, by Nadine Marquand Trintignant, the story of a young couple whose baby daughter dies in a cot death. It had actually happened to the Trintignants themselves while Jean-Louis was in Rome working on *The Conformist* by Bertolucci. Their life is changed by the event. In desperation they shut themselves up at home and refuse to see anybody. In their solitude they are even tempted by suicide. But then, out of an irrepressible instinct of self preservation, they come out of their seclusion and discover the will to live again.

Beside Catherine Deneuve, who acts out her grief in a heart-rending and intense way, Mastroianni produces a performance which is compellingly simple. "I was among the first actors to work with a woman director. It was an extremely enjoyable experience and not a bad film either."

He acts again with Catherine Deneuve in *Liza* by Ferreri from the book *Melampus* by Ennio Flaiano; a writer who creates complex characters that an actor feels at ease with. The Yves Saint-Laurent clothes used in the film create a feeling of ease too; they are clothes which always look good and lend an extremely up-to-date feel to the film, even twenty years on. Giorgio, a comic-strip artist, has retired to a desert island and made a home out of an old bunker. Liza arrives off a yacht, having abandoned her companions with whom she has had a disagreement. Without ever having taken survival classes, Giorgio manages to provide for himself and for his lady alone on the island and even manages to make some sandals for her. But a dog comes between them; Giorgio prefers talking to the dog to talking to her. So she kills the dog and takes its place.

In the bunker, the bare essentials become a sort of style unto themselves. The lack of superfluous things has a double significance. While on the one hand it

A dramatic family scene from It Only Happens to Others, *his first film with Catherine Deneuve.*

is intended to represent the rejection of social well-being, on the other it actually represents the elitist choice of the intellectual who can afford designer art and fashion. Internal space, which can and must be virtually empty, evokes the dilation of space which is the first external sign of affluence.

On a visit to Paris, where his wife and daughter live, Giorgio sits at the Café de Flore with his friend Michel Piccoli, who tells him somthing about the city. They are demolishing Les Halles, changing the face of the city in an attempt to change the inhabitants. In other words, they are trying to repress the cultural pollution of dissent. But what strikes Giorgio most is the noise. He prefers the silence of his island to the acoustic bombardment of the city. When bad weather comes, his canoe is carried away by the tide and there are no more fish, their only source of nourishment.

Giorgio and Liza try to escape in a small aeroplane, but it turns out to be useless and cuts-out half-way down the runway.

The choice of solitude and an almost primordial life made up of instinct, basic physical requirements, a selfless sort of love like the love one might feel for a dog, is no longer adapted to modern man who has been weakened by society and no longer has the capacity to live apart in self-sufficiency. Complete solitude and complete freedom, both personal and social, are possible only in his imagination. Giorgio shows that he is conscious of this when he quotes Marx as saying that the only true representative of the proletarian in ancient times was Spartacus. He is tempted to dissuade Liza from staying with him: "I have decided to live alone on this island, but have my own reasons for doing so: I'm mad".

Ferreri and Flaiano's creation shows not

only Liza reduced to dog-like habits in order to win her man's love; it shows Giorgio too taking on an increasingly canine aspect. But in his case it is not seen in terms of degredation but rather as a process of purification. Mastroianni's performance highlights these canine tendencies and he develops a facial tic whereby he curls his lip and shows his teeth in a sort of canine growl, smooths-down his moustaches and scratches his beard. The combined effect of these mannerisms is to convince us of his complete abandonment of civilized behaviour.

Alex in Roman Polanski's *What?* is another character who has rejected convention. Spying on Nancy (Sydney Rome) from his window he makes a gesture of approval when he sees her naked breasts. Ray-bans, little moustachios and a white bath-robe make up his look this time as he wanders around the seaside villa in Amalfi where the girl has sought refuge from a rapist. "This Italian adventure of Polanski's was not terribly convincing. But I had a really good role in it, a character who was not all there. Who knows what he was suffering from, perhaps syphilis. His hands shook; he could never remember what he had said; he couldn't even remember the other time he had met the girl protagonist and kept on repeating the same thing to her: 'It would be nice to take tea together tomorrow at five o'clock or perhaps six.' It was again a way of satirising the Latin lover, by showing him as someone who really was in a state, a complete idiot, a cretin who didn't know what he was doing most of the time, he was so stuffed full of alcohol or drugs, or who knows what else, suffering real torment with the mosquitoes. But the Italian climate, this mediterranean sun, turned out not to be productive for Polanski; he probably needs a northern climate, different atmospheres. The film lacked grit, it lacked a certain cruelty, it didn't scare you like the script did, which, when you read it, really made

Alex in What?, *a grotesque caricature of the seducer, a figure Marcello repeatedly attacks in his films.*

you terrified about what was going to happen to the girl."

Rather than fear, the film tends to communicate the sense of obsession with sex and its various perversions, treated in a grotesque and derisory fashion. The next morning, Alex takes up his praises again without the least concern for his lack of continuity: "Ah yes, perfect. You see what I really go for is the volume, and the form naturally. I didn't see them very well last night, of course, but they really are first class". "What are?". "Your breasts. If you want some good advice, though; don't sunbathe too much. A dark nipple on a milk-white breast really is a joy to see. I am really quite against sun-bathing." The character is a sado-masochist He gets the girl to whip him while he wears a tiger-skin. Dressed up as a policeman, he whips her in turn, because she has not given him the documents her asks her for. He portrays a

burlesque character, giving constant emphasis to the vulgar aspects of eroticism. "Pure Gold", he exclaims as he slaps the girl's bottom. "Tomorrow, angel, we're going out for the day. See if you can get another bitch to come along will you?" His urge to self-glorification reaches a climax when he proposes to exchange the girl for the picture of *The Medusa's Raft* by Géricault which an art-dealer brings to his house. The picture is great, he feels… as long as it *is* authentic?

On May 28, 1972 Mastroianni and Catherine Deneuve have a child, Chiara. In Italy it is the start of the years of terrorism, and Dino Risi, ever-sensitive to the mood of the day, invites him to play a pharmaceutical manufacturer who is taken hostage by a group of revolutionary students who have just attempted a robbery. The theme and screenplay of *Bite And Run* are by Risi, Ruggero Maccari and

Father Antonelli is a younger version of Don Pietro of Open City. *Here in* Massacre in Rome *Father Antonelli acts out a tragic moment in Italian history.*

Giulio Borsi, the industrialist of Bite and Run, *is a victim of the violence rampant in the late Seventies.*

Bernardino Zapponi. But the Mastroianni-Risi combination yet again does not work out. This is in spite of the fact that Mastroianni manages to be convincing as Giulio Borsi, the despicable businessman who, trapped by the terrorists with his mistress, is willing to stoop to anything to save his own skin.

By way of contrast, in George Pan Cosmatos's *Massacre in Rome*, a super-production which casts Mastroianni and Richard Burton to ensure its success, he plays a priest who chooses to be one of the three hundred and thirty hostages massacred by the Germans in the Fosse Ardeatine on the 24th of March 1944. Padre Pietro

In The Slightly Pregnant Man *with Catherine Deneuve, it's the husband who gets birth pangs.*

Antonelli, director of the Institute for Restoration, is a younger more cultured version of Don Pietro in Rossellini's *Open City*. He courageously stands up to the German colonel, Kappler (Richard Burton): "Art is the only authentic means of communication between one people and another, between one generation and another. Only what is beautiful can save the world, what is beautiful, good and true. And that is a trinity much older than the Church's". He reads Homer and admires Picasso: "Do you know what Picasso said when France surrendered? He said: 'The German generals have beaten the French generals. I am a painter. Let the German painters come here and fight me. I am ready'. And he would have won."

There is nothing he can do in the face of orders from Berlin to take reprisals for the killing of twenty German soldiers who die in the Via Rasella uprising. He does not manage to promote diplomatic action in the Vatican, but he tries everything. He encourages Kappler to reflect on what he is doing: "You call us madmen, utopians. You call a massacre a reprisal and a young, thinking man a partisan. A sick old man, a hostage; a woman who loves, a Communist. The hangman wears a mask, colonel, and you hide behind empty words; you wear a mask with the sole aim of destruction. But we are all human beings, God's creatures on this earth, not the cogs in a machine. Man has the power to choose. You choose, Colonel".

Generous, but rather weighed down by the verbosity of the author and screenwriter, Robert Katz, Padre Antonelli does not give Mastroianni the scope to express himself to full effect. He remains held back by

the robes and role of the mentor which eventually crush him. In a historic reconstruction of the events, it seems that Padre Antonelli is an invented character but is based on the figure of an actual priest who managed to make that sacrifice and take those risks in the Ardeatine massacre that the Pope of the day, Pope Pius XII, and the Vatican did not wish to take. The film did not have an easy release. In 1975, the film's director, author and producer were all taken to court and sued for slander of the memory of Pope Pius XII. The author was sentenced to one year and two months and the director and producer were both sentenced to six months in jail. All went to the court of appeal.

The actor seems much more at home, however, with the light-hearted French film that he makes next with Catherine Deneuve. *A Slightly Pregnant Man* by Jaques Demy has him playing an Italian immigrant who works as a driving instructor. Curly hair, whiskers, moustache; nothing remarkable, really quite an ordinary, even boring sort of man. "If only you had some sense of initiative; if only you did something different now and then," his girlfriend Irene complains. Shortly afterwards, Marco Mazzetti begins to notice some strange symptoms. The doctors announce that he is pregnant. He becomes the talk of the town and is interviewed on television. He talks with a certain naturalness about his situation: "It's a bit like becoming a father; the only difference is that I've done it self-service". Sexual mixup insinuates a sensationalist tone to the newspaper headlines. *The New York Times* headline runs: "Marco Mazzetti is the fourth sex". And *Pravda*: "The revolutionary Marco Mazzetti is the proletarian response to the sexual austerity of Amintore Fanfani".

When he is offered a contract by a prenatal fashion house, he warns them that he is a very ordinary man: "If you need a poet, I must warn you that I am absolutely hopeless". In a direct contradiction of Irene's label of banality, he becomes a famous personality: his adverts cover the bill-boards of the city and his face is on the front cover of every magazine. Just when it seems that it has all been a bluff, Marco goes into labour and gives birth to a child. In Parliament the need for reassurance is felt: "My right honourable colleagues, the news of the recent birth connected to the name of Marco Mazzetti cannot in the least concern us. He is a foreigner. The judgement of professor Kamonski and of the government is categorical and reassuring. It is a one-off case. The constitution and the virile nature of the Frenchman absolutely rule out any possibilty of one of our countrymen giving birth to a child". But a traffic policeman, a salesman, and a factory worker begin to go into labour. Are they all foreigners too?

If acting is a game for Mastroianni, then this film turns out to be more like playtime than most. A humourous comedy which directs its satirical barbs at food pollution and its possibly risky results (Marco always eats roast chicken), it manages at the same time to satirize many aspects of stereotypical feminine behaviour by transferring them to the man. When Marco gets pregnant he wants to get married, and after the birth he worries about not having any milk. While it remains decidedly one of the minor films in his filmography, it serves to emphasize, yet again, the real desire for change that has characterised his career and to reaffirm that quality in Mastroianni which pushes him to seek roles of ever increasing diversity. But in this instance the film is a howling failure and keeps Demy off the set for the next ten years.

The next time Mastroianni meets up with Ferreri and Rafael Azcona, he finds himself in the excellent company of Ugo Tognazzi, Michel Piccoli and Philippe Noiret. "*Blow-Out* is a stupendous example of real collaboration between actors

and director, something like the atmosphere of an army mess, when each actor frees himself of all concern about his character and simply enjoys being with his friends, without caring who gets the best film exposure. A real collaboration is born, an extraordinary team-effort, and the credit for this all goes to Ferreri, who manages to create this atmosphere in which the actors leave aside all the side-effects of stardom and simply become real collaborators." The film receives both Italian and International recognition and is awarded a prize at the 26th Cannes Film Festival in 1973.

Ugo, a restaurant owner, Michel, a television producer, Marcello, an airline pilot and Philippe, a judge, are all old friends.

The four characters meet up in a villa for a gastronomic weekend. They decide to eat themselves to death. The culinary masterpieces, supposedly produced by the expert chef of the group, Ugo, who officiates in this bizarre death rite, are in fact the creation of Fauchon, the famous Parisian luxury food store. Out of the four, Marcello is the erotomane. Right from the start he stands out from the rest. While the others are visiting the house he stays in the gar-

Blow-Out *is a prime example of inspired interaction between actors and director. The actors are Mastroianni, Michel Piccoli, Philippe Noiret, and Ugo Tognazzi.*

With Jean Rochefort in The Bit Player.

den where he caresses a statue in the small of the back. Then he chooses his room singing, together with Michel, "I'll have the Chinese room." While the others go to meet the van which is bringing their supplies, he is in the garage giving fetishistic caresses to the engine of an old open-top car. "Did you know that Bugatti had special shoes made which left his big toe free, like gloves? He really was an artist," he says to Michel. He confronts the funeral rite of the meal with the same self-destructive determination as the others. "And now the party begins," he says, his face expressing deep desperation. He defends himself in front of old photos of nude ugly women: "So you think I am a sex maniac? You are all getting turned on by a funeral". The next morning he complains that he has not

slept. "I'm sorry but I can't stay here things being as they are. With my profession I am used to sleeping all over the place, but I need to make love. Okay, fine: we have taken an oath to shut ourselves up here, but we haven't taken a vow of chastity". He shows the old Bugatti to some children who have been brought by their teacher, Andréa Ferréol, to visit Boileau's linden tree in the garden: "Mr. Bugatti was an artist like a painter or a musician and this car is his work of art." The friends debate a bit and decide to invite some prostitutes. When they arrive, he immediately grabs one of them and, heading towards the bedroom, presents her like a gastronomic speciality to his friends: "Ladies and gentlemen, in the splendour of her flesh". His friends disapprove of his noisy love-making

which disturbs their eating, when they hear him call: "This is your captain calling from the cockpit".

When the girls leave because they find the over-eating too disgusting, Marcello goes to the old car to eat all alone. But at that moment he rebels against a choice which for all of them seems inevitable and shouting "Shit, shit, shit," he throws away the plate of food and stretches out under the car to repair its engine. When he manages to get it going he shouts with joy: "Listen to that music". He invites Andréa to climb aboard and they drive up and down the drive in a symbolic attempt to

escape. He finds a metal cylinder and puts it on his head. It is a touch which reminds us of Mastroianni as Fellini sees him, and in fact Andréa turns to him and addresses him in the manner of his director-friend: "Marcellino, you're beautiful". "Take off your cape," he orders her. He goes to the statue in the garden and caresses it with one hand while he caresses the woman with the other. At the table he winks at her and they go off into the bedroom. Ugo comments: "He really lays some women, that Marcello". But Marcello discovers that the overeating has made him impotent. And it is the deciding factor; he gives up. "You haven't understood a thing; you can't die by eating too much. I'm going." He goes into the bathroom and the tank

breaks covering him in excrement. He starts up the Bugatti and climbs in. Michel, who has been watching him from the window informs the others: "He's gone". But the next day he finds him in the driving seat, rigid, with his eyes wide open and his lips parted. His friends take him into the house and put him in the fridge.

In essence a bulimic film, *Blow-Out* runs on two parallel levels. While on the one hand it highlights some of the more profound aspects of the individual, on the other it also sheds some light on the perversions of society. In the cannibalistic-oral phase in which the four characters are still immersed (which Philippe in particular symbolizes in his morbid attachment to his breast-feeding nurse who still dominates

The Bit Player focuses on the fun of putting on make-up, as we follow a couple of actors chasing after bit parts. "It's a charming film, but it was never shown very much because the distributor went bankrupt. It's the story of a smalltime actor's struggles to create that successful career which he will actually never have. People in my profession really relate to this film."

him), sexual excitement is connected to the eating urge. While we recognise that sexual expression of this phase is eating, it is through exploiting this natural urge that the representatives of the middle-class find release for their death-instinct. By representing a consumer society which is led to self-destruct through excess, Mastroianni presents a role which is a stratification of all his previous roles. For him, death passes through sex, which is also touch, sensation at skin level and voyeurism. The closest point of reference in his previous work is Alex of *What?* Like him, he is weak and superficial and lives in an eternal present. The excessive characterization, highlighted by the braided and bedecked Alitalia uniform he wears, yet again brings to the fore the character of the Latin lover, the eternal Don Giovanni at the edge of the abyss. He is the first one to die, devoured by the ice of his auto-eroticism.

All-round actor, concerned parent, faithless husband, crisis-bound lover, Nicola Monti in *Salut l'artiste* (Hi There, Artist), moves from one role to the next both on and off the screen. While he parades around in the gardens of Versailles dressed as Louis XIV, his ex-wife tells him that their son has run away from home. Worried, but under pressure from work, he hurries onto a set in Paris and gets complained at for being late. In the evening at the Théâtre Gymnase he and a friend, Clément (Jean Rochefort), play two federal agents who enter the scene, say a line and are immediately shot. Later the two friends appear as "The Mysterious Boys," quick change artists.

In a French beret and wearing a moustache, he is playing the part of a fisherman when his son comes to find him. Nicola welcomes him affectionately but ends up giving him a beating. He returns home carrying the cameras his son has stolen which he intends to take back to the shop. "Who is it?" his mistress, Peggy, shouts and he replies: "The duty paparazzo". It is not the only reference to his previous roles; on the wall there is a large photo of him as Rudolf Valentino in *Ciao, Rudy*. The film is both a humourous parody of Mastroianni actor and man, and a behind-the-scenes portrait of a failed actor. Monti is of course of Italian origin. "You can go where you like. Even in Rome you would still be a foreigner," Peggy tells him. "You'd act for anybody, Nicola, you're a fool. You left your wife three years ago and you are still afraid of her leaving you. You're afraid of your children when they raise their voices. With me, with me you are not afraid. It's like my mother says when she sees you on television: with him it's a question of presence. She never says anything else. Ah, Nicola, with you it's a question of absence. You don't mean anything to anybody. You're a fool."

The actor Nicola carries on with his evening performances: his appearances at dinners where they pay him without even looking at him, is clever voice-overs for cartoons, always with his friend Clément, holding his nose to mimic a ridiculous cartoon animal voice. For him, being an actor is like being in the army. "So how are you getting on in civvies?", he asks Clément who has given up his precarious lifestyle for a more secure job in the publicity department of a pasta manufacturer. "*Salut l'artiste* is a beautiful film which I think was distributed in very few places. It is a really nice work by Yves Robert, an interesting director who made his name in Italy with *War of the Buttons*. Around the world it has received some excellent reviews, but we have hardly seen it in Italy; it hasn't found its way in. It is the story of a small-time actor who is willing to take any job in order to survive and to get on the road towards that career that he will never have. It is a very meaningful film for people in my profession."

In Paris, in the Autumn of 1973, he plays General Custer in Marco Ferreri's *Touche pas la femme blanche* (Don't Touch the White Woman). The director sets his parody of a western in the large

With Philippe Noiret.

hole left after the demolition of Les Halles as it seems to him to resemble a large arena where slaves were killed. It is surrounded by "An empire undergoing destruction and reconstruction, a mobile scenography for an eternal story". Ferreri's real stroke of genius was to have set a metaphorical western, which expresses very simply the concepts of God, Country, and Family in a place worthy of its classical traditions. But the chasm in the centre of Paris evokes not only the deserts of Dakota and Arizona at the mouth of Little Big Horn in Montana where General Custer and all his men were massacred by the Indians; it also evokes the stadium where general Pinochet gathers together political prisoners and the pit where the gladiators fight.

Touche pas la femme blanche, a political film in its own way, releases social tensions by giving them a grotesque image and defuses them through the provocative power of laughter. It becomes really hilarious when the conquerers are defeated and Custer is again overthrown and killed by the Indians. Mastroianni-General Custer gallops his horse through the modern Rue Saint Denis heading towards the "Grand Canyon", where there once stood the great pavilions of the architect Baltard. A long-haired wig gathered up in a pony-tail makes him the image of his proverbial enemies in a curious transfer of identity. His personal vanity is emphasized by the way he constantly combs his hair and takes care of his appearance.

A mixture of ancient and modern, the film starts out like a curious procession in which the baffled and amazed passers-by also take part. The story of Custer and the Indians is seen as an epic, a legend which must be re-enacted in a sort of Holy Week rite. Even Ferreri appears in the film as a journalist there to observe and photograph Custer. Mastroianni's right hand man is Mitch, the Indian guide played by Ugo Tognazzi. On returning from a reconnaissance trip, he reports: "There are lots of Indians, lots of Cheyennes, Black-foot, Palestinians." "No Calabresi?", the General asks; "Glory is ours, glory is ours". When Custer meets Catherine Deneuve/Marie de Boismonfrais, an aristocratic Red Cross nurse, he says: "I can't explain it; when I first saw you I had a strange feeling, a premonition or a memory: Scarlett O'Hara in *Gone With The Wind.*"

The deliberately inaccurate reference plays upon the mobile time-scale and on the bogus nature of the character. When the Indians attempt a rebellion, he has them captured and before sentencing them he tells them off: "You must be mad if you think you can stop progress by killing American soldiers. America is your father and mother". "Bravo," says the CIA anthropologist, another modern character who helps to link past and present. "Thank-you," replies the General. "You're welcome," the anthropologist retorts, in a fast-fire repartee reminiscent of the comedian Petrolini. "It means bread for your children. In the name of my government, therefore, you are condemned to death by hanging," the General concludes.

The tension between the Indians, the proletarian minority under-dogs, led by Alain Cuny-Sitting Bull and the Americans, led by Philippe Noiret/General Terry, begins to grow. The poor are divided and fighting among themselves, the conquerors disdainful. "Indians are savages," says Custer. "Therefore to kill them is a laudable action", concludes Marie-Hélène. While they are waiting for the great final battle to begin, the love between the two of them erupts. Custer is a married man and explains to Marie-Hélène: "There is something that has never happened to me before meeting you, Marie-Hélène: falling in love. I do love my wife, of course, but in a different way, like a sister, like a mother, like a daughter. But the feeling you inspire in me, Marie-Hélène, is a feeling of immense love. I have this irrepressible desire to kiss you and hold you passionately in my arms". But he immediately repents: "Marie-Hélène, I must be some kind of animal to have spoken to you in this way. Forgive me. You have nothing to fear, Marie-Hélène, my love is so great that it is open to any sacrifice. Just seeing you is enough. I ask your pardon, Marie-Hélène, I did not mean to offend you. It was a momentary lapse into sensuality".

"*Touche pas la femme blanche*, was an interesting adventure but it had a very cool reception. Maybe, after *Blow-Out* people expected another sensationalist film and here there was only a transposition of epoch, customs and events. It was a surreal film whose satire, perhaps, escaped many people. I know that as actors working together with the director, we found it a very exciting film to make." It is also a curious document of urban restructuring which immortalises on film the destruction of Les Halles and continues the references to the architectural evolution of Paris that Ferreri had inserted into *Liza*.

He returns to Italy in 1974 to make *Allonsanfan* with the Taviani brothers, Paolo and Vittorio, and the film is released in September of that year. His French adventure is for the moment interrupted. But from that time onwards he becomes part of the artistic-intellectual scene in Paris and often goes there to see his daughter and visit his friends. While he has never been involved in politics himself, in the Taviani brothers' film he finds himself playing a revolutionary, albeit a cowardly and self-centred one. As ever, he prefers not to take things too seriously.

"I don't like too much rigidity of opinion. I am a romantic socialist, an old-fashioned one. I deplore labels and imposed ideals. The ideals I care least about are the ideals of the average Italian: God, Country and Family. I realise that the world could find a solution to its problems in a kind of justice according to which even the poorest have the possibility to survive and to live a decent life."

Though he has never been personally involved in politics or political action, in Allonsanfan *he plays a revolutionary in crisis.*

Fulvio Imbriani, the film's protagonist, is a disillusioned revolutionary who, having spent a few years in prison, has lost his faith in the values of liberty and justice which had spread into Europe after the French Revolution. In 1816, when the story starts, he chooses to shut himself up in his private life but cannot manage to shake off his former companions, who try to win him back to the cause, while planning an expedition to liberate the South of Italy. He does not want to get involved in the mad escapade and so decides to lie to them. A real coward, he betrays them several times while pretending agreement, until he is finally found-out by the youngest among them, Allonsanfan, and is tricked and eventually killed, in his turn, by the Bourbons.

The end of revolutionary hopes and the triumph of reaction in a Europe marked by The Congress of Vienna, allows the Taviani brothers to present the current political situation through a historical filter. It is a technique by which the presentation of an exemplary scenario automatically raises questions about the contradictions of the present. Mastroianni constructs the character of Fulvio with a nervous psychology, lost in dreams and nightmares, in a rich and intense chiaro-scuro which is at its best in the scenes with his son, Massimiliano. To celebrate his birthday he plays a violin solo. Then he takes him back to college and stays the night. When the boy has a fevered nightmare, he tells him the frightening story of the bad toad, just so he will be able to console him.

Between September and October he makes *Poopsie*, directed by Giorgio Capitani, once again co-starring with Sophia Loren. With slicked back hair and a small moustache, this time he plays the bad guy, a pimp who is fascinated by Poopsie because of the vague resemblance she bears to Rita Hayworth, his screen idol. The film can be seen almost as a joke that Mastroianni wants to share with his public. He plays the gangster of the title, reaffirming his notorious adaptablity to any kind of role.

The word is out: finally Mastroianni can be cast in bad-guy roles. From *Allonsanfan* to *Poopsie*, to the film he makes next, *The Divine Nymph*, he leaves a trail of low characters. In Giuseppe Patroni Griffi's film, the low-down villain and traitor who has become the exploiter of 'working girls,' takes one step further down the road to iniquity and becomes a rapist and corrupter of minors. The young victim, now a fascinating and attractive grown woman, is Laura Antonelli. Based on the book *La divina fanciulla* (The Divine Girl), it tells the story of the rivalry between two cousins who vie for the love of Manoela Roderighi in the years immediately preceding Fascism. The girl leaves both of them and takes refuge from their suffocating attentions in London. Their reactions to abandonment are very different. Daniele Danì/Terence Stamp puts a pistol to his head and shoots himself. Michele Barra/Marcello Mastroianni, the former corrupter, consoles himself by embracing the cause of the new regime and he becomes a Black-Shirt. Mastroianni very convincingly portrays the sinister character, giving further proof of the refinement of his acting skills. On the set he meets Doris Duranti, a former diva of the fascist regime whom he had already met in 1954 when they acted together in *Tragico ritorno* (Tragic Return), her farewell performance to cinema in that period.

One of his rare bad-guy parts: as Michele Barra in The Divine Nymph *with Laura Antonelli.*

6

The Seventies:
Anger and Utopia

*Don Gaetano, a troubled
accusing priest.*

On the 24th of September *La Dolce Vita* is shown on television with some cuts but again causes discussion. The daily newspapers take up the story of the film, which had been a box-office record breaker and had caused so much disturbance in a provincially-minded Italy which tended to reduce the Ten Commandments to the Sixth. Mastroianni is working on *Down the Ancient Stairs* with the director Mauro Bolognini. The film is taken from a novel by Mario Tobino, a writer-psychiatrist most concerned about the concentration-camp mentality of many mental asylums and about the harrowing existences that many women experience there. Perhaps Bolognini had one of Fellini's unaccomplished projects in mind since he too had wanted to make a film based on one of the writer's other books, *Le libere donne di Magliano* (The Free Women of Magliano) whose leading character was to have been played by Montgomery Clift.

In fact, the character played by Mastroianni in Bolognini's film is a very Fellinian one. He is the chief doctor in a psychiatric hospital at the start of the 1930's who is trying to discover the origin of the virus which causes madness, convinced that once he manages to find the tiny black dot in the blood which is the start of the disease, the disease itself will be curable. In reality his meticulous studies hide his own fear of becoming mad. Opposed to the Freudian ideas of his new assistant he tries to neutralise her influence by including her in his harem. His attempt is unsuccessful. In recompense, casually overhearing the words of a fascist group-leader talking about the racist ideals of the

regime, he realises that the whole world is gradually slipping into a state of general madness.

Professor Bonaccorsi with his moustache and goatee beard is particularly fascinating to women. He is attached to three women in particular – the romantic and

protective Francesca (Lucia Bosè), the sweet and gentle Bianca (Marthe Keller) and the erotic Carla (Barbara Bouchet) – but is also an object of desire for his patients. The line "We are all three of us his," said by one of his mistresses, helps to clarify the situation. They unselfishly share

In Down the Ancient Stairs *his make-up for the part of Professor Bonaccorsi is more or less what Fellini had been planning on for* Mastorna.

him between them and are content merely to belong to him. The film's atmosphere is characterized by an exasperated eroticism, precisely like that of a psychiatric hospital where the inmates release their sexual tensions in a crescendo of abnormal reactions, and by a sense of creeping madness. A madness which moves from the inside to the outside and viceversa, like a sort of contagion which is passed on from social life to the human mind. Mastroianni gives a secure and convincing interpretation of a character whose apparent self-assurance, obsessive eroticism and ostentatious altruism, serve to hide a deep-seated sense of fear and unease. The Locarno Film Festival jury awards the film its special prize.

With *The Sunday Woman*, by Luigi Comencini, Mastroianni makes a leap back to the present. He plays the commissioner

Santamaria, a successful policeman of Roman origin who was transferred to Turin. He goes to investigate the case of a rather dubious architect who has been killed by having his head bashed in with a stone phallus. The film, taken from the book of the same name by Carlo Fruttero and Franco Lucentini, is adapted for the screen by Age and Scarpelli, two authors who invented Italian-style comedy and are also expert crime-writers. They were even asked by Hitchcock to write the screenplay for *The Five R's*, a film which, unfortunately, has never been made.

Santamaria arrives on the scene when it is suspected that two members of the Turin élite may be involved. It is for his well-known tact (he is defined by one of the film's characters as "an almost too-courteous commissioner"), that he is called in to

deal with the delicate investigation. Rather intimidated and ill at ease among the rich society élite, he keeps his jacket well-buttoned even on a stifling summer day. But Anna Carla Dosio (Jacqueline Bisset) – a lady who at first is cast in a slightly suspect light – becomes his ally and succeeds in putting him completely at his ease. She helps him with his investigation and even goes so far as to flirt with him. But their flirtatious repartee after a while gives way to insult. "Don't you ever get tired of being ultra-intelligent all the time, it must be a real effort." "It's an effort that you certainly avoid making." "Using your intelligence

Police Commissioner Santamaria has Jacqueline Bisset's help in solving the murder comitted in The Sunday Woman.

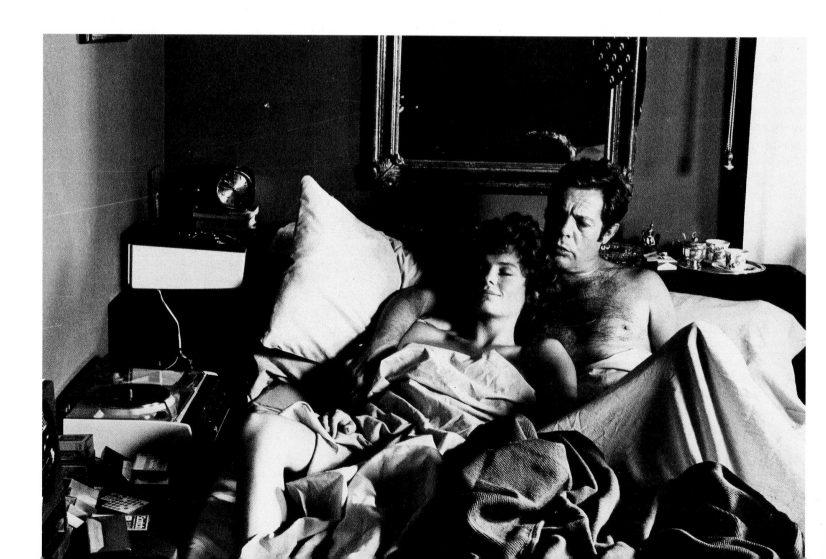

just to kill time is just a load of crap." "Crap?" "Whatever you like: balls, crap, rubbish." "Nice." "You were the one who started being offensive," he says gently placing his hand on hers. But she draws it away. Only right at the end does she finally give in to him, the day before going away on holiday. It is a cruel disappointment to the commissioner who had hoped that it was the start and not the end of the romance. Mastroianni gives a secure and well-paced performance as the experienced commissioner. Acting in situations and circumstances which are natural to him, his performance is completely free of inconsistency or exaggeration.

On the 15th of April 1976, he makes a brief appearance on Italian Channel Two television. The celebrity television presenter, Mike Bongiorno, invites him to appear in his programme, *Ieri e oggi* (Yesterday and Today) with his co-star, Claudia Mori, from the film *Culastrisce nobile veneziano* (Culastrisce, the Noble Venetian) by Flavio Mogherini. The programme presents filmclips of the guests' previous appearances on television and Mastroianni sees himself dancing in *Delia Scala Story* of 1968, and his two previous *Studio One* appearances of 1965 and 1966.

The film about Luca Maria the noble Venetian gives Mastroianni the scope to create some delightfully ironic touches in the character of an eccentric Marquis who continues to believe that he is still living with his wife, who in fact has disappeared in a storm many years previously. In the fairytale, Luca Maria is a lover of eighteenth century music, lives in a splendid Venetian villa and spends his time flying in a hot air balloon. Flora Carabella, Mastroianni's wife, makes a brief appearance as the Marquis's aunt.

In *Todo modo* by Elio Petri, don Gaetano defines himself as "A bad priest, a very bad priest". It is a chance for the actor to take on a character who is full of energy and determination: "The triumph of the

church through the centuries has been due to bad priests. Their evil has served to confirm and exalt saintliness". Mastroianni has already worn priests' robes on two previous occasions. In *The Priest's Wife*, and *Massacre in Rome* he played priests who, in different ways, were meek characters, dedicated to their calling and capable of great sacrifice. Both traditional figures, even if in

Risi's film Don Carlisi gave in first to the temptations of the flesh and then to the temptation of power. But neither was corrupt. In *Todo modo*, which was freely inspired by Leonardo Sciascia's book, Don Gaetano is the spiritual leader of a group of important Christian Democrats who meet in an underground hotel. The first evening they meet, one of them disappears. While

Culastrisce nobile veneziano *(Culastrisce, the Noble Venetian) is the only film in which Flora Carabella appears with her husband.*

123

they are saying the Rosary, a senator is shot. The magistrate seems to have discovered the criminal but the latter is himself soon found dead. All the victims held important posts in some of the major state companies. An anagram of the companies' titles reveals a phrase from one of the works of Ignatious Loyola, which begins: "Todo modo para buscar...". Don Gaetano keeps on with his sermons in which he chastises the rich and powerful: "You are afraid of losing your power, the power which for so many years you have used against men and things. Look at your hands; the power you grasp is burning them".

He rails against them, hurling fire and brimstone, and so instills them with fear that he reduces them to tears: "You should imagine the length, the breadth, the depth of Hell, see the immensity of the flames, the dark flames, the souls of the damned in incandescent bodies, the dark smoke of unending shadows, the burning sulphur, the bodies piled-up on top of one another without a breath of air. The fire in Hell gives no light. The sin of powerful men is more fit for Hell than any other". But his sermons are far removed from the life he actually leads; he is a man of the world who indulges in the sins of the flesh, who smokes in bed luxuriously naked. He asks the President, M., (Gian-Maria Volonté), his antagonist: "Have you ever tried dressing-up as a priest? You should try it sometime. It is a bit like feeling like a woman. In the summer the air circulates freely around your private parts; you don't need to wear any underwear. Priests are half-men, half-women". Tied to power, as are all the men in the basement, he is found dead with the pistol in his hand. It seems to have been suicide and he is immediately suspected of the other murders. To give weight to the argument, a collection of expensive pictures, money, and documents concerning the victims are found in his appartment. But as the notables are leaving

"I'm very fond of Todo modo, *for it was my first chance to play a completely different role from my usual characters."*

A dramatic face-to-face for Mastroianni and Volonté in a violent scene from Todo modo.

the hotel they are all shot one by one. M., the only survivor, cannot stand the suspense of waiting to be killed like the others and orders his chauffeur to shoot him.

"*Todo modo* is a film that I am particularly attached to because in it for the first time I was given a part which was different from my previous roles. This priest was a strong character, fearsome and diabolical; it was a splendid part for an actor and in fact I played the role with great passion. It is a pity that the film didn't meet with much success. It is really uncanny how Sciascia and the film in some way predicted events which were to happen after. I think that a writer like Sciascia must have some sort of antennae, must be able to feel things coming." Mastroianni is of course referring here to an event which takes place in spring 1978, the assassination of the Christian Democrat leader Aldo Moro, an amazing anticipation of events by the writer.

The film has many hurdles to overcome. The screenplay, written by Petri himself with the help of Berto Pelosso, is already ready in May 1974. But the producer, Grimaldi, who is supposed to be financing the film can not find a guaranteed distribution. The film is passed-on to Daniele Senatore, who manages to wangle an agreement with Warner Brothers, and the film looks set to start. The Christian Democrats, however, are opposed to the film. Petri, having already made arrangements with Cinecittà, has to start filming with great difficulty on a basement-set reconstructed in a film studio. The final hurdle comes when an attempt is made to delay the film's release until after the elections on the 30th of May. However, Warner Brothers, who have principally economic concerns in mind, decide to go ahead and the film is finally released on the 30th of April 1976. A protest group defined only as "The Man-Nature Union" immediately forms and denounces the film to the head of the government, then the leader of the house, Aldo Moro, for public defamation. But the denunciation comes to nothing.

The polemic about the film arouses the curiosity of Leonardo Sciascia, and although he is a rare visitor to the cinema as he dislikes closed spaces, he decides to go and see the film. In an interview released at that time he judges it a good film which in the pre-election period acquires exceptional force: "There is a biblical Catholic gloom to it. It is the apocalypse of the DC (Christian Democrats) because, in effect, and we can even say it in religious terms, the DC has sinned against the spirit. *Todo modo* is in fact a fundamentally Pasolinian film, in the sense that the trial that Pasolini wanted to instigate against the ruling DC class has been brought to public 'court' by Petri. A trial as excecution."

On the 28th of June at Saint-Vincent, Mastroianni receives the "Grolla d'oro" for the sum of his work in that season. During the awards ceremony and in front of a large public, Mastroianni accuses the jury of hypocrisy. For it has limited its award description to the fact that Mastroianni "has again made his work worthy of notice in a renewed expressive vein," without mentioning any film by name. It is clear that, following the general acclaim he received for his perfomance in *Todo modo*, the name of Petri's film should have been included in the motivation for the prize, instead of the generic phrase "various films". He does not hesitate to add that the very fact that such an acknowledgment is missing is further proof of how much the film had struck home. His performance has had an explosive quality; he puts everything he has into this performance and in the end creates an almost demoniacal character which remains one of the best of his career. For the role of Don Gaetano he receives yet another coveted prize, the foreign press Golden Globe. Mastroianni has very definite ideas about the creation of a character, especially about what he does not like.

"I have no method. I can't stand the Actor's Studio as an institution; I don't know what it means. It is okay for meeting up with other maniacs like yourself. I don't understand the Stanislavski method. I have never done studies of that sort, which doesn't mean that I am in the right. But what method should you follow? How do you go about it? You think about it. I believe that, if a character really exists, he has a life of his own; and he doesn't remain in larva form but comes out. Sometimes in a film, a guy might be called Mario, but that doesn't mean to say that he has a soul; he is only a silhouette, a puppet. If on the other hand the character has been thought-out, conceived, written really well, I believe that the experienced actor does nothing more than, to use the usual chameleon image, rest on this character and assume his colour and appearance. It is the charac-

*Shown with Susan Starsberg at a reception at the
Actors' Studio, New York, 1962.*

ter himself who creeps into the shell of the actor, into this womb which is ready to receive him and conceive him. You think about him; there is no need to go into the library with your script. You think about him in the most unlikely moments, even eating a plate of spaghetti you sometimes find yourself thinking : what would the character do now, how would he move? It is like when you fall in love; you think constantly about the person you are in love with, and it is almost as though you begin to resemble that person. It is the same thing for an actor. It isn't me who takes possession of a character; it is he who takes possession of me. And I find myself taking on looks and attitudes that perhaps he might have. Then I keep myself open. It is like when an actor has to play a mad person and goes into a mental hospital to

study the mentally disturbed: I don't believe in that sort of thing. I don't like it; it seems like an imitation. If the character has a kind of madness it will come out and that character will be able to use me; I will be the means through which he will express his madness too. Anyhow, haven't we all got a small streak of madness in us?"

In *Signore e signori, buonanotte* (Ladies and Gentlemen, Goodnight), in which he plays a parody of a television presenter, he again steps out of the mainstream of opinion and is made to pay for his non-conformism with eleven months' unemployment. The film (which brings together nearly all the leading figures of Italian cinema in the Cooperative entitled "The 15th of May") aims to be a satire of a day in a television studio. But it ends up directing its barbs at the police, the church and also

Mastroianni is a television journalist in Signore e signori buonanotte; *Monica Guerritore is his assistant. "Television has a fantastic potential for sporting events, concerts, political news, and coverage of disasters. Think of the job it did in showing us the first man to walk on the moon. When it's used in any other way, television is just a surrogate."*

the army, bringing out their less savoury aspects. Among those taking part, and made ugly to the point of seeming like monsters, we find some of Italy's top stars: Vittorio Gassman, Nino Manfredi, Ugo Tognazzi and Paolo Villaggio.

The second half of the seventies introduces an element of economic difficulty into Mastroianni's life. The Italian tax office is biting at his heels to get him to

make back payments of tax, arguing that his previous contributions had been insufficient in relation to the lifestyle he has led. The actor argues that half his yearly income is being swallowed up by tax. He also confesses in an intervierw made at the time: "I have never become rich in my head. The ex-poor person is usually an excellent administrator but I have always managed to out-step myself. I have managed my money like a poor man, a parvenu, who is afraid that he will not have enough time to spend all the money he has managed to earn all of a sudden. I don't say that what I pay is too much; it's just that I would like to know what journalists, publishers, MP's and government ministers pay. We actors are public figures; why don't they become more public too?".

As a public figure, Mastroianni, even though he is in need of money, will not accecpt just any role. As an artist who has always created a favourable impression of the Italians on the international stage, he is not willing to sell himself: "I still find it difficult to just go ahead and make a fool of myself". The offer he receives from Ettore Scola, after eleven months without work, justifies the wait, however. *A Special Day* sees him in the role of a homosexual radio presenter who is persecuted by the fascist regime for his non-conformism.

"*A Special Day* is a film which it was hard to get made because when the distributors received the script they raised some objections: "There's nothing in it. And

"Look at the list: I've been a homosexual, a pregnant man, and an impotent one. There's almost a masochistic pleasure in attacking and demolishing your own stereotyped star image, in saying, in effect: 'I'm not the person you think. I am. I've got a lot of defects, and I'm going to show you one of them right now'. I'm an actor; so I act a lot of different roles, not just the star one, which is less interesting than the other characters I can play."

Once again we see Marcello and Sophia acting together, this time playing a rather different sort of couple.

Sophia Loren and Mastroianni again; aren't they getting on a bit?" The sad thing is that not even this has served to show that a script is just a rough idea and that you have to believe in the quality of the director and the actors. You have to have faith. If we always want there to be erotic scenes or at some point for the cavalry to arrive or something, well that really is the end of cinema. This film is a classic example; work on it started six months after it was due to because there was so much difficulty in concluding the deal. And just look at the result."

In Rome on the 10th of January, 1938, a whole area of the city is deserted; the inhabitants have all gone to take part in a rally for the arrival of Hitler in Italy. Gabriele, a radio announcer, has not moved from his desk where he is writing addresses. There is a pistol on his desk. In a gesture of rage he throws both envelopes and pistol on the floor. At that moment the doorbell rings. It is Antonietta/Sophia Loren, a woman with a large family who has stayed at home, as usual, to look after the house. She is trying to catch a parakeet which has escaped from its cage. It is the woman's interruption that makes him overcome his moment of desperation and urge to commit suicide. Gabriele bursts out laughing and explains to the dumbfounded woman: "Life is made up of many different moments and every now and then the moment to laugh comes, unexpectedly like a sneeze". He starts to dance the Rhumba; using steps drawn on the floor, he teaches it to Antonietta. And he sings: "Beautiful girls in love buy your fresh oranges; they have the taste of kisses".

Later, invited to the woman's apartment to have a cup of coffee, he stands on a child's skateboard to steal a chocolate and hides the wrapper in his pocket. He admires a scrap-book in which the woman has made a collection of pictures of Mussolini with excerpts from his speeches. When he reads "Irreconcilable with female psychology and physiology, genius is an exclusively masculine quality," he tells her about his mother. "My mother was not a man but she was a genius. She used to write and paint and she worked as an accountant; it was she who kept the family going." On the terrace while he is helping her to bring in the washing, he is seized by a desire to confess and tells her why he has been dismissed by the radio company:

"There is a phrase in your album which reads 'a man must be a husband, a father and a soldier'. I am neither a husband a father nor a soldier". "What do you mean?" "They didn't give me the sack at the radio station because of my voice. Defeatist and useless with depraved tendencies was what they said." "I don't understand." "You understand very well,

I'm like that," he says making an effeminate gesture with his hand to indicate that he is gay. Antonietta slaps his face and he shouts: "What did you expect, what did you expect? Kisses, love-bites, fondling, hands up your skirt? That's what you have been expecting since this morning is it? That's what a man has to do when he's alone with a woman. Answer me! After all, men are all the same, aren't they? You have to make them feel it because this is the most important muscle. Isn't that it? Well I'm sorry, my dear, this time you got it wrong, you got it all wrong. I am not that big virile man you were hoping for. I'm a poof. That's what they call us: poofters."

His declaration is charged with suffering for the injustice of a regime that has made him give up work, friends and a whole way of life, forcing him to live on the margins of society. When Antonietta goes to tell him that she is so sorry for what has happened, she tells him how she has been exploited by her family and betrayed by her husband, and Gabriele consoles her. In a moment of physical closeness in which they both try to block out their solitude, Gabriele and Antonietta express an intimate common suffering and understanding. With his hair combed back from his clean-shaven face, Mastroianni gives life to a virile and courageous homosexual. He builds the character up from small habitual gestures characteristic of a bachelor, adding ever-so-slightly affected body movements. His performance, which moves from muted overtones to outbursts of rage and desperation, is always expertly controlled and natural and earns him an Oscar nomination. But he is sure that he will not receive the award, as he confesses in an interview made at the time.

"If they award a prize to a new actor like John Travolta, it means that they make him into a new star, a million-dollar actor, someone people will pay to see for a year or two. If they award a prize to someone like me, what do they get out of it, the Americans? They'd have to be really generous to do that, real artists. When I was nominated for the Oscar for *Divorce Italian Style*, Joe Levine did everything he could: he organized a huge election campaign for me. And they gave the prize to Gregory Peck, who very elegantly said at the rostrum: 'Thank you for the Oscar, but I must say that it was Mastroianni who deserved it'. I am not going to win this Oscar, but it is still a pleasure to have been nominated. Seen in practical terms, it means work. Seen in terms of what it means for me as an actor, it highlights the fact that my character roles have always been my best. Perhaps my physique is that of the galant hero, but I have always felt more at ease when I have been able to interpret the characteristics of an individual rather than simply having to represent his physical attractiveness."

In the second half of 1977 he is in two films. In *Wifemistress* by Marco Vicario he plays a rich turn-of-the-century landowner who is wrongly accused of murder. While he hides and is presumed dead, his wife takes over the business and discovers that he has led a double life. In the film, Mastroianni manages to give credibility to a character who without him would have remained vague and uncertain, immersed as he is in lines and situations which lack depth.

In *Double Murder*, a murder-mystery by the crime-writer, Steno, he plays a police-commissioner. In fact he is a mediocre cop who is punished for having made an error by being sent to work in the archive department. But then, by chance, he is assigned to the case of a double-homicide. And of course he manages to unravel the mystery. His patient and humble policeman is a finely detailed creation and in many ways resembles his character in *The Sunday Woman*. Between takes, he flies to New York with Sophia Loren where they are interviewed by Dick Cavett on Chan-

"To be a Latin lover you have to be infallible. And I'm not."

He's playing a police commissioner again, this time for a witty mystery tale called Double Murder.

A photo with Carrol Baker in Hollywood. "I kept gettinng offers from America to play the usual Latin lover… especially when I was younger. And I kept telling them no and that, since I didn't speak a word of English, a deaf and dumb sheriff would be about the best I'd be able to do. They couldn't understand that, of course. I wanted to make fun of the sheriff figure, who is absolutely mythological for them."

nel 13. When he is asked, yet again, about his image as a latin lover he replies: "To be a Latin lover, a man, above all, has to be a great fucker". "A what?" Cavett asks, amazed and scandalized. "Fucker," replies Mastroianni. To clarify his point he goes on: "To be a Latin lover you need to be infallible. And I'm not infallible; I often foul up." The episode is pounced-on by the newspapers and every daily carries a story of Mastroianni's 'foul-up.' *The New York Post* runs a two-column front-page article: "Love Italian-Style". And the *New York Times* makes a political issue of the incident by opening a discussion on the need for television censorship. The week following the television interview he is interviewed again in the presence of six hundred high-school teachers who defend him for having dared to pronounce a swear-word on television. But perhaps what had shocked the Americans most was not so much the language he had used to express himself, but the fact that he had demolished a Mastroianni-myth that the Americans had long cherished.

On his return to Rome on the 10th of October he is invited to appear on the television show *Bontà loro* (Thanks to You!) hosted by the well-loved Maurizio Costanzo. He arrives unshaven and wearing a pair of jeans, explaining his untidy looks by saying that he is working on a film. The rebel glint in his eye, however, gives the lie to his words and it is clear that his appearance is a deliberate provocation. In response to the inevitable enquiry about the incident on American television he says: "If I am ever asked what is the secret fascination of the Latin lover I will always reply: his penis. I will go on saying that a real Latin lover never fails; he is a faultless fucker. I, on the other hand, am full of faults and failures. I simply consider myself to be a great appreciator of women. Women are an extraordinary source of motivation to me. I need a woman to work, to think, to live. If I haven't got a woman and I find myself alone, I am half a man. Nowadays, partly thanks to the feminist movement, women are more important, more stimulating, more involved,

more complicated. But the newspapers still have this voracious desire for scandal. As soon as you go out with a woman they photograph you. Why don't they go and pry into the lives of a minister's wife or the wife of the draughstman downstairs? It really is a form of persecution. You end up having no private life at all".

In Marco Ferreri's *Bye Bye Monkey*, women are just what the character Luigi wants and cannot get. In November, Mastroianni leaves again for New York to play the role without the slightest idea of what it is. "I knew nothing about *Bye Bye Monkey* when Ferreri called me to join him in New York. We invented my character day by day, rediscovering the pleasure of working on the trail of something, a spirit of adventure I have always enjoyed in Ferreri's films. By observing me in those surroundings, and making suggestions, Ferreri managed little by little to carve out a really good character, in a film which I find excellent."

All the characters in Ferreri's film live in Old Battery Park, at the lower end of Manhattan: Gérard Depardieu/Lafayette who adopts a monkey to be his son; Mastroianni/Luigi, an old man who grows tomatoes among the skyscrapers; James Coco/Flaxman, who runs a wax museum dedicated to ancient Rome; Gail Lawrence/Angelica who is expecting a son; Geraldine Fitzgerald who rejects Luigi's declarations of love and Avon Long/Miko, an old black man who is convinced that he will become a great photographer. One day these charac-

He built up the character of Luigi in Bye, Bye Monkey
*on a day-to-day basis, without looking at the script
beforehand.*

ters, all of them in some way living on the margins of society, find the huge carcass of an ape on the beach and, hidden between its feet, a tiny chimpanzee. It is Luigi who picks it up but has to pass it on immediately to Lafayette because he is seized by an allergic attack. As well as working in the wax museum and as the electrician in a small theatre, Lafayette also acts as Luigi's protector and nursemaid.

The old ex-patriot, romantic and disillu-sioned, part tramp, part gentleman down on his luck, is nostalgic about Italy but has decided never to return even though he occasionally thinks about buying the tick-et: "It's a pity that they are all Communists there now, and I am a property-owner; house and garden, that's what I've got. I really don't think I would like to end up in a collective farm. And then, of course, I am an anarchist individualist". He goes dressed in dark clothing to Lafayette's house.

"You're elegant, today," the young man says to him. "This is the outfit I will wear in my coffin and so I like to give it an airing now and then". "You're a poet, Luigi," the other replies. But his first instinct had been to tell him off, and he announces: "I'm not going to look after you any more".

Luigi is a survivor who feels at ease beside the corpse of the great ape, symbol of an apocalypse. The film is the setting for a clash between the younger and older gen-erations; and the scenario of the end of the world is as evocative as that in *Touchez pas la femme blanche*, because, as Ferreri says, "In cinema, scene and space are essential elements; they are cinema itself." Spurned by women, but still vital and passionate, Luigi gives way to tears of bitterness and desperation. When he is rejected by Mrs. Toland who instead makes love to Lafayette, he cannot hold back his bitter feelings, and shouts: "You only do it with young men, eh? Is that it? Remember it's you who are going through the menopause, not me. Dirty bitch, they're all the same. Everything fine for you. Whore. They don't know that I've got a raging beast here between my legs. I never get a chance to fuck anyone. It's not fair; what am I doing in this country anyway?"

Not even Lafayette's girl-friends, who play the part of mothers in the theatre, take him seriously as a man. Too much in the old style. He tries to make a joke of it: "I am a gentleman and I'm always careful. It was my generation that invented the pill. Why don't you go on the pill?" But, in reality, he feels out of it: "Nobody listens to me any more". Entirely absorbed in his soliutude, Luigi sits down in his small gar-den which lies suffocated between the skyscrapers. With his long grey hair, unkempt beard, glasses and a wooden staff in his hand, he is rather like a peasant or a country priest, and it is he who, half child, half old man, really understands the final catastrophe, which is, above all, the repres-sion that the individual human being suffers when deprived of his natural origins and incorporated into so-called civilization. Mastroianni's melancholic face and subdued voice give shape to the character, his interpretation moving between desperation and bursts of half-forgotten joy.

In January, 1978, he is in Florence making *Stay As You Are* by Alberto Lattuada. "It is a sentimental story about an old man who meets a young girl, a story which is as old as time. It is also a theme which has been used many times in the cinema, but I feel that Lattuada managed to exploit it with a certain grace and lightness. It is the portrait of a mature man with all his cynicism and lassitude who is not even shaken out of himself when he meets an intelligent and beautiful young girl. So it is not limited to the simple sentimental story but there is this element of character study in it too, together with a note of suspense as the man has the horrible suspicion that the girl

is in fact his own daughter. However, in spite of the man's case of unresolved paternity, I think that it is not this that leads him to reject the possibilty of a relationship so much as his own world-weariness. A man of fifty no longer has the wild moments and the generosity of spirit that he had at twenty or thirty, he is caught-up in a kind of inertia which he rarely escapes from."

The character of Giulio, a married architect who falls in love with his daughter's friend, Francesca (Nastassjia Kinski), could in some ways resemble Mastroianni, or at least represent an aspect of men of this generation. He is not stupid; on the contrary he is rather sensitive, but he is

In Stay As You Are *Mastroianni plays the lover to a very young Nastassja Kinski, one of Lattuada's many adolescent discoveries.*

lacking in a certain sense of enthusiasm. He would prefer a love affair on the level of fantasy. It is the first time that Mastroianni acts a love affair with an adolescent. He confesses that very young girls do not interest him very much; he finds them insipid, egocentric, hard-work, and feels that they want constant attention, compliments and protection. Above all, he says, he would not know what to talk to them about.

On the 31st of March, he takes part in an Italian television production of Sartre's *Les Mains Sales* in Milan, directed by Elio Petri. Sartre's play marks Mastroianni's debut in television and he plays the part of Hoederer. "A character I really like, theatrical, really effective and above all a real scoundrel." During his career he has played mainly introspective subjective roles to the point of coming to personify the typical middle-class, middle-aged man in crisis in the seventies. But *Les Mains Sales* requires something different as he has to try to represent the unresolved conflict between political activism and existential individualism. Sartre's play has very rarely been staged. After the premiere on the 2nd of April 1948, there was such an uproar from his own comrades, who accused him of anti-Communist sentiment, that Sartre was obliged to forbid future performances. In the summer of 1977, when Petri first started to think about the project, the veto was still in force. But in the end Sartre gave permission for his play to be translated by Petri and performed in Italy.

For Mastroianni it is the occasion of a long-awaited return to the theatre, even if it is through the medium of television. At the start of the seventies he had thrown out a sort of appeal which had, however, fallen on deaf ears: "I would like to go back to the theatre for a commedia dell'arte production with masks and dialects. A really Italian product for export, signed by Giorgio Strehler. I think I would only go back to the theatre for a production of this kind.

Who knows if Strehler would be interested?" After the press-conference he goes straight to the airport and flies to Los Angeles for the Oscar ceremony. But his Oscar nomination for *A Special Day* goes no further, as he had predicted. The following Monday he is already in the studios of the CTC (Cutural Telecinematographic Centre) working on Sartre's play.

"*Les Mains Sales* was a new experience for me. I like finding new directions especially in the company of friends like Petri. To me the idea of producing Sartre's play three decades after it was written is rather interesting. The re-presentation of the text in the light of three decades of events which have probably very much changed the judgement of the Left, which was originally plainly negative, was also a way of lifting the charge of betrayal which had then been levelled against Sartre. Seeing it again today you realise that lots of things have changed, and that judgement of Sartre and this work has also changed. The only thing I did not like about this experience was the almost ministerial air one breathes in television, like an office. I felt suffocated acting underground, I couldn't breathe. Okay, I know you sometimes work outside for television, but it is very rare; and then the whole television system is different. It was a bit mournful. You had to go to the cash desk to get paid and go to the office to sign your contract; all new things for me. I was used to the way of organising or rather disorganising things that we have in the cinema."

On the 17th of June he is awarded the "Grolla d'oro" at Saint Vincent for his roles in *A Special Day* and *Bye Bye Monkey*. That summer, he takes part in *Traffic Jam*, filmed at Cinecittà during a baking heatwave. Luigi Comencini's film, which features many international actors in different episodes, sees Mastroianni in the role of a famous film star who is saved from a traffic jam by a crafty peasant. He offers him hospitality, feeds him, offers him his bed and

even throws his own pregnant wife in on the bargain, in the hope that he will get something concrete out of it. But the actor again knocks down the celebrated Latin lover image and plays the part of the puffed-up ham actor who has little interest in sex. And so he disappoints the passionate expectations of his admirer who expects to find the virile man of his screen publicity.

In December, Lina Wertmuller's *Blood Feud* arrives at the cinema. Mastroianni plays the socialist lawyer, Rosario Maria Spallone. At the start of the twenties he finds himself in disagreement with the political climate of the time and leaves

Right: *In* Traffic Jam *he is a worn-out ham-actor who has little interest in sex.*
Below: *For Sartre's* Les Mains Sales *Mastroianni becomes Hoederer, a brilliant theatre-role which he is very fond of. "He's really a great scoundrel."*

Bearded in Blood Feud.

Rome to return to his native Sicily. Grandiloquent and rhetorical, he sings its praises to a young companion as he looks out of his car window: "Beautiful, truly beautiful. The Greek conquerers fell in love with it immediately and it became the flower of their foreign colonies. Beautiful and desperate. Look here, look at the problem of the exploitation of minors, and that is only one of its problems. Do you know how much suffering and injustice has for centuries humiliated this poor country of mine? This is Sicily; its bitter people are hardened by privation but they also have an unpredictable streak of madness. Do you know that when the Sicilian *fasci* were born – *fascio* is a word that scoundrel Mussolini stole from our peasants' associations – things occurred here that had never been seen before. My father, who was a landowner, called the police, and do you know what the sulphur workers did? They stripped them. Four policemen dressed only in their underpants. It destroyed them. A naked policeman doesn't frighten anyone."

This long speech immediately gives us a good idea of what sort of character Mastroianni is playing. With his long beard and untidy hair, he plays an eloquent lawyer and passionate lover who prefers talk to action. He bears a strong resemblance to Mangiafuoco, the puppet-master in *Pinocchio*. The speech also presents the film: a love-triangle which is at once full-blooded and extremist, like a melodrama (which the music taken from Bellini's *Norma* serves to highlight) or Neapolitan drama in which the three figures love, hate and finally kill one another. Mastroianni, co-starring here with Giancarlo Giannini and Sophia Loren, does not manage to get beyond the heavy caricatural mask imposed on him by the director ancd remains inaccessible behind his make-up. The dialogues, too, distance the audience from the story, delivered as they are in a dialect which even the actors themselves do not understand. Before making Wertmuller's film, Mastroianni had been going to play the lead part in the film version of Attilio Veraldi's *L'uomo di conseguenza* (A Man of Consequence), the sequel to *Mazetta* which had featured Nino Manfredi. Mastroianni discussed the prospect at length with the director, Sergio Corbucci, before definitively giving it up. He did not feel willing to re-interpret the investigator, Sasà Jovine, created by Manfredi in the earlier film. The story also involved an element of incest, a touchy subject, even though it had been referred to in *Stay As*

Giallo napoletano seems to be half by Hitchcock and half by Totò. Mastroianni is a strolling violinist.

You Are. He still has difficulty throwing off the great lover image. Even at an age when it would seem more natural to cast him in the role of father, there is still a tendency to cast him in the role of father-lover. In place of the film taken from Veraldi's book he works with Corbucci on another story which he is much more in tune with. *Giallo Napoletano* (Neapolitan Mystery) is another story set in Naples, in which he plays a travelling musician who has a strange adventure.

In the style of Hitchcock and Totò, the film is part comedy, part mystery, and sees Mastroianni in the role of a mandolin player with long curly hair, a small moustache, a french beret and a crippled leg who performs in restaurants to earn his liv-

ing. "Dry Thigh" is the nick-name used for him by his father, an old man made bitter by his ill-luck at the games of chance he is addicted to, played by Peppino De Filippo. It is precisely his father's debts that lead Raffaele-Mastroianni to take up the shady-sounding job of an early-morning serenade. First the girl who has driven him to the spot is shot from the window under which he is playing, and then a black man falls from it to the ground. He naturally gets caught-up in the investigations into the mystery and is charged by the inspector on the case. Renato Pozzetto, the inspector in question, defines the mystery as "A problem of the South which I intend to solve." Mastroianni gets entangled in all kinds of adventures and at one point risks drowning with Ornella Muti on a yacht anchored in port. He also dresses up as a woman in an attempt to escape the assasins who have already destroyed his house and tried to murder him by throwing him off a rooftop and tampering with his car's brakes.

Of course it is he, and not the police inspector, who eventually gets to the bottom of the complicated plot and uncovers the guilty party, a suspicious orchestra director masterfully interpreted by Michel Piccoli. Mastroianni is completely at home in the delicately biting humour of a traditional Italian-Style comedy and creates a likeable and witty character, bringing out all his refined talent for comedy.

In 1979 he works on two films which are released the following year with only a month between them: *La terrazza* (The Terrace) by Ettore Scola and *City of Women* by Federico Fellini. Scola's film portrays the plight of Mastroianni's generation of men, now in their sixties, who are under-

Shown with Ettore Scola when they are working on La terrazza. *"If you've got a problem, you'll always find a willing and attentive listener in Ettore.*

valued, often superceded by younger men, and in crisis in their relationships with women. Mastroianni's character is called Luigi, a journalist who still insists on typing his articles on an old typewriter while the rest of the office have entered the computer age. His colleagues on the editorial committee take him off the leading article on the National strike because he is too accommodating and predictable a colum-

Group photo from La terrazza.

nist. On the terrace where he is dining with a group of old friends – The Rt. Hon. Vittorio Gassman, the producer Ugo Tognazzi, the screenwriter Jean-Louis Trintignant, the television official, Serge Reggiani, and their wives and ex-wives – he attempts to strike up a conversation with a girl. "You young people complain about not having a future because of us, because of the past. But if you want to eliminate us, you must get to know us. Look: here is the past. Look," he says opening his arms to present himself.

He tries to win back the wife who has left him, but he is fighting a losing battle. His laziness gives way to an apathy which

cannot be attributed solely to the hot Scirocco wind blowing through Rome. Rather it is due to "work that you feel you can do without effort, without worry or excitement, ageing cells, people who don't understand you or, rather, whom you don't understand."

Sacked by the newspaper, he is reduced to eating alone on his desk, playing with sandwiches stuck on forks like a famous scene in one of Charlie Chaplin's films. When he meets up again with his friends on the terrace, he is wearing dark glasses in mourning: "This is what makes me superior to all of you. At least I make some attempt to camouflage myself". In the

world of cinema seen as a sort of salon peopled by friends-enemies-accomplices, it is the women, with their strength and initiative, that are the cause of the mens' crises. Others present in the salon are Age, Leo Benvenuti, Ugo Gregoretti, Lucio Lombardo Radice, Francesco Maselli, Mino Monicelli, Claudio Sesteri and Lucio Villari, like a large cinema family photograph. Mastroianni's character occasionally moves into an excess of literaryness. He is too stiffly constructed and it is only Mastroianni's skill as an actor that makes him live and breathe. In spite of this the actor remains distant from the character as though they do not completely belong together.

When Fellini first started to think about making *City of Women*, it seemed as though there would be no part in it for Mastroianni. A rumour was still going round that the two old friends were going to get together to make *Il viaggio di G. Mastorna*. It has now been fifteen years since Mastroianni last played a role in one of Fellini's films, and they have only met on the set during a brief appearance Mastroianni made in the film *Roma*. "I played myself sitting in a restaurant in Trastevere, a matter of a few seconds of filming and that was it." The scene was cut in the final version. They work together in an amusing photo-session for French *Vogue* in which Fellini dresses Mastroianni as Mandrake, a magician in an evening jacket whom Fellini used in the film *Intervista*. Snaporaz, the character he plays in *City of Women* should have been "a funny absent-minded little man in the style of Buster Keaton," like Dustin Hoffman, Fellini's first choice. Instead, once again he dresses Mastroianni up in Fellini's own clothes and courageously sends him on.

The film takes its inspiration from Bernardino Zapponi's idea for *Duetto d'amore* (Love Duet), a film Fellini should have made with Ingmar Bergman. From 1975 onwards, one producer gives way to the next and the film does not manage to get off the ground. In the end, in 1979, Renzo Rossellini decides to finance it through Gaumont Italia. The film is interrupted at the end of July due to the sudden death of Ettore Manni, who had been playing the role of Katzone. On the 10th of August Gaumont suspends filming and dismisses the whole team. Filming starts

Surrounded by soubrettes in City of Women.

again on the 24th of September but is once more interrupted because Mastroianni falls ill and has to undergo four operations for a stye which will not heal. On the 12th of November Mastroianni's mother dies. It is only on the 29th of November, at a cost of over seven billion lire, that the film is finally finished. When it is presented at the Cannes Film Festival on the 19th of May 1980 it is not as successful as had been hoped.

A train enters a long Freudian tunnel and Mastroianni/Snaporaz is dreaming in his sleep. A lady sitting opposite him looks at him invitingly. The train stops and the lady gets off. Snaporaz follows her off the train into the open countryside, talking continually to himself: "Eh, old Snaporaz, you can't give it up, can you? Who knows why I carry on behaving like a fool at my age. Smic, smac smic, smac". But after a brief kiss, the lady disappears again. Snaporaz, on her trail, arrives at the Hotel Miramare, where a feminist congress is being held. Grey-haired and with black-rimmed spectacles, he moves with a furtive air, trying not to be noticed by the angry women. But it is all useless as the lady he has been following unmasks him: "The eyes of that man who is moving among us with his falsely respectful face saying he wants to be informed, to get to know us better because only by getting to know us better can he change his relationship with us (and of all his false, hypocrital justifications this is the most despicable). I repeat: the eyes of this man are the same old male eyes, deforming everything they see, bright mirrors of mockery and derision".

According to the feminists, Fellini makes use of women in this episode as a simple pretext to continue to recount "his bestiary, his circus, his neurotic fore-play". The "lugubrious, obscure, tired-out caliph" has no intention of learning anything about women. It is they who have attained a superior level of consciousness and have identified him as a clown and an alien. The

director's intention here, as in his previous films, is to create a lucid expression of his fears and neuroses by making use of his childhood memories and the dominant questions of the day.

Saved by Donatella, Mastroianni shakily crosses an ice-rink on which his feminist antagonists are gathered, then falls down some stairs. He ends-up in the heating-system workshop and the lady proprietor offers to take him to the station. But in the

In Katzone's gallery of erotic souvenirs.

countryside she tries to rape him. He gets away but runs into a group of punk girls and has to escape from them too. Hiding in a wood, he arrives at the house of an ex-school friend, Katzone, who is celebrating, that night, his ten thousandth mistress.

Inside the villa, which is furnished like a mausoleum, he finds a marble bust of the owner's mother and a gallery of niches housing the ex-mistresses' photographs which, when illuminated, emit the sounds of their orgasms. He finds his wife sitting on the edge of a crypt, almost as a sad necessity, and she chastises him for treating her as a refuge or mother-figure. Katzone's party is lugubrious and mournful, an involved play on the love-death theme.

Mastroianni is the embodiment of the director's ideas as he moves through a series of film events which are apparently discontinuous, but intensely creative. In the meeting with Katzone, Fellini confesses to the unproductive and superficial relationship he has with women. He does so in a sort of magical game to the sound of a mediterranean instrument. But the real centre of attraction, the centre of gravity almost, is the vagina of Katzone's mistress which mysteriously attracts the coins that are thrown towards it.

Mastroianni meets up again with Donatella and another soubrette, and they perform a tap dance and a Charleston together to the music of "Lola." He climbs onto the big bed with them but they melt away and his wife appears in their place and climbs on top of him. Escaping under the bed he finds the entrance to a red velvet taboga. He lets himself go on the merry-go-round of memory. He sees the maid whose legs he caressed, hiding under the table when he was a little boy; the fish-wife; the nurse at the health spa; the girl motor-bike riders of 'Death's Highway;' and the lady on the beach. Then on the cinema-bed the children get excited watching some of the great film-stars from the silent films: Garbo's face, Jayne Mansfield's backside. He then finds himself in a cage among the feminists. He is in a basement which has echoes of Latin American political prisons, where men are punished for being male. They interrogate him: "What do you want here? What is the biological difference between men and women? Have you ever known the Real Woman? What are you doing nosing around in a world you don't understand, that doesn't belong to you? What made you decide to be born male? Have you ever explored your female side?" His female judges wear the same mountain masks as the Italian terrorists,the Red Brigade; and they continue to fire questions at him without bothering to wait for a response. "How can I manage to reply? You see I'm a bit confused. Let's conclude like this: thank you very much and see you next time. You are all very nice ladies but the surroundings are not exactly..."

After reading him an enormous list of his crimes they set him free. But he does not want to go, he wants to see what there is behind it all, he wants to find out once and for all whether this ideal woman really does exist. He finds himself dressed in his nightshirt and dressing-gown in the middle of an arena. The feminists throw flowers to him from the raised tiers. He talks to himself: "Now we have gone this far she can't not show herself; she must appear, this spectre I know does not exist. She is a stranger, forever elsewhere, an unearthly shadow that you can't get hold of, she is ruinous". Trying to get closer to this phantom, he climbs onto an enormous balloon in the shape of a woman, with a crown of lights around her head like the Madonna. From below a terrorist shoots the balloon and it starts to deflate. Snaporaz finds himself back on the train.

Mastroianni moves through the film with an air of amusement. He likes acting among women and even during the most dramatic moments does not really seem to be afraid of them. Only at one point, when he is unstably balanced on his ice-skates and he sees them practicing martial arts on the dummy of a man, does he seem to feel threatened by them. His performance, made up of half-smiles, flirtation, and consternation, as well as moments of biterness, rage, joy and vitality, shows just how much in harmony he is with Fellini. He gives proof of the director's skill at drawing-out his best performances; but above all he demonstrates a willingness to identify with a man who claims to be in crisis, but who, in spite of his fragility, has managed to find an unstable equilibrium in being simply as he is.

An actor's career usually has more unachieved projects than it has finished works. Working, as actors do, with the body and the mind, they must feel that they can identify with the characters they are to impersonate. And then the cinema world with all its economic difficulties, often makes projects slow to achieve and an actor's aspirations sometimes remain left to one side. For Mastroianni, at the end of the seventies, there are still quite a few projects that he has not yet managed to realize.

"For an actor it is easy to dream-up projects; a new idea comes to you about every half-hour. It is one of the merits, or perhaps the defects of the profession. Actors live in a fantasy world, in a world of fairy-tale, and any excuse is good enough to come up with a new story. I have had a lot of fun with my brother Ruggero, who is a film editor not an actor, dreaming up the idea of doing a spoof of those American films where there are always two brilliant brothers. At one time, because we knew Petri and were good friends, we put forward the idea of doing a film called *Necrophilia* (it was while I was making *8½*), before Dario Argenti's films became popular. It was going to be a sort of parody of the films of Vincent Price, an actor whom we found really funny. *Necrophilia* was a sort of spoof horror-film; and we had imagined a swimming-pool full of black-puddings, tripe bath-robes, and shady figures played by Buazzelli and Panelli, who stole bodies from the underground passages of a clinic. But Petri did not even take the project into consideration. Our next idea was a western, at a time when the spaghetti western had not yet come into being. This other project was called *Los Ruspantos* and it was the story of two brothers who had a bad reputation and descended on the villages and stole everything out of the kitchens and pantries. It was adolescent humour, really; a way of seeing everything in parody. Petri never took any notice of our ideas, and we really regret never having been able to do films like this.

But I think that there have always been many more projects in hand than finished films. It would take too long to talk about them all, and I can only really talk about those that meant the most to me. There was a script written by Age and Scarpelli about *Cosa nostra* (Our Business), which was going to be directed by Monicelli. It was a film about the Mafia seen from the Italian point of view, a film which was very ironic about the whole thing. The Mafia boss was a homosexual and I was a Sicilian tailor that they had trained up and sent to America, because I came from the same village as the Mafia boss. They sent me as a stowaway on a boat, and as soon as I arrived, the American police sent me back again. Then I managed to get back into the country and the Mafia boss fell in love with me. Shirley MacLaine was going to play the role of a police informer, a prostitute-type character who in fact worked for the police or was a police agent.

Another project that was really nice was a film with Hitchcock which should have been filmed at the Waldorf Astoria in Rome. On that occasion I actually met Hitchcock. I remember being rather disappointed in him because when I mentioned *Psycho* and said that I had really liked it, he replied that in fact it had been a very successful film and that it had financed twelve thousand head of cattle for him. I didn't expect such a crudely practical answer and I was rather put off.

There was another project with Marco Ferreri based on a novel called *Piotrus*. It

On roller-skates and scared stiff.

was a very beautiful story about a man who put himself up for sale in a market in Palestine. We would have liked to have shot the film in a town like New York. Again with Ferreri we were going to make *L'aquilone di combattimento* (The Fighting Eagle), a film set in Chinatown, San Francisco. We even made a trip to America to plan it, but nothing came of it. It was the story of a man of our time with this contemporary sense of disorientation who goes off on a sort of journey through Chinatown led by the hand by a little Chinese girl who is more lucid and direct than he is, the representative of a civilization which is more advanced than our own."

7

Are We as We are, or as We are Seen to Be?

La pelle.

During the eighties, Italian cinema experienced a change of direction. It abandoned, or was abandoned by its realistic, epic, externally directed, socially aware tendencies and turned instead towards the drama of feeling and sentiment, which after all has always been the subject of entertainment. For Mastroianni it was nothing new as even in films which regard social matters, he has always tended to carve out for himself, a personal space in which the psychological experience of the individual is of central significance even when we (and he) could see the laughable side as well. He was not insensitive, however, to the political difficulties Italy suffered during the seventies. His collaboration in works like *Todo modo*, *Les mains sales* and *Allonfonsan* testify to his awareness of the realities of Italian life at the time. A tragic reality characterised by the desire for change which turned to armed conflict. The roles Mastroianni took-on from 1980 onwards seem to express a desire to look to the past in an attempt to find out who he is, to confront his own place in history, to get some idea of the past both as an individual and as part of a collectivity.

On the 18th of August, work starts on *La pelle* (Skin) by Liliana Cavani, first at the Roman Cinecittà studios and later in Naples. The film is loosely adapted from Curzio Malaparte's book of the same name and its events take place in Naples during 1943 when the American, French and English troops have already passed through the city. In the Babel of languages created by the various occupations, Malaparte/Mastroianni acts as a liason officer between the American army and the Italian authori-

ties. His job, which is anything but simple, is to smooth relations between the foreigners and the Neapolitans. In the devastated city, where young girls prostitute themselves to earn a living and mothers sell their children for a few lire, the war has destroyed not only the physical framework of life, but also its moral structure. Malaparte, who observes with a ruthless lucidity the realities of a situation which he can do nothing to improve, skilfully carries out his job of facilitating the conquering army's departure for Rome, preparing the way for General Cork/Burt Lancaster and his fifth division to be the first to arrive in the capital city.

With Amedeo Nazzari and his wife Irene Genna. "I had an enormous admiration for him. When we were young, he was our hero, a warm, open character, with a strong personality. Perhaps, at the end, he didn't adapt to changing times: he didn't see that the time for heroes was past and that characters now had to reveal their limitations, joke about themselves, even cruelly; for Italian-style comedy was developing."

The Italian version of the film uses dubbed voice-overs for all the parts and as a consequence destroys the central idea of the protagonist-interpreter. Mastroianni himself has very strong feelings about the indiscriminate use of dubbing:

"Abroad, people are so used to hearing an actor's voice and reading the sub-titles that they get annoyed if they hear another actor's voice dubbed on top of it. I remember one morning there was a showing in New York of *A Special Day* for a conference of school teachers who were going to give their pupils a lesson about the film. After the film, one of the teachers asked me: 'Why have you been dubbed in English?' And I replied: 'Madam, I speak English very badly. This is a radio presenter, he

must speak perfect English in the dubbing.' 'But wouldn't it have been better for you to speak in Italian with sub-titles? We know your voice and it's not nice to hear somebody else's.' It's the same in France where you can choose to see a film either in the original language or in the dubbed version. But only the people in the country go to see the dubbed version. In the big cities they choose to see it in Italian, English, Japanese, German, or whatever other language it might be in with sub-titles. But back here we don't do it because people say that Italians are not used to it. We have always dubbed everything. For Italians it is normal for a Japanese person to speak Italian; they don't even notice; they are so used to it. People think that if

La pelle: "*Curzio Malaparte had so many facets to his personality: strange, ambiguous, provocative. Fascinating for some; loathsome for others. There were people who considered him a good writer while others felt he was only a journalist taking notes. The kind of man who'd be quick to duel… or throw himself into a passionate love-affair. But in his book* La Pelle *his character is described quite differently, not so dramatic, a sober, normal character, typical of certain Italian types, polite, cultivated, sharp, ironic, but also a bit sorrowful*".

films are shown in their original language with sub-titles then nobody will go to the cinema. But I'm not so sure because the majority of people who go to the cinema are young people and young people today, at least fifty per cent of them, already know English because they learn it at school and on holiday and listen to English songs. It really would be something else. An actor's voice is so important. Take Marlon Brando's voice for instance: he actually has a rather adolescent-sounding voice but in Italy he has always been dubbed with a deep masculine voice which gives a completely different impression. One of the striking things about Brando is to see this imposing physical presence, I don't mean as he is now but as he was as a young man, and then to hear this fragile-sounding voice. It was really this contrast that made the character rather intriguing."

His hair slicked-back, gigolo-style, guiding the conquerors through this post-war inferno he is perhaps himself the least capable of all of them of feeling indignation at the horrors around him. He remains too meek and defeated a witness to the scene, tending to blame the conquerors

"We tried to get a vague physical resemblance; only my hairstyle was an exact copy, but, then again, it was a typical look in that period. If Cavani chose me for the role it was because she wanted to correct an American sterotype of Italians by presenting an Italian who was well-mannered, refined, polite and likeable."

In Hollywood, 1966. "What did I have to do with Hollywood? When they offered me the usual Latin-lover role, I didn't know how to go about refusing directly, so I answered: 'OK. So next Tuesday you'll have to get Giulio over here'. 'Who's Giulio?' 'My barber.' 'Who?' the interpreter asked. 'Yes, because, you see, I always go to Giulio to have my hair cut. He's got a little house in the hills outside Rome, and on Monday, when barbershops are closed in Italy, I go over to his place and he takes out a good prosciutto, good wine - and I really need that. He could come over every Tuesday.' The producer thought I was joking. But he was wrong. It seemed to me like a perfectly logical request for an American star."

rather than the conquered. But the friendly, communicative side of his nature wins through and he ends up representing not the real Malaparte but the kind of individual that Malaparte would probably have liked to have been.

Oltre la porta (Beyond the Door), the film Mastroianni makes the following year, again with Liliana Cavani, is also located in Naples; but this time it is a city where the monsters of the subconscious mind roam over a city devastated now even by the eruption of Vesuvius. Enrico hides behind his large sunglasses and beard. He stalks Nina (Eleonora Giorgi) his step-daughter (or possibly his daughter) with whom he has an incestuous relationship. The young girl believes she has freed herself from the morbid relationship she has with him by marrying Matthew, a young American. The film starts out in Marrakesh, where Nina is staying so that she can be close to her father, who is in prison, charged with the murder of his wife. Nina goes to visit

him every day and takes him clean clothes, books and food. "Have you brought some cigarettes?" "Have you smoked them all already?" "What's this; are you rationing my cigarettes now?" "No. It's just that I wish you would smoke less." Here again we have the *leitmotif* of the cigarette and the accompanying female protests.

While he plays the harsh, suspicious father and jealous lover, it is really Nina who has him under her thumb. The truth about the death of the wife, Nina's mother, is only revealed right at the end, like the end of a murder-mystery. Enrico was her second husband and when she discovered him in bed with Nina she committed suicide and laid the blame on him in a letter she sent to her mother. Enrico continues to protest his innocence but stays in prison under the accusation of the mother-in-law. When he manages to meet her and talk to her he discovers that she has long ago discovered his innocence. But the letter she sent had been intercepted by Nina who

preferred to keep him in prison where they could only see one another. Finally released, he immediately goes to find Nina. Once more she is unable to resist the fatal attraction which holds them together and she leaves her husband and goes off with him.

The story of a double ransom, in which Nina holds Enrico physically imprisoned while Enrico holds Nina psychologically imprisoned, *Oltre la porta* is intended to tell the story of a constricting and sick relationship. The director as usual had sought to represent the most extreme of situations and also to encorage Mastroianni to become particularly involved in the part assigned to him. The role of a sinister and unbalanced character who is ready to rape his step-daughter is a new challenge to Mastroianni and he draws out certain expressions of harshness and perversion seldom seen before. But the film is a disappointment. "We did not manage to produce something that was convincing to the public. It's a pity really because Liliana Cavani and I had worked well together."

Between the two films with Liliana Cavani, who is the third female director he has worked with after Nadine Trintignant and Lina Wertmuller, he also works in the mists of winter-time Pavia on Dino Risi's *Fantasma d'amore* (Ghost of Love). Based on a novel by Mino Milano, it tells the story of a well-off, comfortable and com-

"Oltre la porta *is the story of a young girl who treats two men like puppets: the older man who is her lover, and a young American engineer whom she later marries. The story has a mysterious element* which, unfortunately, we didn't manage to get over to the public. Too bad, really, because I felt I was able to work very well with Liliana Cavani as director."

placent business consultant who unexpectedly meets up again with a woman from his past. Anna/Romy Schneider, whom he had at one time passionately loved, appears to him at first plain and pathetic due to illness, and then in later meetings young and beautiful again, as she had once been. Nino-Mastroianni learns from a doctor friend that Anna is in fact dead but he refuses to believe it, so real is the woman he sees before him. The ghost of his lost love is perhaps death beckoning him towards a sort of sweet madness. It is precisely this madness which liberates Nino from a life of boredom and from a mother-

ing, pedantic and colourless wife, and provides Mastroianni with the chance to underline the real dimensions of the average man by depicting in this role "the infinite complexities of the ordinary individual."

"*Fantasma d'amore* was not an easy film to make. It was a less inspired product than the director's previous works. You can't make a masterpiece every time. A success every time just wouldn't be natural. Making mistakes is part of the daily round. Why should we always be the same? It would become a bit frightening because someone might end up believing that they

"Fantasma d'amore *is a less inspired film than those I'd done with Risi before. It was a hard film to make, but you can't make a masterpiece every time. It's not a big problem if you don't have a success every time; otherwise you might end up believing you're really exceptional. And I feel that would be very bad for you; we musn't forget we're just actors, who aren't really 'creating' anything."*

were infallible. To make only good films and exceptional films would be the ideal. If every now and then you are in a film which is not a success, it's nothing serious. If it didn't happen from time to time, you could start thinking that you really are someting special and that would not be a good thing. Don't forget that we're just actors; we're not creators. I have always felt great admiration for poets, painters, great musicians. They are real artists. We actors are people who have a certain sensitivity and the ability to collaborate with a director to help him to create a character or situation; but we are not the beginning and the end of the product. Actors have never been ranked among the artists. We are simply extremely sensitive artisans; that's the best definition I can think of. Be careful here, though: too often we are impressed by things like the 'Artists' Entrance' to the theatre for example. It is something that has always made me laugh, not out of false modesty but because I feel that I have a reasonable capacity for self-irony, for seeing the ironic side of things. But even the way I am talking now is just another way of showing off, another way of taking people in. It's like in football when a player seems to be running away from the play, into the empty back field; then he gets off a suprise kick, and expects applause for it, too. So even as I protest my modesty, there is an element of vanity. Ah, yes, I admit it. Well, at my age there is no point in hiding the fact that this, too, is a ruse. You say these things in order to be contradicted, for the pleasure of hearing someone say, 'Oh, but that's not true at all!'"

At the end of 1981, and in the first few months of 1982, he makes *Il mondo nuovo* (The New World) with Ettore Scola at Cinecittà. Giacomo Casanova, old and ill, gout-ridden and weak-bladdered. "I don't know if you have noticed but I am also a bit deaf," he says to Restif de la Bretonne. This is to be one of Mastroianni's memorable character-roles. It is not difficult to

Il mondo nuovo. "*An actor has to be a bit naïve; that way he believes in his role and throws himself into it. There's a good anecdote about Gary Cooper that illustrates this. Gary Cooper was standing in front of the fireplace staring at the flames. His mother asked: 'What are you thinking about, Gary?'* And he answered: 'Nothing, Mom'. 'You could be a great actor,' she commented. Certainly you have to have some empty places in you; they'll be filled up by the characters you portray. If you didn't have space ready, there'd be an awful lot of internal collisions.*"

admire this character with his made-up face, rouged lips and delicately painted beauty-spot, his ready intelligence, spirit of observation and rich cutural knowledge . Nor does it surprise us too much that in spite of his age he still holds a certain charm for the ladies. The Cavalier de Seingalt, alias Giacomo Casanova, is travelling from Paris to Metz on the very day that Louis XVI is fleeing the capital to escape the revolution, and on the same road. But Casanova's carriage soon breaks down, but fortunately he is rescued by the daily stage-coach which happens to pass and pick him up from where he is sitting at the side of the road. He finds himself in illustrious company. His fellow passengers include Restif de la Bretonne/Jean-Louis Barrault, the Comtesse de la Borde/Hanna Schygulla, Tom Paine/Harvey Keitel, the rich widow/Andréa Ferréol and the opera singer/Laura Betti. During the journey Casanova manages to guess the other travellers' reasons for making the journey, prove his gallantry to the ladies and even sing a duet from Mozart's *Don Giovanni* with the opera singer; Casanova as Leporello.

As a result of his flirtatious repartee, he manages to make the rich widow fall in

Old Casanova is one of the unforgettable portrayals in the actor's career.

love with him, but in the end has to give her up. "Madam, while what you now call sheer folly some time ago was sheer wisdom, at sixty-six years of age one acquires another kind of wisdom which does not bring happiness but at least avoids tension. I do thank you for your offer, believe me, and, between the two of us, only I shall have anything to regret. It is not this old man who has just now taken your breath away, but his name, his reputation, his past. All things which nowadays no longer exist." He fascinates the young countess with whom he exchanges glances of mutual admiration. Even the countess's hairdresser, Jacob/Jean-Claude Brialy, falls in love with him and is not rejected: "Never exclude anything on principle," he says as he kisses the hairdresser's lips.

For a moment he suspects that he is Restif de la Bretonne's father-in-law, since the latter has married the daughter of a hostess called Nanette, who claims to have been one of his mistresses. He soon realises that she is mistaken, but decides to carry on pretending all the same out of "a desire for intrigue, gallantry and a sense of theatre". When they make a stop in a posthouse he adjusts his make-up, re-applies his lipstick and beauty-spot and for a moment removes his wig, displaying the sparse grey hair which will become characteristic of his role in *Ginger and Fred*.

The film, which at first lasts for two and a half hours and is then shortened to two, is presented on the 27th of April in the non-competitive section of the "Prix René Clair" It appears in the original French version with the title *La nuit de Varennes* and then on the 16th of May at the Cannes Festival. The journey ends in Varennes where the travellers discover that the King has been arrested and taken back to Paris to be tried. But Casanova's flight ends before this, when the Comte de Waldstein's gendarmes arrive to take him back to the castle where he must continue to play his role as a sort of court jester.

La nuit de Varennes was the last screenplay written by Sergio Amidei before he died. The journey towards the new world is based, like *A Special Day*, on the relationship between the individual human being and important historical events. For Mastroianni, a master of self-irony and intelligent professionalism, it remains one of those performances which have illuminated the various stages of his career. One is almost tempted to believe that he felt a certain amount of amused identification with the character of the old but intellectually still brilliant Casanova.

In the summer of 1982, he makes *Storia di Piera* (Piera's Story) with Marco Ferreri. The events are those jointly told by the actress Piera degli Esposti and the writer Dacia Maraini in the book of the same name. They tell the life story of the actress Piera from her birth to her first stage successes. Mastroianni plays the part of Lorenzo, the father, a communist union leader who is often away from home. From childhood on, Piera/ Isabelle Huppert has had a sensually charged and complicit relationship with her mother, Eugenia/Hanna Schygulla. For her part, the mother is an amoral individual, ingenuous and unbalanced, whose only way of protesting against the female condition is through sex; and for these nymphomaniac tendencies she has several times been subjected to electric shock treatment. She spends her nights at the station or on the beach with some casual lover. Piera goes for her to bring her home. Lorenzo is disorientated by his wife's behaviour and tries to cope with the situation, sometimes by beating her up, sometimes by holding in and suppressing his jealousy and at other times by giving in to complete apathy.

He is soon worn-down by the situation and is little by little pushed out of the party, first by being transfered to another region, and finally by being pensioned off. Suddenly old and spent, he is taken into a hospice where he eventually dies. The film covers the whole course of the character's life and we see him as a vigorous and healthy man showing his son a picture of a woman in a newspaper: "Nice thighs; she'll probably have a nice bum too, if you'll excuse the expression". Later we see him playing the harmonica in the silver-white jacket his wife has bought for him, a jacket more suited to a Vaudeville performer, but he is playing the song "Bandiera Rossa" (The Red Flag). There is a wonderful scene between him and his daughter, where he is helping her to rehearse her first amateur roles: "calmly now with a measured tone". When he washes Eugenia he says to his daughter, "Your mother's skin is like velvet". As an old man, we see him complaining to his daughter: "I've got too much time now. I don't know what to do with myself. These ghosts, you know, follow me. I've got all these visions in my head. Before, when I worked for the party, I had hundreds of loves: I had the red flag; I had Eugenia. Now the red flag has pensioned me off, and Eugenia is taking my life". At the end, in hospital, he can no longer even adjust his cuff-links. But he continues to have a very free and open relationship with his daughter. They kiss one another like two lovers and Piera masturbates him and shows him her naked genitals: "Eugenia's was more beautiful; I could make love to her for hours without ever satisfying her".

The character is built-up on whispered tones and very skilfully refined. By now, for Mastroianni, working with Ferreri is an enjoyable habit, even if he's not playing the protagonist. The film is released in Italy on February 4th and is presented at the Cannes film festival in May. In June Mastroianni receives a "David di Donatello" award for his career.

As soon as he finishes the film with Ferreri he flies to Brazil to make *Gabriela* with Bruno Barreto.

"It was a nice experience, but the film was not a success, perhaps because there was not enough heat, not enough sweat. The director was a young man who had already made *Donna Flor e i suoi mariti* (Donna Flora and her Husbands) from another novel by Jorge Amado. When he offered me the part, I thought it was a great idea. I didn't know that *Gabriela* had already been made into a soap opera starring Sonia Braga. It's not that it bothered me much, but the director, having been asked by Metro Goldwyn Meyer to make a screen version of the story, decided not to set it in Baia, the most authentic part of Brazil with the port and the market where the author had set the story and they had shot the soap opera, but in a small eighteenth century village called Parati. This little old village is one of the few of its type still remaining in the area between Rio de Janiero and San Paulo; but it looks like a set for a musical comedy; there is something fairytale-like about it. And when you look at the distance – I went there in a private jet and it took about an hour and a half – it's like setting a Sicilian story in Brianza or even further North, in Switzerland. It's a completely different atmosphere.

If Barreta really had made a musical comedy, perhaps it would have been all right, but for a film which depends upon the forces of nature and the expression of the dark, deeper instincts of the characters it really did lack the sweat, the heat, the flies, the carrion by the roadside. The director took the decision so as not to risk seeming as though he was simply doing a remake, a screen version of what they had already done on television. It was a pity, though, because *Gabriela* is a nice story. If he had made it somewhere else, perhaps it would have worked. I've been to Salvador, which is the capital of the Baia region and it's almost like being in Naples. People selling all kinds of things by the side of the road, an incredible confusion, stray dogs, prostitutes, necklaces, coffin shops with all their little lamps lit-up, churches with a thousand lighted candles. I had never been to Brazil before so I don't feel disappointed about making the film. It gave me the chance to see a new country and to meet different kinds of people and that's always a positive experience. All thanks to the cinema!"

Nassib Saad is a Brazilian whose father was an Arab and whose mother was a Neapolitan. The story is set in Brazil in 1925. Nassib, the owner of the Vesuvius bar, needs a cook; and so he buys one at the slave market. Gabriela/Sonia Braga turns out to be an excellent cook and she ends up making the bar-owner fall in love with her. They have a perfect love story until Nassib starts to become jealous of the attentions of the other men in the bar. So he decides to marry her and keep her shut up in the house. He wants to make her into a bourgeois housewife, dress her up in elegant, restricting clothes and send her to boring conferences, while he gradually loses interest in her. Gabriela still loves him but feels suffocated and neglected and so she ends up making love to a young man. When he discovers them together Nassib decides to put an end to their union and has their marriage annulled. But their love is stronger than other circumstances and shortly after they separate they start-up their love affair again, at the point where it had been interrupted by marriage. Mastroianni's performance is always measured and exact, and he seems to make use of experience gained in earlier light comedy roles and in particular his role in *Divorce Italian Style*.

L'armata ritorna (The Army Returns) was a hard film project to organize; and getting it off the ground was slow going. The idea for the film took shape many years before it was actually made. The offer to make this film arrived from France while I was working on *Bye Bye Monkey* with Ferreri. *Il generale dell'armata morta* (The General of the Dead Army) by Ismail Kadare, who is perhaps the most important Albanian writer, was a beautiful book which at that time had only appeared in France, where it had very good reviews, whereas in Italy it was not known at all and was only published many years later, I think just the day before the film was released. A young French producer had acquired the rights but he hadn't done anything with them, so that in the end Michel Piccoli, who had been offered it like I had and had read the book and fallen in love with it, decided to take the rights off him and make the film himself. While we were talking about the project, Ferreri, who also thought it was a beautiful book, thought that Luciano Tovoli would be a good director for the film. He was the director of photography for *Bye Bye Monkey* and had shown a lot of interest in directing this film. Tovoli went to Albania with Piccoli, who had even learnt a little Albanian; they wanted to get permission to make the film there, because that was where the events took place. Permission was granted, but right at the last minute, just a month before filming was due to start, it seems that the Albanian authorities changed their minds without giving any reason. A difficult country to get into and get out of, as recent events confirm. But Piccoli was heartbroken because he had already spent the money. At that point we decided to go and have a look at a place in Abruzzo where the mountains are a bit like the mountains in Albania. And so in the high plains of the Gran Sasso, where you can't see a soul, and there are no houses or anything, we shot the film, which was a debut for Sergio Castellitto. I have always looked on that particular book and film with a great deal of interest, and it was a positive experience for me."

General Ariosto/Mastroianni receives an order to recover the remains of all the Italian soldiers killed in Albania during the Second World War. In particular he is charged to find the remains of Colonel Salvatore Di Brenni who disappeared with his entire Blue Battalion. Betsy (Anouk Aimée), the Colonel's widow, asks him to find her husband's remains because only by burying him in the family grave can she hope to free herself from the memories which haunt her. The military chaplain (Michel Piccoli), Betsy's friend, also leaves with Ariosto. Their search goes on for months but they find no trace of the Blue Battalion. When they finally find the place, Di Brenni's remains are not there. It is only at a wedding feast in a small village miles from anywhere that Ariosto and the chaplain find out the truth. Di Brenni had been held prisoner and then killed by the mother of a girl whom he had raped. The girl had afterwards hung herself out of despair. Disgusted, Ariosto throws the bones of the colonel into the river but he is then forced to ask a German officer, who is in Albania for the same motive as he is, for a skeleton like the colonel's to take back to Italy.

Mastroianni's performance moves from moments of military rigidity to moments of weakness or crafty behaviour in which he is much more appealing. His acting is perhaps at its best during the scenes of his enforced cohabitation with Piccoli when, for example, in a fever, he has a nightmare about the horrors of war and, wrapped in a blanket and with a beret on his head, he takes to his bottle of cognac. Or when he furtively telephones the countess, Betsy. But perhaps his best moment, which alone serves to give real substance to the character, is when he draws a human tibia and fibula on a piece of beer-soaked paper: "look how elegant the fibula is, like a clarinet," to explain to the German officer the differences between the five hundred bones in the human body.

At the end of 1983, Mastroianni plays the part of Henry IV in a film directed by Marco Bellocchio and freely adapted by Tonino Guerra from the play of the same name by Luigi Pirandello. Many years before the action takes place, the young Henry falls from his horse in a fancy dress parade; and when he regains consciousness he believes that he really is the person he is dressed as. His madness begins when he

sees Matilde (Claudia Cardinale), the girl he loves, in the arms of a rival. But he then carries on being (or pretending to be?) mad, and is indulged by friends and family until one day they decide to try out a strange experiment with the help of a psychiatrist. They decide to present him with the daughter of the woman he once loved, who is the image of her mother, in the hope that the shock will bring him round and put him in touch with reality again. But Henry is not to be tricked and, instead, in a fit of rage, tries to kill Matilde/Claudia Cardinale's lover. His action convinces everyone that he really is mad.

Left alone with his little group of young

followers, he lets out his frustration: "They are only afraid of this: that I can tear off their masks and show them what disguises they wear. As if it was not I who had forced them to dress up this way so that I can enjoy playing the madman". With his beard, moustache, long hair and his cheeks reddened with rouge, he feels at home in the guise of a medieval emperor. But like the castle clock which stopped twenty years ago, it seems that the years have stopped going forward for him too. His outbreaks of rage and the crafty look in his eye seem to be telling us that he is still a young man.

"*Henry IV* is an important part for any actor and most would like to do it at least

"I've never done a theatre version of Henry IV, *though he's a character that allows the actor an extraordinary virtuoso performance. For the cinema version I completely agreed with Bellocchio that the interpretation should be more intimate, since the big screen so magnifies everything you do that you need to underline the character's inner thoughts and development if you want to present his madness… or presumed madness."*

once in their life. In this leading role, the actor is on stage all the time, pulling the strings of the whole performance and moving the other characters like pawns in a game of which he is the master. But perhaps not even this is the most important thing. Henry IV must not seem like an actor pretending to be someone who is acting; he must really be that man there who is so enjoying himself acting a grand part. He enjoys himself and he suffers. He is completely absorbed. You can't help

applauding him. Pirandello's text includes some virtuoso moments when the actor really can pull out all the stops. We made the film character more subtle, a closer, more intimate portrait. At first Henry IV may seem an unpleasant sort of person because he refuses to accept the rules of society, but in the end he grows on you because he is a crafty devil at heart who manages to live all alone in a huge castle where he has his own court and spends his time making fun of everybody. We couldn't

Cin-cin. *"The film eliminated the play's harshness, the note of treachery, the hard-edged vision, the violence. It became a light comedy. Alcoholism is hardly a problem any more in the film version, and the two leading characters don't end up as tramps. In both versions I play an Italian immigrant: the theatre production co-starred Natasha Parry, a fine actress and wife of the director Peter Brooks; the film co-starred Julie Andrews, cinema actress with a long line of successes to her credit."*

manage to take him too seriously. All interpretations of Pirandello have their good and bad points and ours is certainly not the only one possible. In reality his stories are neither comic nor dramatic; they are more grotesque. There is also a sneer. Mad? He uses madness to say what he wants to say, like a kind of passport. There is a line in *Henry IV*: 'With one word, you can destroy a person'. It's true. One word used badly can upset us, make us think about things. Are we really how we think we are or how others see us? The experience of doing *Henry IV* was another of those experiences that has helped me to reflect upon the nature of my profession. An actor does not become an actor without a reason. He tries to complete himself through the character he is playing, using it to fill up the empty spots in his culture and memory, in his mind and feelings. But then, what do I know about it?"

After acting in the cinematic adaptation of Pirandello's play, on the 7th of January 1984, he is on stage at the Théâtre Montparnasse, in *Tchin-tchin* (Cheers). He appears in this play until the 29th March, giving over eighty performances. The play, which Mastroianni would have liked to stage ten years previously with Anna Magnani, is directed by Peter Brook. The co-starring role is taken by Natasha Parry, Brook's wife. The project had taken shape when Mastroianni met the director in Quiberon at a thalassotherapy centre where he goes to rest between jobs. Once again he is the star, or rather co-star, as the entire action revolves around the two central characters Cesareo and Pamela, an Italian man and an English woman whose partners are having a love affair together. They meet up to devise a way of getting their unfaithful partners back. While they give vent to their mutual frustrations, they both attempt to drown their troubles in drink. Cesareo becomes poetic about the word drink, and like Cyrano on his nose, weaves an entire poem around it:

"Don't you find it boring always saying drink a glass? You could say drink and leave it at that. Take a full glass and drown in it. Or if you really have to say drink something you could say: 'I'll take my little dose of medicine,' to make people feel sorry for you like a child. Or you could say: 'Let's have a drop. Let's have a few pints'. Even though it sounds a bit vulgar in French. Think of a light, sparkling, fresh wine with the perfume of the countryside in it. Let's leave it at that. You could even say, 'Let's get pissed' or 'Let's wet our whistle,' like my bricklayer friends. It's straightforward but perhaps a bit macho. You might say, 'Let's ruin our health', or some other such phrase, to hide your fears and difficulties. You could even pedantically say: 'Let us offer libations.' It's dignified ritual. 'Let's offer libations' takes us with dignity to the level of ancient rites."

The play's success makes Mastroianni think that it could be made into a good film. All the more so since in the sixties Harold Hecht, a producer associated with Burt Lancaster, proposed that Mastroianni make a film of it in Hollywood. The producer even went to Rome to reach an agreement, but then he disappeared.

"When I was doing the play in Paris, I thought that the story of two cuckolds, not to mince words, would have had a good reception as a film. But nobody was interested. Then three years ago, Arturo La Pegna remembered the Parisian performance and suggested we make a film. I was delighted and accepted his proposal. So this story about the meeting between an Italian emigré who had made his fortune in the construction business and an English lady, the wife of a Society doctor, was made into a film. This time, having chosen Julie Andrews, who didn't speak French, for the female part, and Gene Saks, who could guarantee the commercial distribution of the film, as the director, the film was made in English. In comparison with the original script, the film version has taken out a lot

of the harshness, perfidy and even violence. The characters come from a better social class. It was converted into a sort of light comedy. Alcohol is still an element in the male role, but is eliminated from the female role."

The film is shot in the winter of 1990, between Paris (many of the scenes are shot in the Musée Rodin, a sort of temple of love), Quiberon, where Cesareo goes to dry out, and Biarritz. It is released in Italy with very little publicity half way through June, 1991 when the cinema season is virtually over. Naturally it falls flat.

In 1984, Mastroianni gets together with Mario Monicelli again to make *The Two Lives of Mattia Pascal*. The film is loosely based on Pirandello's novel *Il fu Mattia Pascal* (The Former Mattia Pascal). Two versions were made: a long version for television and a shorter version for the cinema. It was a very costly production and involved not only the Italian state television company RAI Uno but also a whole range of European television companies: Antenne 2, Telemünchen, TVE, Channel 4 and Rtsi.

It is only when his father dies that Mattia Pascal, a well-off bachelor who lives on his private income, realises that he has been robbed of all his money by the administrator, Malagna. Even Olive, the bailiff's daughter whom he has fallen in love with, prefers to marry Malagna, who has taken care of her whole family. He meets Romilda, one of the administrator's relations, and marries her. But he and his mother are tyrannised by his wife and mother-in-law, and his life becomes more and more miserable. He finds a job at the local library but when his mother dies he decides to leave. He tries out his luck in the casinos in Monte Carlo and wins. When he goes back home to show off his new-found wealth to his wife he arrives just in time to attend his own funeral; everyone has assumed that he is dead. So he leaves for Rome and obtains false documents as Adriano Meis. In his new life he meets Adriana Paleari, his landlord's daughter, and falls in love with her. But he is blackmailed by the girl's brother-in-law who suspects something and so they leave for Venice together. They live in the Grand Hotel and he squanders all his money. He tries his luck on the tables again but this time he loses. He decides to go back to Miragno, where everyone believes he is dead and his wife has re-married. When he gets there the community accepts him back by pretending that he has not returned. And so a scandal is avoided and he can continue his meaningless life, his only refuge being the old mice-infested library.

"It is always good working with Monicelli. It's a pleasure to work with him; he's intelligent, brisk, and he has an acute sense of irony. I like him very much and admire him as a director. I had a good time working on the film. But there isn't really much to say about the film itself. It's a bit like saying to an office worker, 'So what did you do last month, then?' And he replies: 'Well, I did the accounts.' It's the same for us, only now and then does something different come up. If not it's just routine, a fantastic routine, but routine all the same. *C'est mon métier*, as the French say: it's my job."

His meeting with Jack Lemmon in 1985 in *Macaroni* is precisely one of those occasions which go beyond the routine of the job. "I met him in Hollywood the first time I went there in 1962. He was making *Irma la douce* with Shirley Mac Laine. They took me to meet him on the set, but it was just a polite exchange really. I was pleased to meet him. Then I met him again in New York in 1982. I was making *Oltre la porta* in Marrakesh and I was invited to take part in *A Night of a Thousand Stars*, the proceeds of which were to be donated to a home for retired American actors. Everybody was there and I met Jack Lemmon in the theatre. I had arrived after an extremely long journey from Marrakesh and when I got there, there was only Coca-Cola, orange juice and mineral water to drink because they were not serving any alcoholic drinks before the show otherwise everyone would have got drunk. He was so kind as to go out and get me a whisky from a bar and bring it to me. Jack Lemmon is as nice a person in real life as he is on the screen, a really adorable man. Everybody knows that he is talented, but it is his kind nature and his modesty that make him so lovable, so precious. And then he is intelligent, too. He adapted straight away to the Italian way of working which is the opposite to the Hollywood way. And going around Naples is hellish; but he never complained once. He gets his big book of crosswords, sits down in a corner and does his crosswords; and when you call him, there he is, ready to go. He never complained about anything, never. He really is fantastic."

When Robert Traven/Jack Lemmon and Antonio Jasiello/Marcello Mastroianni first meet they do not get on but things soon change. Robert, the Vice-President of an airline company, arrives in Naples on a business trip. He is immediately pounced on by Antonio who shows him a photo taken in 1946. But he does not recognise the girl in the photo and gives Antonio short shrift. Then he remembers; when he was a soldier in the Fifth Brigade he had been engaged to Antonio's sister. He goes to find him to apologise. Antonio, who is an archivist at the Banco di Napoli, pretends coolness but hides behind the desk to give vent to a wave of joy. Traven is warmly welcomed by Antonio's family, almost as if he were a long-lost distant relative. He is amazed by such a warm reception and asks Antonio for an explanation. And so Antonio tells Traven that all these years he has himself written letters to his heartbroken sister, pretending to be him and inventing a whole series of magnificent adventures. Traven is captivated and wants to carry the story on. Soon a firm friendship develops between them.

Traven forgets about the anxiety of a profession which has taken up so much of his time that his marriage has failed and ended in divorce. He discovers that in spite of seeming unremarkable, Antonio in fact has a vivid and fertile imagination. He finds him sitting at a table drinking coffee and talking while he writes: "What a rascal, a real son of a bitch". He is curious and asks Antonio to explain: "Who are you mad at?" "I'm writing a scene for my new play and I have let myself be carried away by the bad character. I don't stop him from doing what he wants. On the contrary I let myself be led by his psychology. Do you see what I mean? Even Chekhov wrote like this." They revert to childhood together, laughing till they cry when they get sugar all over their noses from eating a rumbaba. Robert goes to a performance of one of Antonio's plays, where he is dressed in the style of *The Pizza Triangle* and has taken the place of one of the actors who has fallen ill. They spend the evening together in complete harmony. Antonio is only apparently the crazier of the two and has to hold Robert back when he climbs up on a framework of tubes and can not get down. In the end the American friend has the chance to show his generosity by helping Antonio's son who has got involved with the Neapolitan underworld. But the ending is tragic: while they are sitting on the beach, Antonio dies, with his head leaning against a boat and his last cigarette still in his hand.

Robert does not give up hope. Antonio has told him that he has already died twice before and woken up at one o'clock the following day. And so he waits with the widow and the whole family expecting to hear the bell attached to Antonio's wrist ring. The story, written by Scola, Maccari and Scarpelli, has the flavour of Eduardo De Filippo's bitter Neapolitan fables and ends on a note of hope not only for Antonio but for the whole city. The final images open out onto a panorama of the roofs of

With Jack Lemmon in Macaroni.

Naples and while we watch we seem to hear a bell distantly ringing.

Macaroni is released at the end of October 1985 in Italy and abroad in three different editions. An Italian version for the Italian market. An English version to be distributed in the United States by Paramount Pictures. And a third version in which Jack Lemmon speaks in English and Mastroianni speaks partly in Neapolitan and partly in English, when he is talking to Lemmon. The third and most successful version has, of course, very rare showings. The film is chosen to represent Italy at the 1986 Oscar awards beating Fellini's *Ginger and Fred* and Liliana Cavani's *Interno Berlinese* (Inside Berlin). But the film is received with a certain scepticism in the United States.

"When the film was released, the Americans accused us of being presumptuous. 'So now an American has to go to Naples, a city full of Camorristi and poverty, to learn how to live. Don't make us laugh!' Of course it was not our intention at all to teach an American how to live by going on a trip to Naples. Our intention was simply to show that it is possible to forget success and all its accompanying neuroses, the problems with your wife, divorce and so on; all the sorts of things that exist here too. We took America as the most advanced, the most forward-looking country to show that a country which by comparison has remained far behind as far as development is concerned, nevertheless has preserved a certain humanity which can be a lesson about life for an American. But it could equally well have been about a Swede or someone from Milan, an Italian executive who might have the same sort of prob-lems, running after the same goals which tires him out physically and psychologically and destroys his personal relationships. It is not about attacking America. On the other hand that way of living, of being content to survive day by day in harmony with your wife and children, if possible, was probably an important lesson for the American returning to his own country."

The two actors, give superb performances in the film. Mastroianni brings real humanity to the part of Antonio. Generous, intelligent, imaginative and full of good, common sense, he manages to be both quietly modest and brimming with bold assurance, though it is an assurance always tempered by irony.

8

When We Were Young and Beautiful

On the 12th of February he starts to make *Ginger and Fred* at Cinecittà with Fellini. The film is written by the director with Tonino Guerra and Tullio Pinelli and tells the story of a couple of dancers who had been famous for imitating Ginger Rogers and Fred Astair. After a thirty-year absence from the stage, Amelia Bonetti and Pippo Botticella appear once more in their famous tap-dancing number on the television programme *Ed ecco a voi* (And Presenting…). Their first meeting occurs at the Manager Palace Hotel when Amelia knocks on her neighbour's door because his snoring keeps her awake. Pippo answers the door wearing his dressing-gown and yawning, unshaven and with his hair in disorder. "Amelia, I hardly recognised you," he says with a raucous laugh.

The next morning he turns up dressed à la Fellini with a checked overcoat draped over his shoulders, a red scarf and a checked hat. Amelia hears his voice through the confusion of impersonators, dwarves and eccentric-looking individuals when he turns to someone and says: "When were you born? Et alors, when the great Fred was tap dancing you were still wetting your bed. You might say that now it's me who wets the bed. And so what? Yes, I admit it does happen sometimes. The prostate. Ooh, Amelia, we've ended up with a bunch of amateurs, dilettanti". "Who are you anyway?", someone asks him. "Imbecile. I am Pippo Botticella. In the business: Fred. I can imitate anything. The *chemin de fer*, a typewriter, a machine-gun," he continues, punctuating his words with dance-steps. He is distract-

ed by the appearance of a woman's back-side on the television: "Chiappa tonda, fava gioconda" (A round butt satisfies your dick). He reads another aphorism he has written in his note-book: "A woman without an ass is like a mountaineer without a mule". But he comments with quick competence on a number Amelia is practicing: "I knew it: you always go wrong at this point. No, not the steps; the *visage*. You smile, but it is the exact opposite that you should be doing; I've told you so a hundred times. It is supposed to be much more subtle. The all-enveloping 'Memory' ends here, drifting away like in a dream". Then he asks her if they have paid her yet.

With a few lines the character is complete. Mastroianni's professional touch gives life to the character of Fred, a failure who has not quite given in and whose noisy buffoonery serves to hide his insecurity and fear. He has never told Ginger that he suffered so much when they parted that he ended up in a mental asylum. And in the bus on the way to the studios he confesses his fear of death. "It's difficult to sort-out this feeling. But it's as though for some time now things have seemed strange. As though they were trying to say: 'Goodbye, Pippo, goodbye'."

At the entrance to the studios, they see a criminal in hand-cuffs, arriving as guest. For crime is part of the show today. Fred feels a certain sympathy for the captive and, in a wave of anarchic sentiment, exclaims: "We ought to rebel against all this too; because I burn up at the sight of injustice. I burn up". He is a superstitious person and carries a horseshoe in his pocket. But he is no fool, as is evident when he replies to the journalist's stupid

questions by explaining the history of tap-dancing to her: "It is about time we had a serious discussion about tap-dancing because it is not just a dance; it's more than that. When it was first invented, tap-dancing was not a dance but a sort of morse-code for the negroes who invented it. On the cotton-plantations where the the negro slaves worked they couldn't talk among themselves because the master would skin them alive. So what does the negro slave do? He talks to his companions of misfortune with his feet". He criticises a writer's book and ends his comment with one of his aphorisms: "Chiappa di nanetta la fava ti aspetta" (A dwarf's back-side is waiting for a dick).

Yet again Mastroianni's character suggests a double personality to Fellini. He is himself, of course, present in the first person in his physical representation. And then there is the image of Mastroianni seen through all the roles that he has previously interpreted. He recalls Luigi in *Bye Bye Monkey* when he sees a monkey in the corridor and feels the need to get back to the fundamental elements of innocence and instinct. The lover he has played in so many films is referred to when he says: "Now I try to avoid undressing in front of a woman if I can. It's not like it used to be. When I used to undress it was usually followed by a spontaneous round of applause from the fortunate girl". We are even reminded of a Casanova without make-up. There is also an element of the real-life Mastroianni who, twenty years previously, had wanted to give vent to certain feelings on television, as now Pippo says to a worried Amelia: "Just let me go on stage and then you'll really see some-

thing, because tonight I am going to talk. Tonight I am going to tell all. Tonight, I'm going to have it out with sixty million Italians". "What are you going to say?" "Sheep, sheep, sheep. Ah you think I've come here for the eight hundred thousand lire, but I couldn't give a damn about the money. You sheep have invented television. You are all always there, watching the television. Is that all you ever want to listen to? Well tonight you can listen to me."

Ginger and Fred is also an attack against television, or rather against its worst aspects, and from time to time each of the characters seems to want to get out of the TV engagement. But in the end, they can't resist the professional challenge. During make-up it is Amelia who breaks down and wants to go, but she stays on when she realises that it is a chance to make the myth of the two great American dancers live again. In Fellini's film the public is allowed to watch a TV production from the wings. Along with the performers, we wander through a fantastic Fellinian backstage, which becomes a kind of Vanity Fair of adverts and endless talkshows. While they are waiting to go on the air, Fred continues to drink and smoke even though smoking is not allowed. Then the lights go out. "What are we doing here, Amelia? We must be mad. Let's go before the lights come back on." "Fool" she replies through angry tears. He spreads out his handkerchief so that she can sit down and suggests that the black-

out is part of an assassination attempt. And there in the dark they make their confessions. Pippo tells her about his feeling of having been abandoned when she left him; and Amelia admits that she had only accepted the proposal to appear on television so that she could see him again.

But now their love story is over. "We are a couple of ghosts who arrive in the dark and go away again," says Fred. But while they try to make their escape the light returns and illuminates Fred. "Telly addicts!" he shouts, making an obscene gesture. They start dancing. Fred is out of breath and lets Ginger lead him. When he does the claqué he slips and falls. But, circus-like, they start all over again. Their show of bravado immediately wins the

Ginger and Fred. *"When Fellini said, 'Shave his hair off', everybody told me had ruined me. 'What do you mean, ruined me? Wait and see what a great role this is.' In fact Pippo was a beautiful part. Hell, he's a real desperate case."*

With his daughter Chiara on the set for I soliti ignoti vent'anni dopo. *"I think you can always feel close to your children if you can just adapt to their life-style. Or at least let them know that you care for them. And let them really understand that. It's hard."*

audience's approval. When Fred accompanies Amelia to the station he tells her that he is going to stay in Rome to try to become a television presenter. In the meantime he accepts some money from her while he is waiting to be paid for the television appearance.

With faith in Fellini's genius, Mastroianni has dared to play a physically decrepit and profoundly pathetic character. "When Fellini said to me: 'Lets cut off your hair,' lots of people said to me, 'He's ruined you.' But I knew it would work. 'What do you mean, he's ruined me? This is a beautiful role. Wait and see.' And in fact Pippo is a complex individual with his rich and painful humanity. Hell, he's a real desperate case."

The film's premiere is held at the Palais de Chaillot in Paris on the 13th of January, 1986. It is released in Italy on the 22nd of January after a gala première at the Teatro Sistina in Rome. It is also presented in a non-competitive section of the Berlin Film Festival and is well-received.

In spite of missing the Oscar, it wins Mastroianni a "Nastro d'argento" and a "David di Donatello", the two most prestigious Italian film awards.

I soliti ignoti vent'anni dopo (The Big Deal On Madonna Street, Twenty Years On), which he makes in 1985, is "a joke, a game" for Mastroianni. The film takes its cue from Monicelli's masterpiece and uses some of the original actors, but can be appreciated even without seeing the original film. It opens with the closing scene from *The Big Deal On Madonna Street* when Peppe/Vittorio Gassman asks Tiberio/ Marcello Mastroianni as he is getting onto a tram, "So when will I see you next?" "Never. In fact it would be better if we pretended never to have met," he

replies. But unfortunately, according to the script of the new film written by Todini with Age and Suso Cecchi d'Amico, Tiberio does not keep his word and thanks to Peppe has ended up in prison. When he gets out he discovers that Rome is a completely diffferent city from the one he remembers. His wife, Teresa, is living with someone else and his son, Brunino, has gone to work in Milan. Living on the poverty-line and sleeping in an old car, he decides to dress up as a woman to take part in Peppe's latest scheme. But when Peppe recognises him he laughs so much that it brings on a fatal apopleptic fit. And so Tiberio takes-over Peppe's business himself.

With his small band which includes his

"In O Melissokomos *I played a Greek and I dubbed myself in Greek because I wanted my own voice to be heard. Besides, my name was originally Greek, 'Mastrojanni'; the cinema changed the 'j' to 'i'. So people accepted my Greek dubbing, even with my strange accent; in spite of everything, audiences preferred hearing my real voice."*

son, a girl with a baby, Ferribotte and an old woman, he sets off for Yugoslavia to run a money racket. And he leads the whole affair with true grit. He is entirely at his ease as the leader of the group, embittered by life's misfortunes, and gives a convincing interpretation of a humiliat-

ed character, more recklessly desperate than purely comic, but always thoroughly entertaining.

Between April and May in 1986 he works in Athens and various parts of northern Greece on Theo Anghelopulos's *O Melissokomos* (The Beekeeper). It turns out to be one of the most dangerous adventures of Mastroianni's career. This is true especially of the final scene, when Spiros, the central character, allows his bees to sting him to death.

"The scene with the bees is left right until the end, which made me comment to the director: 'Oh, I see. If I end up in hospital, it doesn't matter anyway because the film is finished'. 'No, no don't you worry; these are very intelligent bees. We are going to put a few hives with some rogue bees on one side and some hives with the good bees that produce honey on the other. When you knock all the hives over, the rogue bees will go over to the other hives to steal the honey and you will be in the middle and they won't touch you. I won't even put my mask on'. We shot the scene at sunset, when bees are less agressive. Production distributed masks to the whole team. Anghelopulos didn't put his on, perhaps to encourage me. Then they got everyone to move away and left me there on my own. It started with a long close-up in which you were supposed to realise that I decide to use my bees to commit suicide. When he said 'Action,' I saw him shoot off across the field, like a rabbit, with a bee on his head. He's bald so you could see it very clearly. All the time I was there trying to express my psychological anguish, I was watching him out of the corner of my eye. When he said 'Stop' and asked me, 'Well, how did it go?', I said 'Fine,' because I didn't want to do the scene again. In reality, when I got up and pushed and kicked over the hives, the bees went mad and stung me a lot, especially on the back of the neck. I was surprised; can it be possible that those little creatures know that your weak-spot is the brain?

We had to repeat the scene for three days on the run. On the third day, they took the trouble to call a doctor with some cortisone at the ready. Somebody said to me: 'Why do you bother taking such risks?' But we were in Greece, not Hollywood, where you can call up the bees on remote control. You just had to go for it. And then I was led on by a form of vanity that only actors have. I thought to myself: "When the public see this scene, they'll understand that it is me exposing myself, so it will be a triumph, if nothing else of a tamer who is unlucky'. The beekeeeper used to say to me, 'Don't move, don't make any quick movements. The

bees won't sting you if you react calmly'. but when a bee is crawling accross your neck, it is an instinctive thing to react. I fell to the ground and the camera panned out on the countryside and sea and then came back to me breathing my last breaths. The only thing I would criticise Anghelopus for is for not taking a shot of me from below, from under a cloud of four or five thousand bees against the sky. He wanted to do one of those slow sequences he is famous for. So the scene lost some of its effect because of that and he had to add sound effects to make up for it. I had taken all those risks for nothing."

The film recounts Spiros' last trip. After his daughter's marriage, he has left wife, job and hometown, on a small truck loaded with beehives, off to wherever flowers bloom, just as his beekeeper father had done before him. He is a gloomy, taciturn man, living on his memories. Then, at a petrol pump, he meets a young girl, who lives uprooted from personal history and memory. At first, they can hardly tolerate each other's company. Gradually, however, Spiros feels a growing curiosity about this girl, and she, in her turn, tries to seduce him. The growing mutual interest changes into a violent attraction, which culminates in a love scene enacted on the stage of an unused cinema. Then their two paths separate; the girl will continue her aimless hitch-hiking. Meanwhile, Spiros' travels have led him to visit old friends, meet up with his wife, and hunt for his other daughter. He is ready for the last stop on his journey, the scene in which he arranges to be killed by his bees.

"It was a really positive experience. A hard film, though, because there is not much urban development in Greece. Greece has had almost five hundred years of Turkish rule; yet no traces remain of their civilization. I remember that the car I had then, a virtually new Volkswagen which had only done one thousand five

hundred kilometres, had seventeen thousand kilometres on the clock when we finished making the film. It was a particularly complicated film to make. For instance, if we wanted to show a shot of a monument or a fountain or some detail or other which in some way represented Greece, we sometimes had to travel two hundred kilometres between a shot of me and a shot of me with my partner against this background. The countryside is unremarkable, without history or interest. Even the dubbing was done in an unusual way. We didn't do it in front of the screen with a reading stand but in the places where the scenes were shot. Anghelopulos was in despair because he couldn't find a Greek actor to dub me. So I said to him: 'You stand next to me and tell me what to say and I'll just repeat it, like we do in Italy with actors we have taken off the street.' And so I did the dubbing in Greek, something which has hardly ever been mentioned. I mean, in a country where Italian actors are dubbed and I dub myself in Greek, I ought to be given a medal. We set out with only one Nagra recorder and one microphone. We worked for months. When we started the film there were still signs of snow and when we went back to

Michail Vasiljević Platonov in Player-Piano. *"When I acted in* Player-Piano *I suggested that we get the RAI (Italian Radio and TV Network) to shoot the play for television. Nikita was ready to do it for television; and I mean really do it right, not just using a television camera to shoot what was going on on stage. But they weren't interested. Thought it would be too boring. Why does this only happen in our country? Don't these people ever go abroad? Don't they know there's a whole television division in France just to film plays put on in the theatre? In England we saw the complete works of Shakespeare on television."*

do the dubbing it was summer and the birds were singing. The driver had to throw stones at them to try to shoo them away. The whole film was reconstructed in Greek without my ever seeing the scenes. We did one phrase a bit faster, then another a bit slower, and then it was all mixed in editing. What a hassle!"

Mastroianni is the narrative mechanism of the film and he is present in it from the first to the last scene. This emblematic character in search of death, entirely closed-in on himself, gradually slips more and more towards total silence and seems to carry with him all the world's suffering. As in all his successful works, he abandons himself completely to the part. The film has also produced an excellent relationship between actor and director and in spite of the episode with the bees Mastroianni decides to work with Anghelopulos again. This comes about in 1990 when they make the film *Il passo sospeso della cicogna* (The Stork's Suspended Tread) in a small town in northern Greece between Turkey and Albania. It is very cold and Mastroianni falls ill during filming. Unfortunately it is not the only misfortune to befall the film. The bishop of the town, who sees Anghelopulos as a subversive, tries to create problems for them by getting the people of the town to interfere with the filming. Not content with this, he excommunicates the director and all the actors.

Made before the Gulf War, the film now has a real topical value. A journalist arrives in an abandoned border town to interview its new resident population, refugees of all kinds: Turks, Kurds, Albanians, who are living there in the hope of finding a better life elsewhere. While he is watching the footage he has made in the town, he thinks he recognises a Greek ex-politician (Mastroianni), who disappeared at the end of the Colonels' regime. The inquiry shifts its objectives and begins to look into the case of this enigmatic indi-

On the set for Dark Eyes *with Marthe Keller and Nikita Michalkov. "Michalkov is great with his actors, perhaps because he's an actor himself. In addition, he's an Italian-style director, which is the most interesting thing for me. He intervenes during the action, gives orders, has a lot of imagination. This doesn't happen with either French or English directors; so I really felt right at home working with him."*

vidual. The journalist follows the man and meets his wife (Jeanne Moreau). He thinks he might get a scoop out of the story but events take things out of his hands. Mastroianni has given up everything in public life and has even left his wife so as not to leave any trace of his whereabouts. The man remains shrouded in mystery. His uncertain character is suspended in time and space; it is like the stork's tread, standing suspended on one leg, caught between advance and retreat. The film is presented in Cannes in 1991 and is released in France on the fourth of December of that year.

In 1986, straight after working with Anghelopulos for the first time, Mastroianni meets and works with another director he greatly admires: Nikita Michalkov. The idea of making a film with the Russian director comes to Mastroianni and the producer Silvia d'Amico Bendicò, while they are working on *I soliti ignoti vent'anni dopo*. Mastroianni is not familiar with many of Michalkov's films but those he does know he greatly admires, especially *Oblomov*, which he has always dreamt of acting in.

He had had to refuse the offer to do Platanov in Chekhov's *Player-Piano* under Visconti's direction, because he was making *La Dolce Vita* at the time. They write to Michalkov asking him if he would like to do a film with Mastroianni. A month later he gets in touch by telephone saying that he will be in Paris at the end of November 1985. Mastroianni is in New York but agrees to go to Paris to meet him. When they meet they take to one another immediately but they do not decide to make a film straight away. They arrange to meet again in Moscow at Christmas. A few days after they meet, on New Years Eve, they decide to do Chekhov. Michalkov and his collaborator Alexander Adabascian start work while the producer contacts the Soviet authorities, who express their agreement. In February,

at a Paris meeting including the other screenwriter, Suso Cecchi d'Amico, a final screenplay is outlined, amidst the usual problematic discussions over the film's financing. In the end, the production is financed by the RAI, which usually takes an interest in quality programmes, and Adriana Cinematografica. But it is only after the intervention of Sacis that the project gets off the ground.

Shooting begins on the 4th of August in Leningrad where the first part of Romano-Mastroianni's journey takes place. On the August bank holiday the

whole team transfers to Kostroma under torrential rain. Kostroma, a beautiful town on the Volga four hundred kilometres North-East of Moscow, is one of the old Russian towns which form the so-called "Golden Ring", the pearl of which is the capital. But since the early 1900's, only two other Italians had arrived before the troupe of *Black Eyes*. The team then moves onto a turn-of-the-century boat which goes from Leningrad to lake Ladoga. Here the meeting between Romano and the Russian businessman take place. The film then moves to Michalkov's dacia

With Elena Soforova. "We both stayed friends with Nikita after the film was finished, and I even worked in the theatre with him. He was invited to direct a play in Italy and got in touch with me right away.

He said: 'Let's share another adventure'. And I answered: 'With great pleasure'. So we did Player-Piano. *And I hope some day we'll get to work together again."*

near Moscow where Romano's journey ends. Filming continues in Italy in the spa towns of Montecatini and Frascati, where Romano and Elisa/Silvana Mangano's villa is, and where the production rebuilds a part of the old spa.

The story draws its inspiration from some of Chekhov's short stories, notably *The Lady with the Dog*. Travelling on a steam-boat, Romano, an old Italian gentleman, tells his life story to the Russian businessman. His marriage to Elisa, a very rich girl, his brilliant studies in architecture which have come to nothing, his wife's economic crisis, their gradual estrangement, the meeting with Anna, the Russian lady he fell in love with, their separation and his desire to see her again. Using a friend's request as an excuse he sets off to Russia to find Anna. He eventually finds her and decides to leave his wife and start a new life with her. But first he must go back to Italy to explain things. When he arrives he loses heart and no longer has the courage to go through with his plan. He stays at home for a while but then leaves his wife for good and goes to work on the steam-boat. The Russian businessman listens and then tells his story confessing that after many years of waiting he has finally found happiness by marrying the woman who until then had refused him. His new wife is Anna.

"I got on with Michalkov straight away because he is friendly, good fun, lively and a really brilliant director. He started to think about what kind of story I could interpret in the Soviet Union which would justify my Italian nationality. And he managed, with the help of his screenwriter Adabascian and Suso Cecchi d'Amico, to come up with a character who was entirely credible, interpreted by me in his country. And so there are lots of elements in Romano which are like me, which I know really well. Drawing a little of its inspiration from *The Lady With The Dog* and from a film made from it, they

thought up a story in which the lady goes to Montecatini to take the waters and there meets an Italian who will then go to Russia to find her. So that's how the film came about. I know the character very well: so imaginative, light and superficial, not bad but simply so incapable of real action that he ends in total defeat. He has a beautiful house, a beautiful family; but he ends up as a waiter on a boat: a failure."

The film is a great success. Apart from an Oscar nomination, Mastroianni receives a best actor award in Cannes, a "Nastro d'argento", a "David di Donatello" and a "Ciak d'oro". Mastroianni plays the part of Romano as if he had known him for years. He has become more complex, more subtle, enriching the role with all the characters he has played so far. Lazy, weak, dishonest, passionate, intrepid, faithful, crazy and clownish he ends the film in the desperation of remorse.

"I have lived every day as though it were just a trial, a rehearsal for the real thing. I have had everything and nothing. My house, my family and even my daughter, who is the spitting image of me, have never really been mine. I don't remember a thing. What if I died this very moment and God Almighty asked me, 'Well, Romano, what can you tell me about your life?'. The lullaby my mother used to sing to me when I was very small, Elisa's face that first night, and the Russian mist."

After such successful beginnings and the creation of a film which, in spite of its sad ending, gives real satisfaction, the two accomplices get together a second time. When the film is released in September 1987 they are already rehearsing *Pianola meccanica* (Player-Piano) at the Teatro Argentina in Rome. Mastroianni's return to the theatre sees him in this play by Chekhov, an old love of his. In fact the Russian playwright is very close to him in spirit, and the character he plays,

Platonov, like all the author's characters, seems to be made of air, is hard to get hold of, even close-to you hardly recognise him. He hides behind an ironic smile and a paradoxical quip. At times he is tragically self-destructive and at others buffoon-like and ridiculous. *Pianola meccanica*, loosely based on *Platonov* and other stories which Michalkov has already used in the film, is a real success. It stays at the Teatro Argentina until December 6th. From December 12th to the 20th, it is on stage at the Théâtre Bobigny in Paris; from December 23rd to January 17th at the Carcano in Milan; and from January 23rd to February 7th it is again staged in Rome, this time at the Brancaccio Theatre. The tour ends in Turin where *Pianola* is put on at the Teatro Nuovo from February 12th to the 21st of that month.

The project of completing a Chekhov trilogy is never realised. Mastroianni should have played the part of the writer Trigorin in a French version of *The Seagull* which was going to be directed by Michalkov's brother, Andrej Konchalovskij; but the idea remains just that. A further disappointment comes when the RAI does not take up the offer of producing *Pianola meccanica* for the television as he and the play's organizers had originally planned.

While he is making the film with Michalkov he is approached by Egidio Eronico who asks him if he would be interested in making a film on the life of the architect, Mario Ridolfi. Mastroianni had always had a lot of respect and esteem for Ridolfi, who had been one of his teachers at the Istituto Tecnico. But *L'uomo sotto la cascata* (The Man under the Waterfall), which takes its name from the Waterfalls in the Marmore where the architect was exiled, never comes to anything.

In the same year, 1986, he plays himself making a television advert for the

As Mandrake in Intervista. *"I'm made-up like a big puppet. It's a joke about me."*

stain-remover Smak, in Fellini's film *Interview*. In reality, the actor has never worked in adverts, aside from some publicity done in Japan. In this Fellini joke, Mastroianni, as ever, is self-deprecating about his work: "I'm dressed up like a big doll. It's a big joke about me. It is really supposed to show me as though I have had plastic surgery. Anita (Ekberg) looks at me and

says: 'Show me your scars'. They show me smoking, and asleep in my car, like an old man. I am an actor who is past it, in Cinecittà to make an advert. In the scene with Anita, we are shown as two people who are really out of it . At the same time we are shown when we were young and beautiful in *La Dolce Vita* when we were dancing and I said to her, 'Who are you? The moon, my mother, who are you?' I saw a tear run down Anita's face when she saw those images. Men don't mind that much, but for a woman it can't be very nice. While they showed us together in the film, the camera showed us behind the screen too and I was saying the same words, 'the moon, the earth, my mother, my mistress'; and then I said, 'Have you got a glass of Grappa?', a sign of our decadence. And she replies, 'Fuck-off.' Of course there was a reaction. Someone said to me: 'How cruel'. Why is it cruel? It is profoundly human, because that's the way things are, and then, I think that so long as you can laugh at yourself there is still some hope, you can still survive. Irony is very important."

It is the first time that Fellini goes on screen himself instead of asking Mastroianni to play him. While a group of Japanese journalists film him for an interview, he gets on with his normal every-day activities with his usual team, and at the same time re-evokes the time when he was a young journalist. Mastroianni, dressed as Mandrake, suddenly appears, when a gust of wind blows open a window and we see him as he disappears upwards in a lift. "Hey, Snaporaz," Fellini calls to him. And he says, "Hi there, team. In trouble again. The usual money problems. There's nothing left in the coffers. Couldn't be worse. Sexual problems? Never fear; Mandrake's here. With a wave of my magic wand all your equipment will be up and ready to go". Fellini invites him to go with him. They get into the car. Marcello smokes. "Marcello; your cigarette," "Sorry, I forgot," he says and throws it out of the window. But he immediately lights-up again. "Open the window, at least," says Fellini. And Mastroianni says: "I can't breathe in here. I can't breathe if I don't smoke".

The director of the Japanese troupe says he can make him give up in a quarter of an hour. "What are you saying? It's taken me forty years to manage to smoke three packets a day. Do you want me to throw away all that hard work?" Mastroianni turns to Sergio Rubini, the actor who is playing Fellini as a young man.

"Tell me something. Do you have the same violent reaction that he does when I smoke?" "No, but I don't like smoking or drinking." "I hope you at least like women." "Oh yes, very much, but to be honest what I like best is masturbating." "Good solution. It helps concentration, and not only stimulates the imagination but in my opinion also helps to develop a writer's talent." While he is talking, he puts a few eyedrops in his eyes. "Mine, for instance, were real fiction serials. There were always new characters who kept introducing others. How do you do? Have you met my sister and cousins? So pleased to meet you. Where was it that we were going, Federì?" Then he falls asleep. He wakes up at the villa. At the door, Antita Ekberg asks, "Who is it?". But she is suspicious and while she opens the door they hear dogs barking. And Mastroianni says, "What does Anita need dogs for? She's magnificent, she looks like a gladiator."

After they have all said hello and hugged and kissed one another they all go into the house. Mastroianni/Mandrake gives proof of his magical powers. "And now, dear friends, if you will permit me, I would like to present a little game in honour of our hostess. Magic wand, obey my command; bring back the good old days we all remember. Music!". They hang up a sheet and on it we see the shadows of Mastroianni and Anita, dancing to the music from *La Dolce Vita*. As if by magic the scene shifts to the pair's unforgettable dance scene at the Trevi Fountain. Today's Marcello says: "There are so many things I would still like to ask you. For instance, have you got a drop of Grappa?" The film rolls on. Anita wipes-away a tear and Marcello-Mandrake, with another wave of his wand, makes everything disappear. Fellini seems to have assigned him the role of Mandrake to make it seem that he is the real creator of this film, the only one with the magic powers necessary to create the dream or construct the myth. Mastroianni

looks back on his own myth, through the dual filters of age and irony. Rather cruelly, the director attributes all the typical characteristics of age to him. The film wins a prize for the fortieth year of the Cannes Film Festival when it is presented in a non-competetive section. In July it wins the jury's grand prize at the Moscow Film Festival. When it is released in Italy, however, it does not meet with the public acclaim expected.

In May 1987, Mastroianni is in Budapest playing Sandor Rozsnyai in Pal Sandor's *Miss Arizona*. The Italo-Hungarian film is partly financed by Reteitalia. It tells the story of a couple of actor-singers who realise their dream when they manage to set up a music hall called the Arizona, which becomes as famous in Budapest as the Moulin Rouge is in Paris. Their adventure, which reaches its climax when the music hall becomes really successful, ends tragically with the war and the Nazi invasion. Sandor, who has some distant Jewish ancestor, is taken to a concentration camp while all trace of Mitzi is lost.

Filmed in Italy on Lake Garda and in Milan, in Berlin, Vienna, on the Danube and in the streets of Budapest, the film is drastically edited in the cutting studio and as a result suffers from a lack of continuity.

"You can't just cut a thing like that. I think that it was originally about two hours and twenty minutes long and they cut it to less than two hours. When I saw it in Budapest, I kept thinking: 'Where did that come from?' There was no preamble, no run-up, and the character of Mitzi's young lover, played by Urbano Barberini, was almost completely cut. He was supposed to wait for her in her changing room while she was singing, a real love-sick side to his character which is completely missing in the film. I agreed to do the film because I really admire and esteem Hanna Schygulla. She told me that the director had made a really beautiful film called "Daniele Takes the Train", about a boy who goes on a journey. And then I fancied visiting Budapest because I had never been there. To me that is another side to the cinema; I use it to visit places I would never have gone to otherwise. In fact, in spite of the film's lack of success, I really enjoyed myself in Budapest and have very good memories of that time. It's an important thing, and, I might almost say, is more important than the film itself. I take my work seriously, but I am also detached from it, because it is the kind of work that allows you to be a rather special tourist. What should you do? Not take advantage of it? We can't spend all our time in this factory, convinced that we are always making masterpieces. Let's get out of here and go to Brazil, Hungary, Africa, Russia, even if the doughnut sometimes has a hole in it."

At the start of the film, Mastroianni humbly presents himself at an audition as a "Composer, musician, singer, clown and poet" and he acts the clown, playing a piano with missing keys. In the course of the story he is the meek part-Hebrew, part-Italian, part-Hungarian, a maternal and concerned father to Mitzi's son and a strolling player who plays the trumpet. He ends up as the Arizona's highly-acclaimed orchestra-director. The character constantly hides behind a screen of buffoonery and even when he reaches the height of success still maintains that spirit of self-parody.

In September he takes part in six films organized by Ettore Scola and Rai Due to promote six young directors. "I played myself in some brief episodes to lend a hand to the project. In each episode I was making a 'phone call to my lawyer and I was ad-libbing; there was nothing scripted. It was a game which might have been amusing for someone who knows about my relations with my lawyer or for other clients of hers, like Scola. But it was a kind of in-joke and I don't know what

With Hanna Schygulla in Miss Arizona. *"I liked the idea of visiting Budapest, a place I'd never been to. I'm all for this kind of adventure, too; I use my cinema work to discover countries I'd probably never get to otherwise."*

sense it could have had for the public. Scola asked me to do it because it would help this nice scheme of his to help these six young directors. And then the linking elements in all the films were myself and Piazza Navona."

On the 5th of December, *Black Eyes* is shown in the Aula Magna of the University of Rome, "La Sapienza". At the end of the film, Mastroianni holds a conference which is attended by more than two thousand students who give him a standing ovation. For an hour and a half he responds to their questions with the irony, straight-forwardness and humour which have become his trademarks. "Have I any regrets? Why? I've had fun: the villa with the swimming pool like Hollywood stars have, success, satisfaction. I suppose you want to know the down-side. Well I have to say that I have had to sacrifice time with my family, my two daughters. I've played the anxious father with them too of course; 'Put a coat on. You don't eat enough'. It's a game, like the one I have played on the set for more than forty years."

In 1988, in Arpino, a small town near Rome, he works on Ettore Scola's *Splendor*. He plays the part of Jordan, the owner of a cinema which is threatened with closure because of the lack of clients. They want to turn it into a supermarket. Ever since he was a small child he had followed his father, who travelled round the villages with his mobile projector. Then the Splendor was built and people flocked to it. When Jordan inherits the cinema, Chantal/Marina Vlady, a French dancer, arrives and becomes both the cinema-usherette and his mistress. The Fifties are the Splendor's hey-day when the crowds really fill the hall and they often have to put out the sign saying "Standing-room only". Then the new projectionist, Luigi/Massimo Troisi arrives and Chantal becomes his mistress. On the screen, black and white films alternate with films in colour; Amer-

ican alternates with Russian. We return to the present. The hall is being dismantled and the workers are arriving to take away the seats. But a resolute crowd of people advances and sits in the seats preventing them from being removed. Luigi climbs on the stage and says: "Merry Christmas to everyone !". Jordan, below, says: "It's June". "Yes, I know, but these things only happen at Christmas." And as we hear the opening bars of the Candle Waltz, snow falls from the ceiling as in Frank Capra's film *It's a Wonderful Life*.

Splendor runs through the history and the stories of the big screen with narrative ellipses which take the spectator from one period to another, and from one film to another. The owner, Jordan, is a dreamer who is determined to fight against the public's loss of interest and the closing of the hall. He finally decides to combine a strip-tease with the films to try to keep the public interested. But when he sees the rehearsal, he can't stomach it and says: "That's enough; one evening like this and that's fifty years serious work down the drain". And so he sends the dancing girls away. In the end he is forced to sell. But he wants to have one last satisfaction. He gives the buyer ten million lire in exchange for the pleasure of giving him a sound slap in the face in front of the local bigwigs at a meeting of the town's cultural society.

Scola's film is a loving farewell to a kind of cinema which is gradually disappearing. His homage is like those in Giuseppe Tornatore's *New Cinema Paradise*, Luciano's Odorisio's *Via Paradiso* (Paradise Street), and Fellini's project for a film called *Fulgor*, a name homage to a cinema in Rimini. The film's chief merit, however, is to have put Mastroianni on the screen with Massimo Troisi, creating a new film partnership.

"I got on very well with Troisi. If we hadn't hit it off so well we would never have made *What Time Is It?*, a film made

possible because of this good relationship we had established in *Splendor*. *What Time Is It?* is an old idea that Scola had always put to one side. While we were making *Splendor*, I remembered it and said to Ettore: why don't we finally do that story about the father who goes to visit his son who is doing his military service in Civitavecchia? Massimo would make a perfect son in that film. But Scola was signed up to do *Capitan Fracassa*, which he had already twice put off doing and now really had to go through with the deal he had with the producer. So then I talked to Massimo, and said to him: 'It's a nice idea, do you like it?'. 'I like it, I like it,' he said. 'Right. Now all we have to do is twist the director's arm and convince him to do it right away.' Troisi was very witty, I remember, and he came out with some really nice quips. When he was eating lunch once , he said: 'Hmm, this fish is good. In Civitavecchia they do really good fish in that restaurant called The Red Flag, do you remember, Marcello? You're a Communist,' and to Ettore; 'You'd like it at the Red Flag restaurant in Civitavecchia'. That was all he did: just verbal jokes, but every day. So finally Ettore began to take the idea seriously and started to write while we were still filming *Splendor*. We made *What Time Is It?* a few months later. Neither I nor Troisi was in another film between those two, which means that we had got on well. He's intelligent and talented. He is not like anyone else. His way of acting, made up of invention, breaks, syncopated acting, those speeches of his which never seem to end and seem nonsensical but in fact do have a meaning; it is all very interesting. I like it even though it is very different from my way of doing things. I belong to a more traditional line of Italian acting whereas he doesn't seem to follow academic rules; he is more spontaneous. We have a certain laziness in common as individuals, as men. His is perhaps even more developed

With Massimo Troisi in Splendor.

A scene from Splendor.

than mine. I like him for this too. We aren't all full of dynamism but we do have a different, internal dynamism of our own. Ettore is a constant. I think I will carry on working with him. It is one of those positive kinds of friendships which allow you to work because the friendship comes into play in work too. I am not in *Capitan Fracassa* but Troisi is. So I said to them both, turning to Massimo, 'Oh. I see. I've become the wife now, and he's found himself a young lover and abandoned me. But fortunately, like all wives, after so many years I have become more patient and understanding and have learnt to adapt to circumstances. In effect, I'm not jealous, because I know that sooner or later he will come home again.'"

In *What Time Is It?* Mastroianni plays a prominent Roman lawyer who goes to Civitavecchia to see his son who is doing his National Service. In his anxiety to recover a relationship that he has never had with his son; he overwhelms him with

gifts: an Alfa Romeo car and an appartment in a fashionable quarter of Rome. The son is irritated by these gifts but appreciates another small gift his father has brought with him much more. It is his grandfather's Railway watch which has a locomotive etched on it and which the boy remembers always wanting to see, constantly asking the question: "What time is it?"

During the day father and son pass through moments of difficulty and of joy, because although they love one another they are still strangers. Marcello has never found the time to talk to Michele, and Michele has always felt crushed under the weight of his father's importance and has never felt able to compete. Marcello suffers and is jealous when he sees that Michele is more concerned about Cesare, the owner of the bar in the port, than he is about him or when, in the cinema, he wakes up from a nap and finds that his son has gone off and is telephoning some-

one. He writes him a note. "I saw you while you were on the telephone. It has been such a bore, this half-day with me, that you have gone straight away to let-off steam with someone else. I have never seen you look so happy since you were eight years old. I thought that you were all alone in this so-called city, but you have hoards of friends, fishermen, librarians and so on. Well you can go and see them now and I'll just leave you in peace. Bye. Your father."

The father tries to get involved in his son's life, and in some way to live off it vicariously, when he insists on meeting his girlfriend. He is jealous of their close relationship and feels completely excluded. "When a father all of a sudden wants to take an interest in his child, he is pathetic. He wants to know about all those things he has taken no interest in for years. Cramming it all in like some students who don't study all year and then when they get to exam week..." he tells the girlfriend. It is now evening and father and son walk toward the station where Marcello has to take his train, and his son gets on to see him off. "Talking to a stranger is easy, but talking to one's own father is difficult," Michele says. "We have talked about everything and nothing," Marcello replies. But when he gets on the train he asks his son, "What time is it?". And the son proudly takes out his grandfather's watch and tells his father the exact time. Mastroianni is particularly affecting in the role of a father exhausted by a life of hard work, too much drinking and smoking. He identifies with Scola's attempt to give the film an autobiographical tone, and he throws himself into the role of a a father

With Massimo Troisi in Che ora è?. *"I worked really well with Troisi; we understood each other right away and so were able to add our own improvisations to the script. We didn't violate the original screenplay in any way; with the director's permission, we added little touches of our own, because we felt at home with the story and could identify with the characters."*

On the set with Troisi and Scola.

who has given up, a loser. At the Venice Film Festival both Mastroianni and Troisi are presented, ex-aequo, with the Volpi award for the best actor.

The father in *What Time Is It?* is the first of a series of fathers Mastroianni is to play in the nineties. In Giuseppe Tornatores' *Stanno tutti bene* (They Are All Fine), he plays a father in search of his children. His wife dead, he leaves his home in Sicily, and goes on a sort of prilgrimage to visit his offspring, who are too involved in their own lives to be bothered with him any more. From the postcards which arrive from time to time he has formed the impression that they are all happy and well-established. But when he arrives in Naples, Rome, Florence, Milan and Turin it is an entirely different story. Back in Sicily, he goes to his wife's tomb

to talk to, her as he has always done, but he lies to himself and to her saying that they are all well and happy.

Mastroianni has been aged ten years in the film, given a larger nose, false teeth, a face puffed-up with cotton wool, greyed hair, and enormous black-rimmed glasses which magnify his eyes so much that they seem deformed. He is the heart of the story, being both protagonist and the narrating voice-over. Lonely, and with no one to talk to he tries to ask questions which

will create conversation. When he leaves Castelvetrano he greets the Station Master and asks him: "How is your father?" "He's dead". "Say hello to him for me will you? Tell him I'll drop by to see him when I come back". He is only used to talking with his dead wife, and he does not make any distinction between the living and the dead. He has reached that point in life when the boundaries between the two are no longer important.

He also has a brief romantic interlude

Stanno tutti bene.

when he meets Michèle Morgan on the train and she helps him to repair the photo of his children which the guard has stamped by mistake. This is their first film together since the long-ago *Racconti d'estate*. She is travelling with a pensioners' tour group, and when they get off the train at the Romagna riviera, he joins them, ending up at an evening of dancing that finally makes him feel ill. "It's such a long time since I last had a dance." The next morning he kisses her hand and says goodbye. When the film is presented at the 43rd Cannes Film Festival it is well received. Mastroianni is awarded the SNGCI (Sindacato Nazionale Giornalisti Cinematografici Italiani) prize for the best leading actor.

"I had a good time touring Italy for three months to make this film. I enjoyed playing that man; he is a character I really liked. It was a bit uncomfortable because of all the travelling around and those monstrous glasses which made everything misty. I couldn't see the other actors very well and I couldn't even move from one part of the scene to, the other. I had to rehearse first without the glasses and count steps and stairs. Then it was tiring for my eyes, all day long with those thick lenses. It tired my eyes and gave me a headache. But everything went well. Tornatore was always very affectionate, full of attention for me. He is someone who knows this business really well."

In *Verso sera* (Towards Evening) which he makes between the 22nd of May and the 24th of July 1990, he is directed by a very young director, Francesca Archibugi. It is the second time, after *Stanno tutti bene* that he works with Italian cinema's new generation. "Both Tornatore and Archibugi are very talented, they really know this profession well. I work well with them. But that's no surprise. It's not as though you have to wait until you are fifty for your talent to show through. If someone has got talent it shows even when they are twenty. Then you have to know the profession. At twenty-five or thirty, it is normal to be good. I think Fellini was about that age when he made *I vitelloni*. If anything there is real pleasure for someone of my age to work with very young directors. It refreshes and renews you. They are less calligraphic; there is less

need to know about the mechanisms of cinema. The camera virtuoso is less useful nowadays. Today's 'Author's Cinema' is about states of mind and situations: things which don't require a perfect technical knowledge. Thirty or forty years ago, before you could become a director you needed to spend ten years or so as assistant director and learn all the secrets of the camera. You had to know it all really well. Nowadays it is not necessary at all. If someone has some experience, all the bet-

ter: it will be easier for him to confront the making of the film. But if you have got some interesting ideas, you can express them in a less 'calligraphic' manner. And I am not giving a negative sense to the word 'calligraphic' here. In the same way, writers today have a more dynamic approach. Thers is no need any more to say that someone goes to the bar, has a coffee, then he wipes his mouth, then he leaves the bar and crosses over the street and goes through a doorway. From the moment he

puts his cup down we see him already in the appartment opposite. All this still requires narrative technique but it can be done in a more simple way. Certain elaborate camera techniques are no longer so essential. Young beginners may only have been a director's assistant for a short while but if they have interesting, fresh, new, original ideas and they have the strength of character, they may make a few spelling mistakes and have to be content with a more elementary way of writing, but behind that there is a great deal of substance."

The film is an idea developed by Francesca Archibugi, Gloria Malatesta and Claudia Sbarigia for Vittorio Gassman; but when they have to start work on the film, he has other work in hand. Having read the script, Mastroianni falls in love with the character, Professor Ludovico Bruschi, and decides to do the part. Here too, with almost-white hair and gold-rimmed spectacles, they age him a few years.

The film *Verso sera* starts at the end, in effect, when the grandfather, Mastroianni, writes a letter to his granddaughter. "Dear Papere, I am writing you this letter for when you are eighteen. I am trying to imagine what you will be like, what you will be thinking, and what effect this year you have spent together with me and your mother will have had on you. Of course, nothing will be the same as before, not even me, or our country or our world. This is why I want to tell you why 1977 was the happiest and saddest year of my life."

A year previously his son, Oliviero, had

With Sandrine Bonnaire in Verso Sera.

left the child in his care when he separated from his wife (Sandrine Bonnaire). And so Papere becomes part of her grandfather's life: the ordered and methodical life of a retired university professor. While she is at first intrigued and perplexed by this existence, which is so different from the one she is used to, she seems to manage to get used to it until her mother, Stella, arrives. Confused and disoriented, she too decides to stay at the grandfather's house for a while. But the two disagree violently and evntually Stella decides to go. And Papere finds herself alone again with her grandfather.

When he has no news of Stella for a month, he goes to her mother to find out what has happened. The mother tells him that she has had an accident and is in hospital with her leg in plaster. He goes to get her and takes her home. At the hospital a woman says to her, "What a handsome man. Is he your father?"

Father-in-law and daughter-in-law find it impossible to live together, partly too because of a new element in their feelings for one another. Mastroianni's narrating voice reads passages from the long letter to his granddaughter in which are inserted the salient events of the year 1977. Through political battles, drugs and a way of life free from responsibilities and ties, the young people of the day are trying to follow a path which their parents have not been able to prepare them for. The parents, for their part, realise that it is too late to make up for the errors they have made. Professor Bruschi concludes his letter: "I spent the day you moved out with an old giraffe in the zoo. I realised that, like me, he already belonged to memory and that memory is the one thing you can't pass on. I realised, too, that the giraffe and I were neither of us much longer for this world. I have told you this story so that when you are older, you can decide who was in the right, someone like your mother, or a person like me; because

I haven't been able to figure it out." In the film, Mastroianni never resolves the complex relationships with his granddaughter and his daughter-in-law; he spends his time with his mistress, and with a group of friends with whom he plays classical music. His character is constructed in crescendo and shows the development away from a rigidly bourgeois way of living to a re-awakening of feeling and sentiment, with all its consequent complications for his peace and tranquility. He is awarded the "Nastro d'argento" for his performance.

At the 1990 Venice Film Festival he is awarded the "Leone d'oro" for his career. He feels that it marks an important point

With Sandrine Bonnaire and child actress Lara Pranzoni.

in his career, but jokes about its possible significance: "It is a great pleasure with one small reservation. Does this prize for my career mean that my career is now over and I should quietly retire? There is a small grain of suspicion there. Seriously, though, I do think that it is a very nice gesture for which I should thank the festival jury and organizers. Of course if they had given it to me when I was thirty, I wouldn't have this little sneaking doubt."

Le voleur d'enfants. *"Right from the start I felt that this role was written for me. But at first the film was supposed to be done in English with an English director, and I didn't feel comfortable about that. I beat about the bush, without giving any definite confirmation, until finally Sergio Gobbi, a producer working in France, asked me if I was still interested. I was glad to accept, the more so as the film was shot in Paris, where the action of the novel originally took place."*

From the 15th of April to the end of May he is working on *Le voleur d'enfants* (The Child-Stealer) by Christian De Chalonge, in France. The film project has been in the air since February, 1986 when Mastroianni read Jules Supervielle's novel and immediately decided to play Bigua, the lead role. The film will be shot in French as a European co-production. Various directors are contacted; in the end both Mastroianni and the producers are enthusiastic about De Chalonge, whose screenplay, written with Dominique Garnier, perfectly reflects the spirit of the novel. But Marcello, at the time, is scheduled for one film right after another and has no free time until the Spring of 1991. Paris 1925: Colonel Filemone Bigua-Mastroianni a rich Argentine exile, spies on some children on stage from behind the curtain. The little theatre is one of the

favourite places of the old gentleman who, because he can not have children, steals them. He is helped in the enterprise by his wife, Desposoria/Angela Molina, and they have already managed to put together a group of ten or so children whom they lovingly take care of. He entertains them by telling them stories about his exploits in the war and dresses them all the same in clothes he makes himself. At the park he spies on Antoine, a little boy he has sent a wooden ostrich to, and he gets him to follow him.

Up until this point, he has only collected male children and he begins to feel that they need to have a sister. He looks all over the city, hoping to find a girl. Then the puppet-master, Armand/Michel Piccoli, badly in debt, suggests selling him his sixteen-year-old daughter, Gabrielle. All the boys, from the youngest to the oldest,

fall in love with her. Bigua himself is a bit taken too, but he continues to play the father. But Joseph, who is seventeen, one night gives in to temptation and rapes her. When Bigua finds out he throws him out but the boy violently resists. In the struggle that ensues, Bigua feels his strength failing and in desperation throws himself into the Seine. Then he remembers that he is still carrying the will in which he leaves everything to the children and so he returns home. Gabrielle tells him that she is pregnant. The news makes him change his plans and he decides to take the whole family to Argentina so that the grandchild can be born in his native country. Gabrielle gives birth on the ship and Desposoria is overjoyed, as though it were the child she had never been able to have. Armand, meanwhile, films the events.

Loosely adapted from the novel by Jules Supervielle, the film gives Mastroianni the opportunity to play an original character, full of rich undertones, who moves from the paternal to the buffoonish, to the galant to the grotesque, always illuminated by a streak of pure madness.

At the end of the summer, he leaves for the United States, where he starts to rehearse *Used People*, a film directed by Beeban Kidron, an English director in her early thirties. He works with three Oscar-winning actresses: Shirley MacLaine, Jessica Tandy and Katy Bates. Sylvia Sydney and the young Marcia Gay Harden also star. The film is finished in November. It is the sixth time he has been directed by a woman and he is rather pleased by the fact: "I think I must hold the record. In the morning it's nice if there is a kind lady there to take care of you, a protective presence, almost maternal. She asks how I have slept, makes me a cup of coffee and doesn't make me climb the stairs too often."

Shot in New York and Toronto, the film gives us an elated Mastroianni, surrounded by women. It tells the story of a large Jewish family living in New York between 1945 and 1965. The story revolves around Shirley MacLaine, who is at the centre of a large group of grandparents, aunts, uncles, children and cousins. Mastroianni plays the part of an Italo-American who is in love with her. He is a self-made man who tries to impress the lady by quoting from the classics. The very day her husband dies, he arrives at the funeral and asks her to marry him, saying that he has waited twenty-four years for her and can not wait a moment longer.

"After our first day on the set, the children started greeting my arrival in the morning with 'Buongiorno, papà', clinging to me. Like the children, I, too, identified myself with my role. It was a wonderful game, as if I'd become a child again, and was one of them. When the film was over It was hard to leave them."

Acting Is a Game, a Wonderful Game

Mastroianni has always said that for him acting is a game. A complicated and malicious game which takes hold of you and does not let you go. The more you do it the more you want to do it. "I live the actor's profession like a game. A fantastic game. Acting is almost better than making love because it really is intoxicating to take on the appearance, attitudes and psychology of another person. It's what children do. It is the oldest game of all. It is the first game we invent when we play 'You be the policeman and I'll be the gangster. I'll hide over there and you do this.' And you really believe it."

Games mean turning back the calendar, creating a time paralysis, which ancient peoples depicted as a child playing dice. Perhaps this is what Mastroianni feels when he says that the forty years of this career which he has spent 'playing' have gone by so quickly that it hardly seems that he has lived them at all: "Always hidden behind some character, one after another; when have I ever lived life as Marcello Mastroianni?" He immediately qualifies his statement: "I don't want to play the artist who has only lived through others, even though it is a bit like that". Between the reality principle and the pleasure principal,

which are present in many people like an alienated couple who at any moment are ready to leap at one another and tear each other apart, in Mastroianni it is definitely the pleasure principle that wins the day. Very often, though, he is weighed down by guilt complexes: "In the acting profession, without realising it, you are constantly on the run. Often out of cowardice because, not being mature, you are not willing to confront reality. It is easier to tell other peoples' stories, to tell fairytales. But if you do this you avoid fulfilling the duty you have towards yourself, other people and life in general."

With the constant change of roles, one wonders if he ever confuses life on screen with real life and if the characters who take hold of him need to be exorcised in order to leave him in peace. "Sometimes someone might carry on the role of a coward or a scoundrel because it is easy for him. In a certain situation he might say to himself: 'I think I'll play that eccentric person now with his strange way of doing things'. And it might even work. Do you see what I mean? Someone who thinks that they are a bit boring can feel better with some added colour; they can feel more interesting. If I have done it sometimes, I have done it con-

sciously and not because I am dragging this phantom behind me that I can't get rid of."

He is caught up in the game, in other words, but only up to a certain point. It is better if the actor is not capable of criticism because he ought not to be too aware of what he is doing. Diderot wrote the same thing. "You should not expect an actor to be too intelligent or too sensitve because it would end up by blocking him. If he over-develops his abilty to criticise himself, his sense of the ridiculous will paralyse him. An actor must really be a bit naïf because then he believes, he gets involved, he gets into it." In place of the image of the dynamic, agressive actor who gets hold of the script and consumes it, Mastroianni prefers a softer, more reflective image. For him it is a sensation like falling in love. "It's like when you fall in love. You think about your beloved constantly. The relationship between the actor and character involves a curious kind of transfer." This less resolute image brings out the feminine aspects of the process which is constructed entirely from the inside, hidden, but anchored onto the very roots of personality.

Just as the harem image is a basic model in the realms of male fantasy, in Fellini's films, Mastroianni finds himself in a situation of complete liberty, of a kind that he could never experience in everyday life without running into all sorts of insoluble problems and contradictions.

"While I was making *La Dolce Vita* I lived in a state of complete harmony with myself, my defects, vices and inadequacies. I was no longer afraid to show myself as I was. I felt free, deeply free and happy." Without the restriction of having to choose a role for life which is never fully accepted, he manages to use his screen characters to express himself through his own defects and those defects become his very expressive capacities. Life on the set is more real for him than real life. He accepts the roles precisely because they are not him, they are

not in the first person, but instead they are provisional identities behind which he can hide. Only through acting can he manage to change the nature of his reality.

It is a rare thing for Mastroianni to lose his sense of cool and only in one case is he particularly touchy. When he is accused of being a seducer. It is an image which he refuses to accept. "Why do people always ask me about women? I am lazy by nature and I have had more women after me than I have chased after myself. I have never played the role of seducer, even though I have always been surrounded by very beautiful women. It has usually been me who has been seduced. I completely reject this particular label." For him a seducer has to be exceptional. On the screen he is the actor with the capital "A" like Clark Gable and Gary Cooper. In life it is someone who is filled with the desire for conquest, someone who plans his battles well. Mastroianni has never declared war against the opposite sex. He does not feel the need to trap women or to prove his own virility. He is in a state of permanent armistice with women, for he has nothing against them. On the contrary he tends to be on their side and his relations with them are purely non-aggressive.

This mistaken image of the seducer has been one of his biggest disappointments. It is as though all those years he has spent in the public eye have been wasted, because people have not even noticed the person behind the hundreds of masks he has worn. But he is the first to make a joke of this disappointment, hiding again behind a front of good humour. You can never catch him out. He seems to be the least complicated actor in the world and yet, even now, at sixty-seven years of age, he may still have some surprises in store for us. For, as he says, "It's all there: inside". The hundreds of characters he's played, the understatment, self-mockery and irony, that capacity to enter into another personality and possess it.

"When we started shooting I was very worried about working with ten children on the set; twelve, if you count the two bigger children. I was wondering how long it would ever take to make that film, if you consider that working with just one child is usually pretty much of a complication. As I saw it, a child would probably tend to follow his own imagination, doing the opposite of what the director wants. Directing ten of them, I was sure, would be a very tough job. But Christian de Chalonge, the director, was really wonderful: he got them to do everything he wanted, as if they were all playing a game together. They were perfect."

Filmography

1948
I MISERABILI by Riccardo Freda with Gino Cervi, Valentina Cortese.

1949
A TALE OF FIVE CITIES, by Montgomery Tully, Romolo Marcellini with Bonar Colleano, Barbara Kelly, Gina Lollobrigida.

1950
SUNDAY IN AUGUST by Luciano Emmer with Anna Baldini, Franco Interlenghi, Vera Carmi, Massimo Serato.

1950
VITA DA CANI by Steno e Monicelli with Aldo Fabrizi, Gina Lollobrigida, Delia Scala, Tamara Lees.

1950
CUORI SUL MARE by Giorgio Bianchi with Doris Dowling, Jacques Sernas, Charles Vanel.

1950
CONTRO LA LEGGE by Flavio Calzavara with Fulvia Mammi, Tino Buazzelli.

1951
ATTO DI ACCUSA by Giacomo Gentilomo with Lea Padovani, Andrea Checchi.

1951
PARIGI È SEMPRE PARIGI by Luciano Emmer with Aldo Fabrizi, Ave Ninchi, Lucia Bosè.

1952
L'ETERNA CATENA by Anton Giulio Majano with Marco Vicario, Gianna Maria Canale.

1952
GILRS OF THE SPANISH STREET by Luciano Emmer with Lucia Bosè, Cosetta Greco, Eduardo De Filippo.

1952
TRAGICO RITORNO by Pier Luigi Faraldo with Doris Duranti, Franca Marzi, Dante Maggio.

1952
SENSUALITÀ by Clemente Fracassi with Eleonora Rossi-Drago, Amedeo Nazzari.

1952
PENNE NERE by Oreste Biancoli with Marina Vlady Versois, Guido Celano.

1953
GLI EROI DELLA DOMENICA by Mario Camerini with Raf Vallone, Cosetta Greco, Elena Varzi.

1953
IL VIALE DELLA SPERANZA by Dino Risi with Cosetta Greco, Liliana Bonfatti, Maria Pia Casilio.

1953
FEBBRE DI VIVERE by Claudio Gora with Marina Berti, Massimo Serato, Anna Maria Ferrero.

1953
NON È MAI TROPPO TARDI by Filippo Walter Ratti with Isa Barzizza, Paolo Stoppa.

1953
LULÙ by Fernando Cerchio with Valentina Cortese, Jacques Sernas.

1954
CRONACHE DI POVERI AMANTI by Carlo Lizzani with Antonella Lualdi, Cosetta Greco, Anna Maria Ferrero, Adolfo Consolini.

1954
ANATOMY OF LOVE by Alessandro Blasetti, *The Kid* episode with Lea Padovani, Nando Bruno.

1954
SCHIAVA DEL PECCATO by Raffaello Matarazzo with Silvana Pampanini, Camillo Pilotto.

1954
DAYS OF LOVE by Giuseppe De Santis with Marina Vlady, Lucien Gallas.

1954
CASA RICORDI by Carmine Gallone with Paolo Stoppa, Gabriele Ferzetti, Danielle Delorme.

1954
TOO BAD SHE'S BAD by Alessandro Blasetti with Sophia Loren, Vittorio De Sica.

1954
LA PRINCIPESSA DELLE CANARIE by Paolo Moffa with Silvana Pampanini, Gustavo Rojo.

1955
THE MILLER'S BEAUTIFUL WIFE by Mario Camerini with Sophia Loren, Vittorio De Sica.

1955
TAM-TAM MAYUMBE by Gian Gaspare Napolitano with Pedro Armendariz, Kerima.

1955
LUCKY TO BE A WOMAN by Alessandro Blasetti with Sophia Loren, Charles Boyer.

1955
THE BIGAMIST by Luciano Emmer with Franca Valeri Giovanna Ralli, Vittorio De Sica.

1957
THE TAILOR'S MAID by Mario Monicelli with Vittorio De Sica, Marisa Merlini, Memmo Carotenuto.

1957
LA RAGAZZA DELLA SALINA by Franz Cap with Isabelle Corey, Jester Naefe, Peter Carsten.

1957
THE MOST WONDERFUL MOMENT by Luciano Emmer with Giovanna Ralli, Marisa Merlini, Ernesto Calindri.

1957
WHITE NIGHTS by Luchino Visconti with Maria Schell, Jean Marais, Clara Calamai.

1957
IL MEDICO E LO STREGONE by Mario Monicelli with Vittorio De Sica, Marisa Merlini.

1958
UN ETTARO DI CIELO by Aglauco Casadio with Rosanna Schiaffino, Polidor.

1958
THE BIG DEAL ON MADONNA STREET by Mario Monicelli with Vittorio Gassman, Totò, Renato Salvatori, Claudia Cardinale.

1958
GIRLS FOR THE SUMMER by Gianni Franciolini with Michèle Morgan.

1958
AMORI E GUAI by Angelo Dorigo with Richard Basehart, Valentina Cortese, Eloisa Cianni.

1959
WHERE THE HOT WIND BLOWS by Jules Dassin with Gina Lollobrigida, Pierre Brasseur, Melina Mercuri, Yves Montand.

1959
TUTTI INNAMORATI by Giuseppe Orlandini with Jacqueline Sassard, Marisa Merlini, Gabriele Ferzetti.

1959
IL MARITO BELLO (IL NEMICO DI MIA MO-GLIE) by Gianni Puccini with Giovanna Ralli, Vittorio De Sica.

1959
FERDINAND OF NAPLES by Gianni Franciolini with Peppino De Filippo, Eduardo De Filippo, Vittorio De Sica.

1960
LA DOLCE VITA by Federico Fellini with Anita Ekberg, Anouk Aimée. Yvonne Fourneaux, Alain Cuny, Magali Noël.

1960
IL BELL'ANTONIO by Mauro Bolognini with Claudia Cardinale, Pierre Brasseur, Rina Morelli.

1960
LOVE A LA CARTE by Antonio Pietrangeli with Simone Signoret, Sandra Milo, Emmanuelle Riva, Gina Rovere.

1961
THE NIGHT by Michelangelo Antonioni with Jeanne Moreau, Monica Vitti, Bernhard Wicki.

1961
THE LADY KILLER FROM ROME by Elio Petri with Micheline Presle, Cristina Gaioni, Salvo Randone.

1961
PHANTOMS OF ROME by Antonio Pietrangeli with Sandra Milo, Tino Buazzelli, Vittorio Gassman, Eduardo De Filippo.

1961
DIVORCE ITALIAN STYLE by Pietro Germi with Daniela Rocca, Stefania Sandrelli, Leopoldo Trieste.

1962
A VERY PRIVATE AFFAIR by Louis Malle with Brigitte Bardot, Grégoire von Rezzori.

1962
FAMILY DIARY by Valerio Zurlini with Jacques Perrin, Valeria Ciangottini.

1963
8½ by Federico Fellini with Anouk Aimée, Sandra Milo, Claudia Cardinale, Caterina Boratto.

1963
THE ORGANIZERS by Mario Monicelli with Annie Girardot, Renato Salvatori, Bernard Blier, Folco Lulli.

1963
YESTERDAY, TODAY AND TOMORROW by Vittorio De Sica with Sophia Loren, Aldo Giuffré.

1964
MARRIAGE ITALIAN STYLE by Vittorio De Sica with Sophia Loren, Tecla Scarano.

1965
CASANOVA '70 by Mario Monicelli with Virna Lisi, Marisa Mell, Enrico Maria Salerno.

1965
THE TENTH VICTIM by Elio Petri with Ursula Andress, Elsa Martinelli, Massimo Serato.

1965
KISS THE OTHER SHEIK by Marco Ferreri, Eduardo De Filippo, Luciano Salce with Catherine Spaak, Virna Lisi, Pamela Tiffin.

1965
THE MAN WITH THE BALLOONS, by Marco Ferreri with Catherine Spaak, Ugo Tognazzi, William Berger.

1966
IO, IO, IO... E GLI ALTRI by Alessandro Blasetti with Walter Chiari, Gina Lollobrigida, Vittorio De Sica.

1966
THE POPPY IS ALSO A FLOWER by Terence Young with Yul Brinner, Hugh Griffith, Angie Dickinson.

1966
SHOOT LOUD, LOUDER... I DON'T UNDER-STAND, by Eduardo De Filippo with Raquel Welch, Eduardo De Filippo.

1967
THE STRANGER by Luchino Visconti with Anna Karina, Georges Wilson, Bernard Blier, Georges Geret.

1968
A PLACE FOR LOVERS by Vittorio De Sica with Faye Dunaway, Caroline Mortimer.

1969
DIAMONDS FOR BREAKFAST by Christopher Morahan with Rita Tushingham, Elaine Taylor, Maggie Blye.

1970
SUNFLOWERS by Vittorio De Sica with Sophia Loren, Ljudmila Saval'eva, Anna Carena.

1970
THE PIZZA TRIANGLE by Ettore Scola with Monica Vitti, Giancarlo Giannini.

1970
GIOCHI PARTICOLARI by Franco Indovina with Virna Lisi, Timothy Dalton.

1970
LEO THE LAST by John Boorman with Billie Whitelaw, Calvin Lockhart, Vladek Sheybal.

1970
THE PRIEST'S WIFE by Dino Risi with Sophia Loren, Venantino Venantini.

1971
SCIPIONE, DETTO ANCHE L'AFRICANO by Luigi Magni with Ruggero Mastroianni, Vittorio Gassman, Silvana Mangano.

1971
MY NAME IS ROCCO PAPALEO by Ettore Scola with Lauren Hutton, Tom Reed.

1972
...CORREVA L'ANNO DI GRAZIA 1870 by Alfredo Giannetti with Anna Magnani, Mario Carotenuto.

1972
IT ONLY HAPPENS TO OTHERS by Nadine Marquand Trintignant with Catherine Deneuve, Serge Marquand, Dominique Labourier.

1972
LIZA by Marco Ferreri with Catherine Deneuve, Corinne Marchant, Michel Piccoli.

1972
WHAT? by Roman Polanski with Sydne Rome, Hugh Griffith.

1973
BITE AND RUN by Dino Risi with Carole André, Oliver Reed, Lionel Stander.

1973
MASSACRE IN ROME by George Pan Cosmatos with Richard Burton, Delia Boccardo, Leo Mckern.

1973
THE SLIGHTLY PREGNANT MAN by Jacques Demy with Catherine Deneuve, Micheline Presle.

1973
BLOW OUT by Marco Ferreri with Ugo Tognazzi, Michel Piccoli, Philippe Noiret, Andréa Ferréol.

1973
THE BIT PLAYER by Yves Robert with Jean Rochefort, Françoise Fabian, Carla Gravina.

1974
ALLONSANFAN by Paolo e Vittorio Taviani with Lea Massari, Mimsy Farmer, Laura Betti, Claudio Cassinelli.

1974
TOUCHE PAS À LA FEMME BLANCHE by Marco Ferreri with Catherine Deneuve, Michel Piccoli, Ugo Tognazzi, Philippe Noiret, Alain Cuny, Serge Reggiani.

1975
POOPSIE by Giorgio Capitani with Sophia Loren, Aldo Maccione.

1975
THE DIVINE NYMPH by Giuseppe Patroni Griffi with Laura Antonelli, Terence Stamp.

1975
DOWN THE ANCIENT STAIRS by Mauro Bolognini with Françoise Fabian, Martha Keller, Lucia Bosè.

1975
THE SUNDAY WOMAN by Luigi Comencini with Jacqueline Bisset, Jean-Louis Trintignant.

1976
CULASTRISCE NOBILE VENEZIANO by Flavio Mogherini with Claudia Mori, Lino Toffolo.

1976
TODO MODO by Elio Petri with Gian Maria Volonté, Mariangela Melato, Ciccio Ingrassia.

1976
SIGNORE E SIGNORI, BUONANOTTE by Luigi Comencini, Nanni Loy, Luigi Magni, Mario Monicelli, Ettore Scola with Vittorio Gassman, Nino Manfredi, Ugo Tognazzi, Monica Guerritore.

1977
A SPECIAL DAY by Ettore Scola with Sophia Loren, Françoise Berd.

1977
WIFEMISTRESS by Marco Vicario with Laura Antonelli, Leonardo Mann, William Berger.

1977
DOUBLE MURDER by Steno with Agostina Belli, Ursula Andress, Peter Ustinov.

1978
BYE BYE MONKEY by Marco Ferreri with Gérard Depardieu, James Coco, Geraldine Fitzgerald.

1978
STAY AS YOU ARE by Alberto Lattuada with Nastassja Kinski, Francisco Rabal.

1978
BLOOD FEUD by Lina Wertmüller with Sophia Loren, Giancarlo Giannini.

1979
THE TRAFFIC JAM by Luigi Comencini with Alberto Sordi, Annie Girardot, Patrick Dewaere, Gérard Depardieu, Stefania Sandrelli, Ugo Tognazzi.

1979
GIALLO NAPOLETANO by Sergio Corbucci with Ornella Muti, Renato Pozzetto, Michel Piccoli.

1980
LA TERRAZZA by Ettore Scola with Ugo Tognazzi, Vittorio Gassman, Jean-Louis Trintignant, Serge Reggiani, Carla Gravina.

1980
CITY OF WOMEN by Federico Fellini with Anna Prucnal, Bernice Stegers, Éttore Manni.

1981
LA PELLE by Liliana Cavani with Burt Lancaster, Claudia Cardinale, Ken Marshall, Alexandra King.

1981
FANTASMA D'AMORE by Dino Risi with Romy Schneider, Eva Maria Meineke.

1982
LA NUIT DE VARENNES, by Ettore Scola with Jean-Louis Barrault, Hanna Schygulla, Jean-Claude Brialy, Harvey Keitel, Daniel Gelin, Michel Vitold, Andréa Ferréol, Laura Betti.

1982
OLTRE LA PORTA by Liliana Cavani with Tom Berenger, Eleonora Giorgi, Michel Piccoli.

1983
STORIA DI PIERA by Marco Ferreri with Isabelle Huppert, Hanna Schygulla.

1983
GABRIELA by Bruno Barreto with Sonia Braga, Antonio Cantafora, Antonio Pedro, Nelson Xavier.

1983
L'ARMATA RITORNA by Luciano Tovoli with Anouk Aimée, Michel Piccoli, Gerard Klein.

1984
HENRY IV, by Marco Bellocchio with Claudia Cardinale, Leopoldo Trieste, Paolo Bonacelli.

1985
THE TWO LIVES OF MATTIA PASCAL by Mario Monicelli with Flavio Bucci, Laura Morante, Nestor Garay, Alessandro Haber.

1985
MACARONI by Ettore Scola with Jack Lemmon, Isa Danieli, Daria Nicolodi.

1985
GINGER & FRED by Federico Fellini with Giulietta Masina, Franco Fabrizi.

1986
I SOLITI IGNOTI VENT'ANNI DOPO by Amanzio Todini with Vittorio Gassman, Tiberio Murgia, Clelia Rondinella.

1987
THE BEEKEEPER by Theo Angelopulos with Nadia Mourouzi, Serge Reggiani.

1987
DARK EYES by Nikita Michalkov with Vsevolod Larionov, Silvana Mangano, Elena Sofonova.

INTERVISTA by Federico Fellini with Sergio Rubini, Anita Ekberg

1987
MISS ARIZONA by Pal Sandor with Hanna Schygulla, Gâbor Zsôtêr, Alessandra Martines.

1988
SPLENDOR by Ettore Scola with Massimo Troisi, Marina Vlady.

1989
WHAT TIME IS IT? by Ettore Scola with Massimo Troisi, Anne Parillaud.

1990
STANNO TUTTI BENE by Giuseppe Tornatore with Michèle Morgan, Marino Cenna, Roberto Nobile, Leo Gullotta, Valeria Cavalli.

1990
VERSO SERA by Francesca Archibugi with Sandrine Bonnaire, Lara Pranzoni.

1990
CIN CIN by Gene Saks with Julie Andrews.

1990
LE PAS SUSPENDU DE LA CICOGNE by Theo Angelopulos with Jeanne Moreau.

1991
LE VOLEUR D'ENFANTS by Christian by Chalonge with Angela Molina, Michel Piccoli, Virginie Ledoyen.

1991
USED PEOPLE by Beeban Kidron with Shirley Mac Laine, Jessica Tandy, Katy Bates, Sylvia Sidney, Marcia Gay Harden.

PHOTOS

Every possible effort has been made to give correct and detailed photo credits. Obviously not all historic data has been easily accessible or necessarily precise. The author and publisher express their regret for possible errors or omissions and shall be glad to accept any authorized revisions, to be included in future editions. Sincere thanks is also extended to all those whose cooperation made this publication possible.

Agenzia Fotografica Pierluigi 52, 54, 55, 56, 57, 77 (inclusive), 78, 79, 143; A.L.A. Fotocine 98-99; Alonso Avincola 88, 97; Archivio A. Bernardini 110, 114, 115; Archivio Fotografico Ente dello Spettacolo 48; Archivio Fotografico RAI 29; D. Beer 144, 146, 147; Bosio Pressphoto 20 (top right); Franco Castelnovi 26, 31, 36, 39, 46, 47, 58, 59, 60, 62, 65, 86 (bottom), 87, 101,108; Divo Cavicchioli 64, 66, 67; Centro Studi Cinematografici 149, 150, 155, 156, 175 176; Guglielmo Coluzzi 21 (bottom), 89, 92, 93; De Antonis 20 (top left); Dial Press 18, 34; Luciano Emmer (private collection) 27, 28; Foto Civirani 44; Foto Manueli 22; Foto Vaselli 51; Ghibbi Foto 19; Giornalfoto 131; Henry Grossman 68, 126; Tommaso Le Pera 167; Luciano Locatelli 135 (bottom); National Film Archive/Stills Library 24, 25; Renata Pajchel 182, 183, 184. Firmino Palmieri 118; Pietro Pascuttini 75; C. Patriarca 111 (bottom); G.B Poletto 63, 145; Press Photo 21 (top); Rivista del Cinematografo 85, 122, 125, 128; Paul Ronald 40, 41; Tazio Secchiaroli 2-3, 6, 80, 81, 82, 82-83, 90, 91, 94, 95, 96, 105 (left and bottom right), 106, 190-191; Studio Longardi 121; M. Tursi 134, 178, 179; Tv Sorrisi e Canzoni 30, 37, 61, 107, 111 (top), 119, 135 (top), 136.